BASICS OF LIBRARY AUTOMATION, KOHA LIBRARY MANAGEMENT SOFTWARE AND DATA MIGRATION: CHALLENGES WITH CASE STUDIES

BASICS OF LIBRARY AUTOMATION, KOHA LIBRARY MANAGEMENT SOFTWARE AND DATA MIGRATION: CHALLENGES WITH CASE STUDIES

By

Vinod Kumar Mishra

Ess Ess Publications
New Delhi

BASICS OF LIBRARY AUTOMATION, KOHA LIBRARY MANAGEMENT SOFTWARE AND DATA MIGRATION: CHALLENGES WITH CASE STUDIES

ISBN: 978-81-7000-814-9

First Published 2016

Published by:
Ess Ess Publications
4831/24, Ansari Road,
Darya Ganj,
New Delhi-110 002.
INDIA
Phones: 23260807, 41563444
Fax: 41563334
E-mail: info@essessreference.com
www.essessreference.com

Cover Design by *Patch Creative Unit*

Printed and bound in India at Salasar Imaging Systems.

I dedicate this book to my mother, father, spouse, son and daughter who helped me in providing all the comfort of life, motivated and to become a writer of a book. I would also like to dedicate the book to the entire Koha community for developing such excellent software for social development.

Contents

Acknowledgements

This book would not have been possible without the help of so many people in so many ways. I would like to thank all the institutes like IIT Kanpur. IIT Roorkee. ISRO. and NIT Rourkela. who have given me an opportunity to work and explore the knowledge in the field of library and information science. I would like to include a special note of thanks to Prof. Sunil Kumar Sarangi. Director NIT Rourkela. who have given a lot of freedom to work and always motivated to extend the help to needy libraries and guided me in learning so many new things related to LIS. Thanks to Mr. D.P. Tripathi. Assistant Librarian. NIT Rourkela. who have contributed to enhance my technical knowledge and share his ideas during various workshops and implementation of Koha. ILMS at different institutes.

I am also grateful to the entire team of Biju Patnaik Central Library. NIT Rourkela who always appreciated me for the good works and motivated for developing IT based further skills in LIS. Thanks and grateful to the entire Koha community and developers of Koha. ILMS, who have directly and indirectly contributed a lot to this book. The inspiration for writing this book which came from my friends and seniors are priceless who always motivated me from the various corners of the country. At last 1 would like to say thanks to Ms. Prantika Ari. Library Trainee. BPCL, NIT Rourkela for review of my book draft and family members who encouraged and helped me a lot during entire career and co-operated me in learning the new things in odd days/hours.

Preface

The book "Basics of Library Automation, Koha Library Management software, and data migration: challenges with case studies" is an outcome of authors approximately ten years of practical experience in the field of library automation. The idea of writing this book came into mind after gaining rich experience of Koha implementation at various reputed institutes of India and helping libraries abroad through remote login and telephonic supports on a voluntary basis. More than twenty libraries have invited the author for data migration, and implementation of Koha ILMS at their institutes apart from this many workshops has been organized by the author and served as a resource person in workshops as well as delivered many lectures related to library automation and open source solution for libraries.

This book fulfills the academic requirement for all level of students and faculties of Library and information science as well as research scholars who wish to do research in Library Automation and related open source solutions. Apart from above, this is equally written and very useful for Koha workshop trainers, computer professionals, Koha vendors and who wish to implement the Koha software and migrate data from existing software/Excel. The book contains all the basics of library automation, Koha library management system, and data migration skills. Many successful case studies of implementation of the Koha software and migration of data from excel and other software have been included in the book.

This book deald with real practical problems involving in library automation and their solutions for the cost-effective and efficient use of ILMS. The author is sharing his expertise with the various social media and personal website which is available at http://mishravk.com/, the book includes the ideas and tips and tricks of Koha implementations as well as data migrations which were gained from various community support forums. This book is divided into eight chapters and includes bibliography at the end of the book for further studies. One of the main benefits of reading and procuring the book is its accompanying material (LiveDVD of Koha) which is very popular on the entire globe and used by thousands of people for learning Koha as well as implementations in the libraries without any technical issues. Many people from library and information science domain requested the author to share the ideas of library automation, Koha implementations and data migrations in the form of a book so that entire LIS fraternity may get the benefit of huge expertise gained in the said area.

Hence, this book is a complete solution for basics of library automation and developing expertise on Koha, ILMS. The readers are suggested to read the book since chapter one and install the Koha ILMS on any test machine for practicing as per the instructions provided in the book. The current book does not only fulfill the theoretical requirements of LIS professionals as per their academic curriculum in automation, but it also provides a lot of practical materials/instructions for practice and developing IT-based skills.

The book ensures the reader that after consulting the book, they will be able to understand all the basic skills which need to be required for successful implementation of automation tools and techniques in libraries. As the book is written by real practical/working experiences gained by the author in Indian top level institutes/Libraries like IIT's, NIT's and ISRO, etc. hence the content provides the real life problems and their solutions for efficient and successful implementation of automation solutions. Koha has been chosen as it is the world most popular open source solution and libraries are willing to adopt it because of its state of the art features, but due to lack of expertise and knowledge in the said field many libraries are handicapped. Koha has also been incorporated in all level of study in the field of library and information science too, hence keeping all in view author felt the requirement of such book in the public domain which can be used for gaining knowledge in the said field and their implications for the real world.

The book is written in a very simple English language which can be understood by any persons having little knowledge of English. The students of Bachelor/Master of library and information science will get a clear theoretical as well as practical idea about the library automation, Koha, data migrations, etc. as per their academic requirements. Any reader of this book may contact the author in case of any difficulty in understanding the concepts theoretically as well as practically, the author always welcome their feedback to improve the contents. At last author would like to share that the royalty received from this book will be contributed to Koha community for its further development and poor children's of India.

— **Vinod Kumar Mishra**
http://mishravk.com

ABOUT AUTHOR

The author is having rich practical experience in almost all domains of library and information science, worked in worlds leading institutes like Indian Institute of Technology Kanpur and Roorkee, Indian Space Research Organization, and at present working in National Institute of Technology Rourkela, apart from this has worked in ISO certified schools too. The author is having Bachelor of Science, Bachelor and Master of Library and Information Science qualifications from one of the most reputed Banaras Hindu University and did Master in Sociology from Chatrapati Sahu Ji Maharaj University, Kanpur as well as did Diploma in computer applications. Author has contributed many articles in National, International conference, book chapters and Journals as well as delivered invited lectures in the field of library and information science. Author has conducted many workshops in the capacity of Convener/co-convener and invited as a resource person.

Koha software has been implemented by author at various institutes like the Central University of Assam, Central University of Gujrat, Central University of Jammu, Central University of Odisha, Indian Institute of Science Education and Research, Bhopal, etc. Apart from above author is having a wealth of experience on other open source software like DSpace, Joomla, Wordpress, Newgenlib, Ubuntu, etc. The author supports the library for implementation of open source solution for libraries on a voluntary basis not only in India but abroad also via remote logins, community support forums, creating tools like live DVD, etc. Author has developed a website and can be contacted at **http://mishravk.com/** for the assistance of Library and information community with a motto "Empowering Library Profession to Empower Society (ELPES)".

ABOUT BOOK

This book fulfills the academic requirement for all level of students and faculties of Library and information science as well as research scholars who wish to do research in Library Automation and open source solutions. Apart from above, this is equally written and very useful for Koha workshop trainers, computer professionals, Koha vendors and who wish to implement the Koha software and migration of data from existing software/Excel. The book contains all the basics of library automation, Koha library management system, and data migration skills. Many case study has been included in the successful implementation of the Koha software and migration of data from excel and software.

The students of Bachelor/Master of library and information science will get a clear theoretical as well as practical idea about the library automation, Koha, data migrations, etc. as per their academic requirements. As the book is written by real practical/working experiences gained by the author in Indian top level institutes like IIT's, NIT's and ISRO, etc. hence the content provides the real life problems and their solutions for efficient and successful implementation of automation solutions. The book is written in the very simple English language which can be understood by any persons having little knowledge of English. Any reader of this book may contact the author at http://mishravk.com/ in the case of any difficulty in understanding the concepts theoretically as well as practically; author always welcome their feedback to improve the contents.

1

Introduction to Library Automation

1. INTRODUCTION

The automation of human life-related activity is one of the primary requirement and future need to cope with the fast processing of activities with minimum efforts and time. The automation is supposed to be the greatest challenge in each and every activity created/innovated because the implementation of innovation in real life and getting the output in minimum time and efforts is considered to be another challenge. The existing manual or semi-manual activities along with innovations need to automate then only it would see as viable for growing world. The developed and developing countries have better production and information management systems due to automation of processes associated with that. Hence, automation plays the vital role in understanding the growth rate and prospects for any individual and country. Railways, banking, education systems, all type of industries, post offices, libraries, etc. are now a day's very common place where we can see fully or semi-automated systems. Automation not only makes the life ease physically, but it also gives much mental comfort and peace. The current book discusses the automation of libraries which is the heart of any institution and a place for digging in depth preserved knowledge on any particular topics.

The number of Libraries is increasing day by day with the rise of educational and research organizations, industries, banking, etc. hence, the knowledge content and the function of each library are different due to its various types of patrons and their information requirements. The activities of the libraries and information centers are mostly common, but it depends on the type of services provided and demand of the users. The automation of each process of the library seems to be very challenging and necessary to fulfill the information thrust of the users promptly. The current book is written by rich author experience on automation of libraries using open source solution Koha integrated library management software (ILMS). The book will attempt to describe not only the process of automation but the challenges for automation and how to overcome with the situations especially data migrations from existing ILMS to Koha.

1.1. Library Automation

When we start talking about library automation the first thing strike in our mind is "What is Automation"? The term automation, inspired by the earlier word automatic (coming from automaton), was not widely used before 1947 when General Motors established the automation department. It was during this time that industry was rapidly adopting feedback controllers, which was introduced in the 1930s. Feedback control is a control mechanism that uses information from measurements to manipulate a variable to achieve the desired result.

The term automation seems to be very scientific in nature and extensive application in scientific processes and industry, but it plays the vital role in all sphere of human life and socio-economic growth of the country.

Some of the requests of automated processes widely used in:

- Automobiles
- Pharmaceutical Industry
- Mines
- Railways
- Electronics and communication industry
- Hospitals
- Banking
- Education
- Libraries
- Agriculture etc.

Library automation can be only defined as the application of ICT's to library housekeeping operations and users services. The word "automation" has been derived from Greek word "auto mode" means something, which has the power of spontaneous motion or self-movement. The term "automation" was first introduced by D.S. Harder in 1936, who was then with General Motor Company in the U.S. He used the term automation to mean automatic handling of parts between continuous production processes. Now a day's various software and hardware's are being used in the libraries to provide prompt services to the users and minimize the human efforts.

The different meaning of library automation is defined as follows:

a. According to Encyclopedia of Library and Information Science, "automation is the technology concerned with the design and development of process and system that minimize the necessity of human intervention in operation". (Kent, 1977)

b. According to Webster's Third new International Dictionary of English Language Automation is defined as "automatically controlled operation of an apparatus, process/ system by the mechanical or electronic device that takes the place of human organs of observation, effort and decision". (Gove, 1966)

c. According to the Oxford English Dictionary, It defines automation as "application of automatic control to any branch of industry or science by extension, the use of electronic or mechanical devices to replace human labor". (Simpson & Weiner, 1989).

d. According to McGraw-Hill Encyclopedia of Science and Technology, It defines automation as "a coined word having no precise accepted technical meaning but widely used to imply the concept, development, or use of highly automatic machinery or control systems". (McGraw, 1982)

1.2. Objectives of Library Automation

The primary objective of any automated system is to achieve the best quality in minimum time with fewer efforts, so when we talk about the library goals, it revolves around the user services and information handling which may exist in the form of hardcopy or softcopy. Some of the primary objectives can be defined as:

- Storage of huge bibliographic data in minimum space with maximum distribution
- Reduce the cost of data handling and human resource
- Prompt services to the end users
- Better library resource sharing and networking
- Better reputation and ranking of library and information services
- Reduce duplication of work

1.3. Library Automation Costs and Challenges

Change in any system for further development involve costing and future risks which should be well planned and forecasted as well to avoid any significant permanent loss to the existing system. The cost involve in the automation of libraries can be divided into the following broad areas:

- Consultation costs
- Hardware and software purchase
- Data conversion and other system configurations
- Internet connectivity, domain charges, and Public Internet protocol charges
- Networking of computers and other associated hardware
- Power backup
- Human resources
- Annual maintenance costs of the hardware and software
- Access and subscription of databases etc.

Apart from well system design and plan, there is always significant risk of failure or unexpected results which may be categorized as follows concerning library automation:

- Vendor viability
- Managerial support of higher level administration
- Staff attitudes towards training and adoption of new system
- Users awareness and keen to learn using new systems
- Financial assistance and flexibility in budget allocations
- High-level Computer skilled technical manpower

1.4. Area of Automation in Libraries

There may be the various area of automating the library functions depending upon the size, collection, services provided by the library, type of library, etc. Hence the automation requirement of the libraries various from one to another traditionally almost libraries are mainly focusing on their housekeeping operations such as:

Acquisition management

The acquisition involves procurement/purchasing of reading materials for the library as per the recommendations of the users. The whole process requires good managerial skills, accounting procedures, communications with vendors for quality and prompt supply. Therefore, any ILMS should have some basic features of acquisition module which is shown in below diagram. It should be noted that many manual interventions also involve at each step of automation, and that can't be ignored for example manual verification of shipment received, the condition of item received, etc. hence accordingly provisions are given in the automation system to reject the items in case of damage, duplicate, etc.

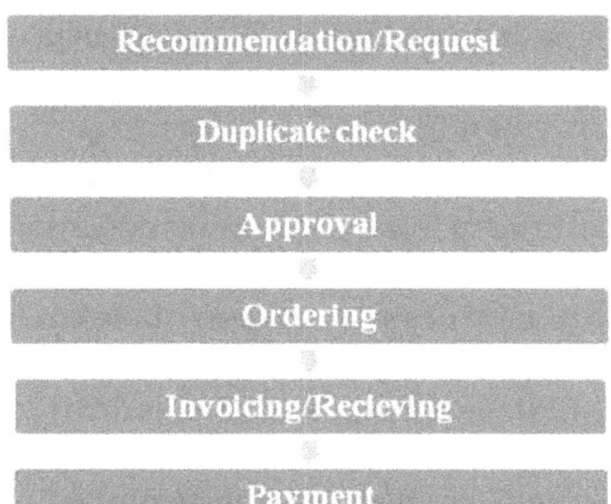

Fig. 1.1. General acquisition process

Periodicals management

Periodicals management is one of the most complicated and complex due to the massive involvement of online resources. Hence, not only print but online resources also need to be maintained with the serial/ periodical management module. Most of the works are similar to the acquisition, but little changes in the procedure are involved as described in the Fig. 1.2.

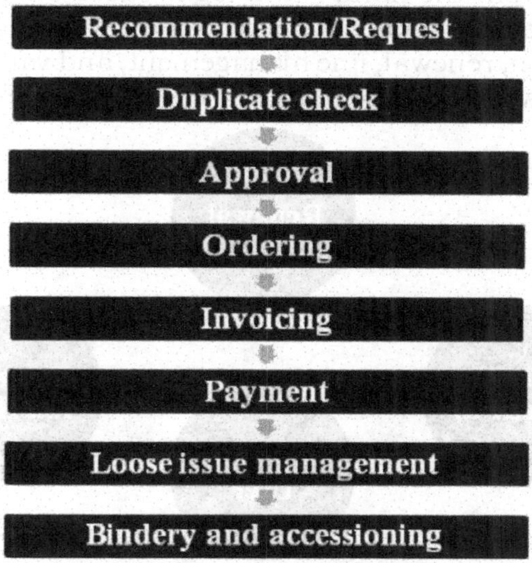

Fig. 1.2. General serial management process

Cataloguing of Library Materials

Cataloging or technical processing of processed documents from acquisition department is sent to the technical section for bibliographic input in a standard format. There are many customized formats provided by ILMS, which May or may not satisfying the international standards like MARC21, etc. The provision should be there to enter the data in customized MARC21 formats for various types of reading materials like DVD, Map, book, serials, etc. This module is having options for retrospective conversion of data, display of new materials, update holdings, options for entry of multiple copies of same books, etc.

Circulation management

Circulation is the division which directly deals with the services of the library and always in front; it reflects the quality and promptness of the library system and services. A modern user expects a lot of state of the art features from the library and login based online facility for their transaction details, recommendations of book, reservation, renewal, fine management, and various other facilities which can be seen in Fig. 1.3.

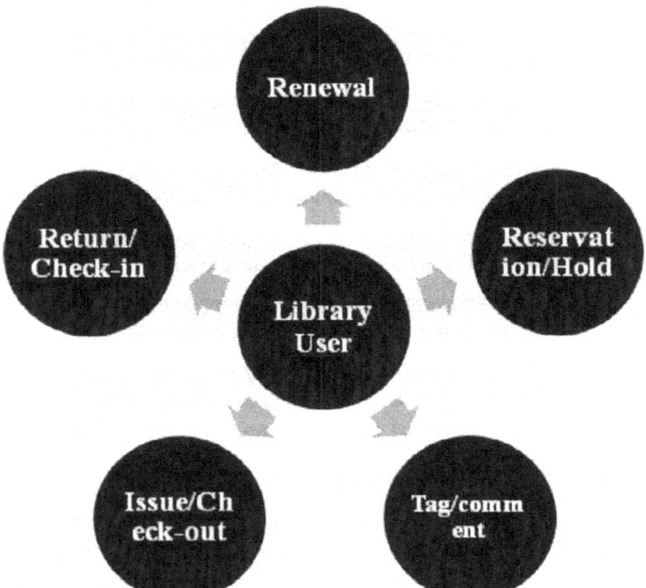

Fig. 1.3. General features in circulation as per user's expectation

Online public library catalogue (OPAC)

Online public library catalog (OPAC) is the windows through which users and people look at the library virtually and discover the various types of reading/

educative materials available with it. Advance web OPAC is now a day's provided by library automation solution systems having a lot of features including web 2.0 and login based transaction details, advance searches, online recommendations, etc. Some of the features of latest OPAC features are demonstrated in the Fig. 1.4.

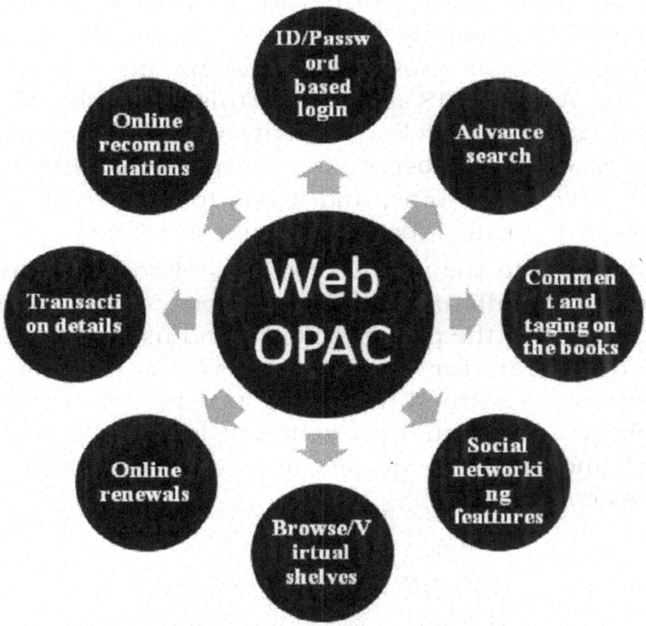

Fig. 1.4. Some Advanced and Standard Features of OPAC

Reporting and Budgeting

Reporting and budgetary management of any software are one of the most important features in any ILMS without which there is no use of a system as reporting is nothing but the output of the system against the input provided by the library. Various types of reports may be needed for routine works, statistics, management, budget monitoring, staff output, and efficiency, etc. The report modules must be flexible and having the facility to get customized reports as per the library requirements.

Budget modules are nothing but it should be properly integrated with all the modules of the ILMS so that centralized budget control can be monitor for various library procurements.

Stock verification

Stock management and verification is very important, especially for audit purpose. Hence, the different ILMS has provided this feature, but it still lacks in many. A good ILMS should have this feature for efficient stock management related activities like bindery, status updates, weed-out, lost books, damaged books, etc. These works take much time, and it has to be carried out in any library during a particular interval of time.

Access to the various modules of software can be divided into staffs and end users majority of the functions is restricted to the personnel only, and users can access the database for fulfilling his/her information requirements without having the privilege to modify the database. The visual presentation is given in Fig. 1.5 which indicates the various library modules and their access control:

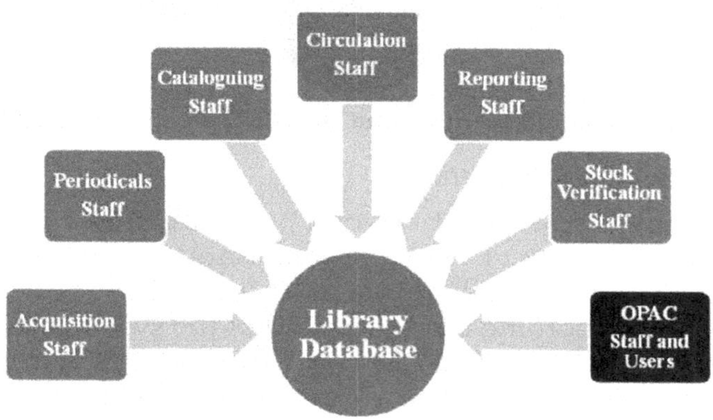

Fig. 1.5. Various modules of software and their access rights

REFERENCES

1. Automation. (n.d.). Retrieved January 15, 2016, from https://en.wikipedia.org/wiki/Automation
2. *https://controls.engin.umich.edu/wiki/index.php/Feedback_control* (accessed on 15/01/2016)
3. Lam, K. T. (n.d.). Issues in Library Automation. Retrieved January 16, 2016, from http://ihome.ust.hk/~lblkt/diploma/libauto/libauto.html
4. Library automation and networking in dental college libraries. (n.d.). Retrieved January 15, 2016, from http://shodhganga.inflibnet.ac.in/bitstream/10603/5661/9/09_chapter 4.pdf
5. UNESCO. (n.d.). Introduction to Library Automation. Retrieved January 15, 2016, from http://www2.unescobkk.org/elib/publications/ICTEIP/MODULE2/EIPICT_MOD2_ppt/EIPICT_MOD2_L1.pdf

2

Planning and Steps of Library Automation

Developing of any new system or revamping the existing system require a lot of planning and efforts, the steps of library automation is no exception because of its complexity especially when the old system is either manual or semi-automated which needs to be removed. The author would like to share the experiences gained by automating many libraries of India and some general procedures to be followed either by using Open source solution or propriety solution. When we start talking about change in the system then most important question came in our and others mind is:

Why Change, When to Change and How to Change?

The above question seems to be very simple but when we start finding the solution of above question then the whole process of getting the appropriate solution becomes the process of automation. The process which takes many days and planning, consultations, management related issues, budgeting, testing, staffing, reporting, etc. is nothing but a complete cycle of steps in automation of libraries. Some of the major steps in planning and final execution of new system are discussed in detail in the following subsections. By practical experience of the author in library automation, it has been observed that six major steps are involved in the execution of the complete library automation task for cost and service effective point of view which is summarized in the Fig. 2.1.

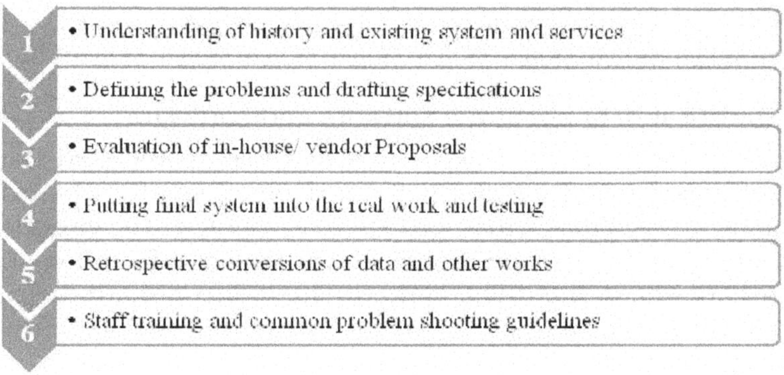

Fig. 2.1. Six Steps of Library Automation

2.1. UNDERSTANDING OF HISTORY AND EXISTING SYSTEM AND SERVICES

Sociological and historical study of any system reveals various decisions taken by the policy makers in the past, and then the correlation with the existing gives more strength and ideas to the implementation of the new system in any sphere of research and developmental study. Following points has been discussed below to know various areas which need to be taken care of such study and their practical implications

Present system and its history

The management and administration of any system are not constant, and it is very dynamic in nature we can see many changes in top level management within a couple of years for better productivity and improvements.

The changes may be sometimes problematic and cause a delay in decision-making processes due to the wrong understanding of the existing system and the reason for creating such environment by the past management. The good manager has to analyze the current practices in the library with the help of existing records and senior colleagues who are serving for many years. Such studies help the management to avoid the duplicate of work and proper understanding the user's expectations and complexity involve.

Statistical data about the software and hardware

Once the historical study has been completed the Information and communication technology (ICT) based software and hardware needs to be evaluated. The various data about the system should be prepared for its cost, manpower in handling, time consumed in procurement, maintenance charges, technical capability and feasibility, etc.

Present housekeeping operations and services

Services and housekeeping operations rendered by any library depends on its type and users, for example, the academic library serves the academic purpose in providing course and research related books/journals as well as other information, public libraries serve the entire nearby community including all age group of people and special libraries deal with specific subjects. The services and other related works of the library changes time to time hence planners must include all those current and prospects in their mind. In general libraries are involve in procurement of library reading materials like books, journals, compact disks etc., technical processing of procured materials, circulation of library materials to users, access to library resources etc. but all such process and the method of execution may not be same for all libraries and it varies to suit local requirements.

Technical available manpower and planners

The human resource is supposed to be the backbone of any system and ignorance of valued human resources result in destroying of any system or delay in execution of planned activities. Library automation planning does not involve only the ICT based skills but it require many clerical and managerial skills too. Decision makers must evaluate the human resources for:

Who is fit for what?

Accordingly the confidence of each such staffs need to be gained, and proper distribution of job-related to automation system planning needs to be distributed. Ignorance of any human resource at this stage will be too dangerous hence most of the time should be devoted to each staff, and the common meeting should be arranged to get their feedback and to know their interest area in such activities.

2.2. DEFINING THE PROBLEMS AND DRAFTING SPECIFICATIONS

System needs change and what are the changes need to be done hence this section revolve around the question:

Need Change but What Changes?

Changes must also be documented, and the reason of change should be explained and justified, what would be the alternatives and the specific requirement to bring positive changes in the system must be demonstrated and forecasted its impact in present and future. The following section describes on the same as we need to explain our requirements in this step.

Description of the specification requirements

The problems and the expected solutions need to be expressed in the form of documents with clear examples so that the software/hardware vendor can easily understand the client requirement and design the system accordingly before delivery. Exhaustive testing of existing system manual or automated need to be done and all the problems should be noted and discussed with management. The people involved in decisions making must clearly specify their requirements keeping in view the present and future requirements. All the specifications gathered from various sections/cell of the library should be properly analyzed and compiled in a systematic way without any duplication of specification and error free.

Setting the priority of specifications

Sometime in the initial stage of library automation, there may be many specifications as per future and current requirements. In such a case priority of the requirements must be set because the vendor may take much time in fulfilling all the demands of the library and customization of ILMS may not be possible on demand basis. Hence, libraries should understand the fact of customization and program the software and made their specifications feasible so that getting work from the system should not be illogical and dependent on only one feature and modules i.e. various substitute solutions should be kept in mind to be adopted in the case of failure of others.

Survey of expected solutions in the market

Now once the specifications have been made properly than library should try to investigate into the market about the solutions on the basis of specifications designed. This exercise is necessary to verify that specifications made by the library are valid or not, and possible solution exists in the market. After getting the idea from the market, necessary changes in the specification need to be incorporated for better solutions.

Proper compilation, evaluation, and testing of specifications

Designing of specification needs to be given more emphasis as this will be the bible for all future correspondences and other technical issues with vendors in executions of the automation process. Once the market survey has been done completely in order to find the possible solutions as per specifications designed in the initial stage, it's the time for evaluation of specifications and it's testing with the current system and future possibility. Any inaccuracy in framing the tender/ quotation document leads to legal issues also if any conflict arises with the vendor. Therefore, all legal and terms and conditions framed must be discussed with purchase/audit/legal departments before floating the tender/call for proposals. Sample specification is added in section 2.7 of this chapter below with special reference to Koha library management system.

2.3. EVALUATION OF IN-HOUSE/ VENDOR PROPOSALS

Floating of tender deadline decided for receiving of proposals vary from Institute to Institute and country to country. But proper time must be given, and quotation needs to be properly advertised through the internet and daily news in order to get proposals from renowned suppliers of hardware/software. Proposals received must be properly evaluated with the help of technical experts as discussed below:

Shorting the Proposals

On closing of the dead line, all the technical experts must gather and evaluate the proposals in terms of specifications asked and other terms and conditions mentioned in the tender document. Proper Excel sheet need to be maintained with each specification and remarks should be noted against each proposal. The proposals should be grouped in rejected and shortlisted for further action to be more careful at this moment re-evaluation should be done again to shortlist error free and biased proposals.

Calling for demonstration of the product and time for final implementation

Proposals may be fanciful and untruthful too so testing of proposals in the real environment is must hence all the shortlisted vendors needs to be invited for demonstration of the proposed model/system. Each vendor should be given proper time to explain their information product and how they satisfy the specifications and other library requirements along with costing of their products etc. During the demonstration care must be taken by the subject specialists and various library department managers to evaluate the presentations.

Analyzing the vendor response, capability and existing client response

In-house internal committee of experts should be now gathered and discuss the vendor's capability on the basis of demonstration of the product, simultaneously existing clients must be contacted to get feedback of the all shortlisted vendors who have demonstrated the product. Area of expertise, their strength of manpower, experience in automation in years, various pricing models, existing clients, etc. must be discussed and truth must be investigated by many means.

Cost, vendors, and negotiation

Costing of any project is major issues but getting proper solutions to the problem should not be compromised hence if the proposed cost is not in accordance with the predicted budget then best three lowest price proposals must be called for final negotiations. The better managerial skilled people should be engaged for negations as per the quality and quantity of the product. Please note that in software industry costing involve in designing the software is not a repetitive expenditure hence once it is designed only maintenance and bug removal need to be done and some customizations as per client requirements. Therefore, negotiations should be started from as much as low price and compared with the other already negotiated product. Ultimately the job is done, and now lowest bid price/ negotiated price should be given the opportunity to handle the project of library automation.

2.4. PUTTING FINAL SYSTEM INTO REAL WORK AND TESTING

On selection of the final proposal, the library should place the order for the hardware/software as soon as possible to avoid any delay in final implementations. Vendors must be given proper time for supply of materials and other associated time as discussed below:

Hardware and software installation

The major task begins with hardware and software installation on site hence proper planning of locations, server room, electric supply, etc. need to be done much in advance. Technical staffs and computer center people should be involved in the installation of systems so they may get the better experience of the same.

Small scale testing and evaluating the installed system

Installations and its functioning need to be tested with sample data. All type of library materials and sample users data should be entered, and whole library housekeeping process must be tested in small scale. Faulty installations and system configurations should be rectified and re-tested till attains the best quality.

2.5. RETROSPECTIVE CONVERSION OF DATA AND OTHER WORKS

Once installation and configuration of the system

are done next work is to migrate the existing data or data input to the new system as per international standards, the actual work of the library starts while retrospective conversion or migration of data from old to new ILMS. Many precaution and standards are applied for better output.

Technical staffs selection for retrospective and standardized data conversions

All professionals may not have expertise on various library standards like MARC21 (Machine-readable catalogue), AACR2 (Anglo-American cataloguing rule), RDA (Resource description and access), Sears list of subject heading, etc. hence data entry must be done by well-qualified staff which is necessary for bibliographic control of the library reading materials.

Bar-coding/tagging of Radio frequency identification (RFID) tags

Bar-coding of each library material or putting RFID tag is another time consuming and standardize work, various type/size of bar-codes are available similarly RFID tags may be of High Frequency (HF) or Ultra high frequency (UHF). Keeping the prospects in changing such type of tools and technology library must select or implement only those which provide flexibility in future to change and adopt the new technology with maximum efficiency.

2.6. STAFF TRAINING AND COMMON PROBLEM SHOOTING GUIDELINES

If a man is hungry for many days and you provide them good tasty foods then it may be useless if he/she does not know what to do with the items provided to him, for example, a man never seen Apple may not eat assuming toxic chemicals inside that. Hence proper guidance needs to be provided about the things which are supplied to the customer, and it is the duty of the client to get proper training on the same.

Training to staffs and Common problem shooting guidelines

Once the system has been configured, installed and some retro conversion has been done, the library must ask the vendor to provide exhaustive training to staffs on each module. Practically each option as per library routine works should be demonstrated and how the reporting's etc. can be customized in case of requirements. Some common problem shooting guidelines and real problematic situations handling tools and techniques should be explained; it makes the library independent of vendor dependency and prompt service to the users without any hurdle. Once everything has been successfully done, and tested library may go for payment to the vendor with withholding some amount for at least six months to see the stability of the system installed and configured.

2.7. SAMPLE TENDER/QUOTATION DOCUMENT WITH SPECIFICATIONS

Library and information centers always face difficulty in designing of the proper specification and certain conditions keeping legal aspects and complexity of materials supplied. It is always advisable to consult various terms and conditions made by other similar institutes while implementing library automation. Specifications made in tender/quotation must be very clear and as per library present and future requirements. An example of detailed tender has been provided here with special reference to floating tender for academic library management software.

Sample Tender / Quotation with specifications for Koha ILMS and RFID

The Central Library, India invites Quotations/ Proposals for supply, testing, and installation of Library

Management Software and Radio frequency identification (RFID) Based Library System, (All the RFID components chosen for complete solution must conform to ISO 15693 / ISO18000-3) in accordance with equipment listed below:

Detailed Specifications of the Solution needed by Central Library of India

Item	***Quantity***
RFID Tags	20,000 Nos.
Staff Station	One
Electronic Article Surveillance Gates(2 EAS pedestals) complete in all respect with necessary accessories	One
RFID Software integrated with Library Application Software	One
Shelf Management System	One
Self Check-in Check-out Units	One
Book Drop	One
Library Management Software, Koha	One
Tagging/Bar-coding of RFID Tags on library publications	2,00,00 books
Migration of data from present system running on MySQL to the new system	2.00.00 Data

Technical Specifications of Library Management Software

S. No	***Requirement***	***Specifications***
		GENERAL REQUIREMENTS
1	**Library Software functions**	The Library software should support all the major library functions listed below: • Acquisition • Cataloguing • Authority control • Circulation • Web OPAC • Serials control • Import/export of records • Reporting • Systems management etc.

2.	**Standards**	Must be an open architecture system and should support various international standards. The system should also support the following Internet standards TCP/IP, SMTP, MIME, HTTP, SSL. Interactions with external systems need to support the following standards: • Record syntaxes: MARC21, UNIMARC, USMARC • ANSI/ISO Z39.50 (ISO 23950) on both server and client • NCIP and SIP2 for RFID Integration • ISO 2709
3.	**Multilingual Capability**	The System should be capable of maintaining multiple languages using UNICODE.
4.	**RFID Support**	The System should have support for NCIP and SIP2 protocol for RFID transactions.
5.	**Barcodes**	The system must be able to handle barcodes in different formats like EAN-13, SICI/SISAC, Codabar.

GENERAL HARDWARE REQUIREMENTS

1.	**Hardware Platform**	The Server should run on UNIX/LINUX/ Windows Platforms
2.	**Backup and recovery**	Hot Backup should be possible, I e. It should be possible to do backup with the system in full operation
3.	**Security**	Verification of users should be done in a secure manner, and it should be possible to set different security setting for users.
4.	**Support**	Problem reports must be logged on the The vendor database. And a live update of the support has to be provided.

APPLICATION SOFTWARE

1.	**Architecture**	The system must be Web-based. The application should not require any proprietary software licenses.
2.	**Database**	The backend database must be robust using Microsoft SQL/Oracle/MySQL/PostgreSQL
3.	**Client Software**	The client operations must be web-based (platform independent).
4.	**Librarian interface**	Librarian interface (client software) must be web-based. The librarian Interface should allow searching Z39.50 servers.

5.	User Interface	The main OPAC interface for the users outside the library must be a web browser, such as Internet Explorer and Firefox.
6.	**Import & Export of Data**	The system must support the import and export of records in MARC21 and other standard formats.
7.	**Reports & Statistics**	Library system must support exhaustive management statistics and reporting functions allowing the library to be able to create their own reports.
		OPAC ACCESS
1.	**OPAC access Links**	It must be possible to allow access to Web-based services both from within the staff client as well as from the Web OPAC.
2.	**OPAC searches**	There must be provisions for different search levels (e.g., simple and advanced) in the OPAC, language filtering, item types, etc.
3.	**Indexing**	All indexes and record displays must be updated in real-time. All fields and sub-fields should be available to be keyword and/or string indexed with flexibility in defining indexes.
4.	**Searchable data**	It should be possible to: • Search a record as a whole (any field) • Specify any variable field to be searched • Boolean search Searching should be possible by, including but not limited to: • Author • Title • Subject • Publisher • Call number • Standard number (e.g., ISBN, ISSN, etc.) • Barcode number • Year Search refinement should be possible by: • Author • Series • Topics • Item type • Location/ branches

		• Place of publication • Availability
5.	**WEB OPAC Customization**	The Web OPAC should support templates so that it can be customized by the library.
		CIRCULATION SYSTEM
6.	**Circulation System**	The following functions must be included in the circulation system: • check-out (charges) • renewals • check-in (discharges) • reservations • fines and fees • statistics and reports
7.	**Patron Record**	The patron record should be in a MARC-like format & The patron record must include fields for the following information: • Name • Member card number • Patron category • Telephone numbers • E-mail address • Alternate contact person • Date of joining • Date of expiry • Notes
8.	**Barcode and patron card Generator**	The system must include a utility can be used to print barcode labels for the library items and patron cards.
		CATALOGUING
1.	**Import of bibliographical records**	The system must be able to import records in the USMARC/MARC21 formats, online through a Z39.50 client which is integrated with the cataloguing (and acquisition) module. The system should have a reservoir for managing imported MARC records so that it can be checked before loading into the database.
2.	**Authority Control**	It must be possible to create and maintain authority control for the following search elements: • personal and corporate names

- conferences
- uniform titles
- series titles
- subjects
- name/title combinations
- publishers

3.	**Data entry**	The system must have full-screen data entry and editing ("empty screen" with MARC header) for cataloguing as well as a number of predefined data entry screens (templates). It must support hidden fields which can be seen in MARC editor but not in the OPAC.
4.	**Output**	It must be possible to export the bibliographic records in standard MARC communications format (ISO2709).

ACQUISITIONS

1.	**Order Initiation**	For titles indented • Check for duplication of titles from 'on order', received and Web OPAC • All data entered at acquisition section be used throughout system • Option to download bibliographic data via z39.50, International databases or vendor supplied electronic catalogues.
2.	**Approval**	• Flexibility in including specific titles in an approval list • Amendments in approval list prior to its printing • Budget and expenditure analysis • Formula based Budget allocation among different units
3.	**Placing Orders**	Firm orders for titles, including for materials received. • Purchase orders printing/ (e)mailing • Title / publisher/ vendor wise order generation • Amendment/ cancellation of order • Incorporation of special delivery statements/ conditions • Standing orders for annual publications • Proposal for prepaid orders

4.	**Receipt of Order**	Procedure to record/ editing the details of items received.
5.	**Invoice Processing**	Includes accessioning of items. • Permits more than one invoice for an order • Allows changes in units' price, variable discount, exchange rate, etc. • Maintains exchange rates of various user defined currencies • Accession number can either be generated automatically by the system, or it can be a user-defined number • Keep up to date order status with relation to titles ordered, received, accessioned. • Updated funds account online
6.	**Order Follow Up**	• Periodic overdue notices/ reminders • Online printing of follow-up notices
7.	**Online Queries**	Acquisition related queries include- • Titles in the process of acquisition • Pending orders, overdue orders and, for the specific order, details of titles ordered, title received, pending titles, its invoices. • List of invoices with the library and invoices with the accounts section and, for a specific invoice, details of items accessioned against it and payment details, if any. • List of vendors, giving titles received 'on approval', pending titles against firm orders, orders placed, invoices received. • Budget analysis of titles in the acquisition process • Order details by accession number/ supply order number
8.	**Reports**	System should be robust enough to generate following requests- • Approval requests form • Purchase order • Overdue/ Follow-up Notice • Budget and expenditure analysis (periodic) • Payment requisition report

- Payments cheque delivery notices
- List of titles on order
- Accession register
- Bill register
- List of recent arrivals, etc.

PERIODICALS

1. **Subscription** New serials initiated, go through the approval process and ordering.
   - Duplicate checking.
   - Prints approval lists Updating of 'Approved' or 'Rejected' titles.
   - Prints Purchase Orders for single or package subscription.
   - Status mandatory
   - Print purchase order by department/ publisher/ vendor wise.
   - Print order for single and package subscription.

2. **Subscription Renewal**
   - Renewal Order Printing either by Department / publisher/ vendor /Centre or Library, based on subscription expiry date.
   - Separate orders for renewals and additional serials.
   - Cancel supply order of single or all titles from particular order.

3. **Subscription Extension** Resulting from claims on missing issues and numbers.
   - Extension specified as a) period extended up to, or b) number of issues not received, or c) last volume/issue number.

4. **Invoice Processing** Both for new subscription and subscription renewal.
   - Allows more than one invoice for an order.
   - Allows changes in subscription, period, volumes, issue nos., frequencies, etc.
   - Accepts supplementary invoices for any title.
   - Accepts and updates subscriptions details.

5. **Receiving Issues**
   - Well designed screens requiring entry of minimum possible data

		• Recording of issues by volume/issue number or date and barcode. • Facility to record receipt of regular issues, various indexes, special issues and additional issues.
6.	**Claims Monitoring**	Makes possible timely follow-up of 'not received', (missing issues and supply not started) overdue and damaged journal numbers. • Provision of claims for each title of package or bundle subscription.
7.	**Binding Control**	Provisions for combining of many loose issues and assigning a single accession number to it.
8.	**Routing and Circulation**	User-defined routing of issues registered, along with circulation of bound volumes and loose issues. • Routing of an issue immediately on arrival may be defined, before it is displayed or circulated. • Integrated with the circulation module • Overdue reminders
9.	**Cataloguing**	Provision of catalogue generation for current journals and serials holdings according to MARC21, CCF, AACRII.
10.	**Online Queries**	Serials-related queries are: • Titles in bindery • Recent arrivals
11.	**Reports**	Reports generated by the Serial System include: • Order form • List of completed volumes • Bindery order • Accession register (for bound volume collection) • Current arrivals • Classified and specialized indexes and lists of serials, as required. • Budget & Expenditure analysis • Missing issues list • List of duplicate issues • Notices for 'not received', 'overdue',

'soiled/damaged' issues

- Subscription renewal order
- New subscription order
- Claim letters for missing and non-supply.
- List of current subscription- Alphabetical, Department wise, Publisher wise, vendor wise.
- List of new titles added and deleted titles for particular year.

Other General Specification

1. Support unlimited data
2. LAN & WAN enabled client/ web server interface.
3. Multi-user, user-friendly and multilingual
4. ANSI Z39.50 Compliant
5. Import present data from MySQL to proposed library software
6. Full data transfer from present software including Indian language data.
7. Extraction of record in any MARC-21 format.
8. Imports/Export facility in ISO/2709/MARC21 format
9. Acquisition module with facility to show book/ journals (either purchase/ complimentary/ exchange)
10. Circulation module with facility to scan member photo on membership card and online reservation, with features to check the status and history of each member online.
11. Serial Control with Selective Dissemination of Information (SDI) and Current Awareness Service (CAS) with back volume maintenance
12. Union Catalogue with multiple access points.
13. Multi-tasking with online help facility
14. Provision for customization of reports.

15. Financial management with different budget heads.
16. Security of Access control as per categorization.
17. Articles indexing and scanning of articles
18. Should support image and multimedia files
19. Automatic currency conversion
20. Duplicate record check
21. Binding record management
22. RSS feed
23. Hyper linking of books
24. Status of user's account from OPAC
25. Metadata (MARC21/Dublin Core)
26. E-resource management
27. Use of preferred RDBMS such as Oracle/SQL Server/ MySQL / Postgress SQL for databases and should be open, not locked to generate further any required report.
28. Centralized acquisition from Central Library for departmental libraries.
29. Report on order/ budget status department wise.
30. XML-based interface for reports.
31. Windows TM based, client server application
32. Unicode TM standard
33. Flexibility to move from one language to another in all subsystems.
34. Multiple search options available in OPAC
35. Multimedia access
36. Backup/ Restore/recovery of complete database.
37. Comprehensive set of parameters to customize the software to meet the library's operational environment.
38. Completely web/ browser based (works on internet/ intranet)

39. Supports windows / Windows NT/ Linux/ Unix
40. Fingerprint devise integration

RFID Device Specifications

The Proposed system must be compatible with the Library Management Software system using SIP 2 and NCIP protocol. No deviation is accepted.

a. *RFID TAGS*

Item	***Specifications***
	Passive Re-writable RFID Tags consisting of a Microchip and antenna, a low acid or good quality self-adhesive RFID Tags having 1024 bits memory; Built-in antitheft control bit with lifetime guarantee.
Dimensions	Books-RFID Tag size 50x50 mm (App.)
Chip Memory	e"1024 bits/ optional 2048
Frequency	13.56 MHz
Standard	Fully compliant with ISO 18000-3 Mode 1 and include both mandatory and optional Commands specified in ISO 15693-3.
Data Rate	Tag to Reader: 26kbps minimum, Reader to Tag: 26 kbps minimum.
Type	Read/Write, Lockable.
Distance for detection	As per ISO18000-3
Operation Mode	Passive
Other features	A single tag for Identification and Anti-theft must be read even if not visible and must be read in any orientation; tamper proof.

b. *Staff station*

Item	***Specifications***
Staff station	Hardware: RFID Reader + Pad Antenna
RFID Reader	Frequency : 13.56 MHz
	Standard : ISO 15693/ 18000-3 compliant
	Weight : Light weight
	Power Supply : 240v±10%/50Hz./rechargeable battery Communication Interface : RS232/ RS485/USB

Pad Antenna	Read/Write Performance: 10" or more Software-: Client software to perform function like tagging; checkout; Check-in; Renewal; label monitoring; sorting, etc.

c. *EAS Gates (with two EAS pedestals)*

Item	***Specifications***
Hardware	Two pedestals (single corridor)
Frequency	13.56 MHz
Chip Compatibility	ISO 15693 or 18000-3
Gate Synchronization	RF protocol
Alarms	Lights and Buzzer located at the top of Pedestal.
People Counter	Should count in and out traffic/bottom Embedded.
Range	Minimum 36" on either side
EAS System	Digital Signal Processor
Pedestal Spacing	36" between pedestals
Power Supply	240v±10%/ 50Hzs

d. *RFID Device Client Software*

Item	***Specifications***
The Software should be able to perform the following necessary actions	• Tagging, Retagging and un-tagging of the books. • Check out, check in, and renewal of multiple books/CD's/loose Issues/journals. • Monitoring information on tag. • Locating a book • Stock Verification.
The software should be able to generate tagging, check out, check in, renewal stock verification reports, etc.	
Software should provide functional security as per user defined	
The System should also have the following provisions	• Periodical Stock checking -The system should be able to run inventory scans at specified time and the ability to generate reports on schedule after every scan. • Access :- One Administrator level access should

	be given, Librarian level access to update the required information in the system for Issue / Receipt / Renewal of Books, etc. and Users level access as required for reports and queries, etc. • The software shall be compatible with Windows and Linux. • The software should have inbuilt keyboard functionality.
Job work	Tagging of Books to be quoted separately

e. *Shelf Management Reader:*

Item	***Specifications***
Shelf management	Hardware: Handheld RFID Reader + Antenna
Frequency	13.56 MHz
Chip Compliance	ISO 15693
Maximum Input Power	1W
Tag Reading Speed	15 books/sec minimum
Memory Card	256-MB or more
Software	Client software (Interface) to perform Function like tagging; Check-out; Check-in; Renewal; label monitoring; sorting, searching, etc

f. *Self Check-In/Check-out Station:*

Item	***Specifications***
Self-check-in/check-out station	Hardware : RFID Reader + Antenna + Kiosk Enclosure
RFID Reader + Antenna	13.56 MHz, ISO 15693/ 18000-3 Compliant.
Touch Screen	20" or Higher Touch Screen TFT Flat Panel. High resolution display.
Printer	High Speed Thermal Slip Printer
Software	Client software to perform function like tagging; checkout; check-in; Renewal; monitoring; sorting etc.

g. *Book Drop:*

Item	***Specifications***
Book drop	Hardware: RFID Reader + Antenna Book Drop Enclosure Receiving Cart Slip Printer

RFID reader	13.56 MHz, ISO 15693/ 18000-3 compliant.
Book Drop	Wood/ Plastic
Receiving Cart	Lightweight
Printer	High Speed Thermal Slip Printer

Prices should be quoted in tabular form only

S. No	Item Description	Counter of Origin	Quantity & Unit	Unit Price	Optional Unit Price	Total Price
1.	RFID Tags		25000			
2.	Staff Station with client device software					
3.	EAS Gates One Nos., (2 Pedestals) including all the accessories					
4.	RFID s/w Integration with Library Software					
5.	Shelf Management System-One					
6.	Self Check-in/Check-out Unit- One					
7.	Book Drop Station-One					
8.	Library Management Software					
9.	Job Work (Fixing Tags, Registering & Accn. No. on Tags)					
10.	Installation & Commissioning and Migration of data from present system (MS access) to new system					
11.	Any Other Item					

Terms and conditions

a. Payment will be given 25% on receipt of order/items, and 25% will be given after satisfactory installation and testing. Rest amount will be released after Six months of all customizations and stability of system provided.

b. Vendor will share and educate on all the customized feature codes of if Koha, ILMS.

c. The middleware must be compatible with existing and any other original equipment manufacturer RFID devices at present or in future.

d. The customized code of open source software (OSS) like Koha features shall be share to the community as patch so that any Koha users can use it around the world.

e. Vender will support the integration of other OEM RFID devices if needed in future.

f. Vender must educate and share the OSS like Koha customized codes to our library/institute staffs.

g. OSS like Koha is open source software hence no additional codes etc. should be inserted without the knowledge of library staffs, and each code/ configurations should be open in such a way that anybody can understand and do modifications without any restrictions.

h. The vendor must quote the prices only for those features which they will customized and not available on OSS like Koha community forums or provided by Koha developers.

REFERENCES

1. Automation. (n.d.). Retrieved January 15, 2016, from https://en.wikipedia.org/wiki/Automation

2. *https://controls.engin.umich.edu/wiki/index.php/Feedback_control* (accessed on 15/01/2016)

3. Lam, K. T. (n.d.). Issues in Library Automation. Retrieved January 16, 2016, from http://ihome.ust.hk/~lblkt/diploma/libauto/libauto.html

4. Library automation and networking in dental college libraries. (n.d.). Retrieved January 15, 2016, from http://shodhganga.inflibnet.ac.in/bitstream/10603/5661/9/09_chapter 4.pdf

5. UNESCO. (n.d.). Introduction to Library Automation. Retrieved January 15, 2016, from http://www2.unescobkk.org/elib/publications/ICTEIP/MODULE2/EIPICT_MOD2_ppt/EIPICT_MOD2_L1.pdf

3
Application of RFID Technology in Libraries

INTRODUCTION TO RFID

Radio frequency identification (RFID) is the latest technology which is now used by the library for automation of the housekeeping operations. Unlike EM (Electro-Mechanical) and RF (Radio Frequency) systems, which have been used in libraries for decades, RFID-based systems move beyond security to become tracking systems that combine security with more efficient tracking of materials throughout the library, including easier and faster charge and discharge, inventorying, and materials handling, It is combination of microchip and radio frequency technologies. The information which is contained / entered in the chips is detected by the radio frequency waves for further processing of carried data.

RFID technology is in use since the 1970s. RFID tags can be active, semi-passive and passive. It is a small device available in many sizes with varying data storage capability. Passive tags don't have internal batteries. RFID reader is a device that can receive and transmit a radio signal. It is built to encode data stored in the tag's microprocessor. Because of the higher cost, active and semi-passive RFID tags are used for valuable asset tracking. The passive RFID tags are used in RFID library management systems

Usage of RFID in libraries

There are many areas/housekeeping operations where RFID technology is used in the libraries which are described below:

Book charging/discharging : This is one of the most used application of RFID in libraries, it provide very fast and accurate transaction of library items, and main advantage is at a time more than one item can be issued/ returned.

Book Drop : This is a drop box where user can just drop their items, and book will be returned with return slips, it can be placed outside the libraries at various remote locations so that users can have opportunity to return the books at any time irrespective of holidays.

Self-issue/return KIOSK : The concept of KIOSK is almost similar to Automatic tailoring machine (ATM) where bank client can withdraw and deposit the amount at any time. However this device is placed inside the library only so that patrons can themselves issue and return the items without the interference of the library staffs, it helps in reducing manpower of the library.

Shelve reader : This device is used for inventory control/stock verification and locating the missing items in the library.

Security (EAS) gate : Electronic article surveillance (EAS) gate is used for security purpose, if a library member attempted to take out the books outside the library without proper issue from the RFID system this gate alarm the library personnel's about possibility of theft. Now a day's these gates also help in counting the total visitors to the library.

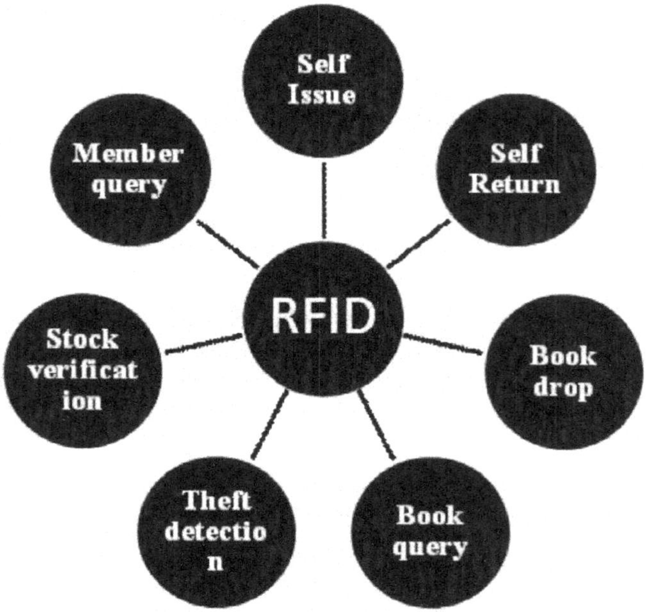

Fig. 3.1. Some application of RFID in libraries

Hardware Components of RFID devices

RFID tags/ transponder : There are three types of tags available in the market namely Low frequency (LF) which covers frequency from 30 KHz to 300 KHz and provide very short read range of approximately 10 cm, High frequency (HF) tags are those tags which work in between 3 to 30 MHz frequencies but most of the HF tags work in 13.56 MHz and it is applicable for libraries. HF RFID is commonly used in ticketing, libraries, payment, and data transfer applications. There are several HF RFID standards in places, such as the ISO 15693 standard and the ECMA-340 and ISO/IEC 18092 standards for Near Field Communication (NFC), a short-range technology that is commonly used for data exchange between devices. Other HF standards include the ISO/ IEC 14443 A and ISO/IEC 14443 standards for MIFARE technology, which used in smart cards and proximity cards, and the JIS X 6319-4 for FeliCa, which is a smart card system commonly used in electronic money cards. Ultra high frequency (UHF) tags cover the 300 MHz to 3 GHz, UHF Gen2 RFID systems in most countries operate between 900 and 915 MHz. The read range of passive UHF systems can be as long as 12 m, and UHF RFID has a faster data transfer rate than LF or HF. UHF RFID is the most sensitive to interference, but many UHF product manufacturers have found ways of designing tags, antennas, and readers to keep performance high even in difficult environments. Passive UHF tags are easier and cheaper to manufacture than LF and HF tags.

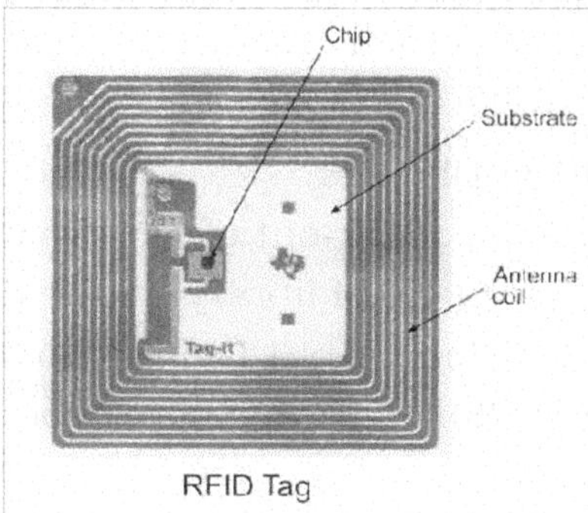

Fig. 3.2 Components of library RFID tag

Readers or Sensors to query the tags : Reader is the main device which detects the signals as soon as it appears in its radio range and decodes the signals for further processing. Hence, reader interrogates the tags and detects the data contained inside the chips and sends it to the system for processing.

Antenna : a device which emits the frequency and connected with the reader as soon as any tag is detected within the range of antenna is charge the tag (passive tag) and get the data to be sent back to attached reader. This is also used as staff station for tagging, retagging of library materials and circulation of books with staff interference.

RFID Label Printer : This is nothing but generally high-speed thermal printer which is used to generate the slips.

Handheld Reader : Device with varying size and models which detect the tags on the shelves and stores the data, it helps in locating and stock verification of library collections.

Self Check Unit : ATM-like device with monitor and printer connected with it an antenna and reader attached with it helps in self-issue/return of books.

Book Drop : a box-like structure with monitor, printer, reader and antenna inside that through which users can just drop their item and it will be returning from their accounts.

Benefits of RFID in Libraries

- Fast check-in/check-out of Library materials
- Increased security of library materials
- Self-check-in/check-out facility to patrons
- Long life of RFID tags in comparison to Bar-code
- Fast stock verification
- Save lot of time and man power to the library
- Ability to locate/search the misplaced books in the library
- Enhance reputation of the library and its services

Drawback of RFID in Libraries

- RFID system implementation may be high-cost affair for small libraries
- Security may be cracked by placing aluminum foil, magnet and wrong alignment of two tags in books.
- Maintenance of RFID devices is very sophisticated and costly
- RFID devices need some basic infrastructure for more effectiveness like wooden rack/shelves, proper

electric wiring beyond RFID devices, etc.

- Proper ventilation and moisture need to be maintained in the libraries
- Due to lack of standard in RFID system changing the RFID vendor is very difficult

REFERENCES

1. Bose, R. W. (n.d.). RFID Technology for Libraries. Retrieved March 01, 2016, from http://www.ala.org/PrinterTemplate.cfm?Section=technotes&Template=/ContentManagement/HTMLDisplay.cfm&ContentID=68138
2. Pandey, P., & Mahajan, K. D. (n.d.). Application of RFID Te chnology in Libraries and Role o f Librarian. Retrieved February 06, 2016, from http://eprints.rclis.org/15253/3/RFID.pdf
3. Shahid, S. M. (n.d.). Use of RFID Technology in Libraries: A New Approach to Circulation, Tracking, Inventorying, and Security of Library Materials. Retrieved February 06, 2016, from http://unllib.unl.edu/LPP/shahid.htm
4. State Library of NSW. (n.d.). A business case framework for RFID in NSW public libraries. Retrieved February 12, 2016, from http://www.sl.nsw.gov.au/sites/default/files/rfid_cost_benefit.pdf

4

Software for Library Automation

The automation processes is having its own advantages and disadvantages which has been discussed and explained in previous chapters. When we talk about the automation, some software and hardware cames in our mind out of which software is the major component in entire automation system development because it is the tool which instructs the various associated hardware for execution of the desired work. The mechanization of all the manual works started with the advent of the computer and related technologies since after year 1960s. History of library automation also goes long back, and it also took many decades to come into the present shape. There are various tools and technology of automation solutions exists now a day's which need to be utilized and properly exploited as discussed in next sections.

4.1. HISTORY OF LIBRARY AUTOMATION

Before computerization of library housekeeping operations, all the works were performed manually like sending orders by post on paper, invoicing, making of library catalogue cards with all the bibliographic details of the books, circulation with various methods like Browne charging system, three card systems, a collection of library fines with local bills, etc. Now the entire seen has been changed and all the processes have been integrated with the help of automation systems in such a way that duplicate works has been completely removed, and the work done by others can be accessed in another module of ILMS for further processing, users need not to visit the library for checking transaction details etc. due to online web OPAC. The entire automation or computerization of libraries can be categorized in following groups:

The 1960s: The Influence of Computer Technologies

Coincidently MARC was invented along with the computer and various groups started sharing their MARC catalogue among libraries to reduce the duplicate works and prompt user services.

1970s–1980s: the early integrated library system

During this decades lot of improvements took place in computer system specially the storage and other techniques due to which Integrated library system has been developed for automated circulation and reminders, acquisitions and other housekeeping operations.

1990s–2000s: the growth of the Internet

Internet era came into existence, and people from remote places started communicating with their clients, similarly in libraries web OPAC services have been started, and many online service facilities came into force during these decades.

The mid-2000s–Present: increasing costs and customer dissatisfaction

A huge number of vendors and ILMS came into the market for the supply of library hardware and software which includes open source solutions to propriety solutions. Costing on the implementation of automation systems increased due to many features involved in ILMS as per users demand and interest of the libraries. Many libraries were unable to afford these technologies because of prices and complexity involve in their managements as well. Almost every large sized library have implemented the automatic process with the help of software solutions which may be partial implementations, this can be specially seen in developing county libraries.

2010s–Present: the rise of cloud-based solutions

The use of cloud-based library management systems has increased drastically since the rise of "cloud" technology started. Some common management systems include Insignia, Libramatic, OCLC WorldShare, Alma, Aura Software and Librarika. Many modern cloud-based solutions allow automated cataloging by scanning a book's ISBN. This technology was pioneered by Libramatic, although it is currently in use by systems such as Librarika and Insignia. Many libraries started to take cloud services for installation of ILMS remotely like Amazon services this is to decrease the cost of hardware and its maintenance.

4.2. CRITERIA FOR SELECTING LIBRARY SOFTWARE

Now a days we have seen many ILMS exist in the market propriety to open source solutions for automation of the libraries, local to national and national to international solutions available today. Libraries have to survey and see the demonstration of products as per their library requirements. Some of the criteria's we must consider before selection of any ILMS are:

- Open source or propriety solution is now the first option to consider
- National or International developer
- Supports after sale
- Hardware support and dependency

- Operating system (Linux/Windows) and other associated software
- Relational database management system like MySQL, Oracle, etc.
- Programming language on which source code is written
- Costing and maintenance charges
- Training and documentation available
- Security and stability
- Modules available and Up gradation
- Modern features like web2.0
- RFID integrations
- Data handling capacity and vendor locking

Apart from above, there are many other criteria which must be considered before selection of software like, some clients, terms and conditions of the vendor, experience of vender in the automation field, etc.

4.3. POPULAR LIBRARY MANAGEMENT SOFTWARE

Computer technology in the age of Google is increasing with much pace and competition hence, the skilled peoples are developing the information products to beat the market for high gain, so they are coming with modern effective solutions in Library automation system developments. In comparison to the software in 1970 to 2000 now seen has been completely changed from most popular old software CDS/ISIS to latest Koha, Chameleon, etc. Some of the most popular software's are listed below:

Table 4.1. Popular software's

Software Name	***Developer***	***Brief description***
Koha	Open source software	Handling all type of libraries word wide popular, International standards, most popular OSS.

Newgenlib	Open Source Software	Basically for academic libraries
Evergreen	Open source software	An open source enterprise-class library automation system that helps libraries manage, catalog, and circulate materials.
Alice for windows	Alice	Windows based software for medium size libraries.
Librarian	CR2 Technologies Limited	It is a next generation library management system designed for small to large libraries. Library manager software uses established thoughtfully created design and development principles. Digital library software showcases library's individual strengths while freeing staff from routine functions.
Liberty	Softlink America	A web-based library and information management automation system available on our servers or yours.
Libsys7	Libsys corporation	A modular web-based library automation system with the acquisition, cataloging, circulation, indexing and other modules.
Millennium	Innovative Interfaces	Millennium is the Web- and Java-based automated library system that integrates future-forward technologies.
SirsiDynix Symphony	SirsiDynix	Integrated library management systems for total management of library operations.
SOUL	Inflibnet	Specially developed for University Libraries
Cyberlibrary	Open Source solution	Open Source Library Management System having all the modules
Virtua	VTLS	One of the most popular propriety solution for all size libraries
Alexandria	COMPanion	Alexandria library software efficiently manages libraries and gives your patrons the

		ability to search your catalog from anywhere
Mandarin	Mandarin Library Automation	It helps single libraries, libraries with multiple sites and school districts save time with one-point installation, maintenance, and updates.
Winisis	Unesco	Software for customized data entry and retrieval.
Ex Libris Alma	ProQuest Group	Ex Libris Alma supports the entire suite of library operations—selection, acquisition, metadata management, digitization, and fulfillment—for the full spectrum of library materials, regardless of format or location.
ABCD	Unesco	Based on CDS/ISIS to develop ILMS

4.4. OPEN SOURCE VS. PROPRIETY SOFTWARE

The internet brought people close to each other and social networking created greater opportunity for collaborative works among the people living at any corner of the globe. Due to the advancement of such technology open source software's are now very popular among the community, and now it is replacing many propriety solutions including Windows operating system to Linux based system like Ubuntu, Debian, Fedora, etc. Many libraries are replacing propriety solutions because of its limitations and high cost, some of the difference between both are tabulated below:

Table 4.2. Open source vs. propriety software

Open source solutions	*Propriety Solution*
Source code is open to all	Source code is only available with vendor
Available under General public license	Licensing policy is commercial
Free support by community	Support on payment basis
Use open standards	Standards are confined to vendors knowledge

No locking of data and limitations	Data locking and lot of limitations restricted on payment basis
Fewer bugs and faster fix	Bug may be more and time for fixing is much
Frequent updates and free of cost	Updates are mainly on demand and charge basis.
Maintained by huge number of community	Limited to few company staffs
Build as per common library requirements but can be customized	Customized as per client requirements
More security since its tested word wide	Security is less
Stability and scalability are very high	Stability and scalability are less
No guarantee of timely community support	Vendor is bound to support due to agreement
Innovation and the new feature are more due to the participation of various types of professionals.	Innovation and features are restricted to clients requirements
Redistribution and modifications	Can't distribute and modify

In recent years, numerous open source software have emerged as viable alternatives to costly proprietary and commercial products. Open source software s are gaining popularity. However, both types of solutions have advantages & disadvantages depending upon the application features they provide. Propriety has a long lasting stand in the computing era. Open source is fast gaining acceptability and is the future of e-learning. Many world class institutes have adopted Open source especially in libraries like DSpace, Eprint, Koha, Newgenlib, Joomla, Drupal, etc. for digitization, automation and content management in libraries.

REFERENCES

1. Anandraj. L. (n.d.). Historical development of library automation. Retrieved January 17, 2016, from http://www.slideshare.net/anujessy/library-automation-history-anandrajl

2. Best Library Management Software. (n.d.). Retrieved February 19, 2016, from http://www.softwaresuggest.com/library-management-software
3. Comparison of open-source and closed-source software. (n.d.). Retrieved February 23, 2016, from https://en.wikipedia.org/wiki/Comparison_of_open-source_and_closed-source_software
4. Criteria for evaluation of library software packages. (n.d.). Retrieved February 17, 2016, from http://liswiki.org/wiki/Criteria_for_evaluation_of_library_software_packages
5. Criteria for Selection and Evaluation of Library Software Packages. (n.d.). Retrieved January 17, 2016, from http://www.netugc.com/criteria-for-selection-and-evaluation-of-library-software-packages
6. GreeNET. (n.d.). Open Source vs. Proprietary Software. Retrieved February 22, 2016, from http://www.gn.apc.org/support/open-source-vs-proprietary-software
7. Husain, S., & Ansari, M. A. (n.d.). Library automation software packages in India: A study of the cataloguing modules of Alice for W indows, Libsys and V virtual. *Annals of Library and Information Studies, 54*, 146-151. Retrieved February 20, 2016, from http://egranthalaya.nic.in/ALIS.pdf
8. Integrated library system. (n.d.). Retrieved January 17, 2016, from https://en.wikipedia.org/wiki/Integrated_library_system
9. Jackson, J. (n.d.). Open Source vs. Proprietary Software. Retrieved February 22, 2016, from http://www.pcworld.com/article/243136/open_source_vs_proprietary_software.html
10. Malwad, N. M. (1995). Selection Criteria for Library Automation Software. *DESIDOC Bulletin of Information Technology, 15*(2), 17-26. Retrieved from http://publications.drdo.gov.in/ojs/index.php/djlit/article/viewFile/3179/1699
11. Optimus information. (n.d.). Open-Source vs. Proprietary Software Pros and Cons. Retrieved February 22, 2016, from http://www.optimusinfo.com/downloads/white-paper/open-source-vs-proprietary-software-pros-and-cons.pdf
12. Pankaja, N., & PK, M. R. (2013). Proprietary Software versus

Open Source Software for E ducation. *American Journal of Engineering Research (AJER), 02*(07), 124-130. Retrieved February 24, 2016, from http://www.ajer.org/papers/v2(7)/O027124130.pdf

13. Patil, S. K. (n.d.). Criteria for evaluating a Library house-keeping software. Retrieved February 17, 2016, from http://www.slideshare.net/libsoul/criteria-for-evaluating-a-library-housekeeping-software

14. Top Library Automation Software Products. (n.d.). Retrieved February 17, 2016, from http://www.capterra.com/library-automation-software/

5

Basics of Koha Library Management Software

Koha a beautiful name comes from a local language of New Zealand Maori which means for a gift or donation. It is the world most popular integrated library management system developed initially by Katipo communication for the Horowhenua Library Trust in New Zealand, and the first installation went live in January 2000. Koha is a fully featured, scalable library management system. Development is sponsored by libraries of varying types and sizes, volunteers, and support companies worldwide. Koha is very active open source project. According to ohloh, it has a very large, active development team and a mature, well-established codebase.

Koha is a true enterprise-class ILS with comprehensive functionality including basic and advance options. Koha includes modules for circulation, cataloging, authority control, acquisitions, serials, reserves, lists, patron management, branch relationships, and more. Koha uses a Relational database management system (RDBMS) coupled with an external search engine to provide powerful searching that is truly scalable library standards compliant. It is built using library standards and protocols that ensure interoperability between Koha and other systems and technologies while supporting existing workflows and tools. Web-based Interfaces, Koha OPAC, circulation management and self-checkout interfaces are all based on standards-compliant World Wide Web technologies–XHTML, CSS and Javascript–making Koha a truly platform-independent solution. Koha is distributed under the Free Software General Public License (GPL) version 3 or later. Some of the major features of Koha ILMS are as follows:

- Supports International Standards & Protocol such as MARC 21, z39.50, etc.
- Supports Import/Export data compatible with MARC
- Multilingual & Strong Web OPAC
- Comprehensive advance search
- Flexibility to customize online public access catalogue according to your library needs
- OPAC can be used as Content Management System
- Printing functions for barcode labels, patron cards and reports
- Virtual Book Shelf & Course Reserve
- Supports copy cataloguing
- Provision to have branch libraries and Items transfers
- Budget & Fund Management
- Customizable Data Entry Sheet (In different framework) & supports import/export MARC framework
- No platform dependency. It can run on Linux, Windows, etc.
- It uses MySQL as backend RDBMS and Apache Web server (Open Source Software)

- Support Multiple Instances (One can create more than one library with different database)

Koha is developed by the community support that spread all over the world; many new ideas are shared on the various Koha forums and Bugzilla (a platform where all new features are requested, and any bug available in the current or old versions is reported. Various venders and libraries when work together than many new features come up, highly experiences team of Koha developers work on each feature and test it well before the release of new features and versions. Some of the major advantages of Koha, ILMS are:

Ability to modify to fit local needs : Since its source code is available it can be customized to suit local needs.

No restriction on use : No vendors restrictions on how the software is used.

Cost : There is no charge for the software itself. But some commercial firms charge the nominal fee for training, customizations, implementation, etc.

Free Exchange of Technology : All Koha users can share the customized codes for mutual benefits.

Stable Technologies : Koha is tested and has demonstrated both stability and scalability, used in thousands of libraries worldwide.

Sharing Technologies : The libraries involve in using Koha share their expertise regarding technical man power and development of solutions fits many libraries.

Support : Koha source code is open which is developed and supported by many libraries so it can be modified as and when to require. Therefore, its development does not depend on the single vendor as in the case of proprietary ILMS.

Upgradation : Koha is frequently upgraded with latest technologies and provide better solutions in comparison to commercial software.

Apart from many advantages author's experiences does not found any serious disadvantage in the implementation of Koha in comparison to other OSS or propriety solution. Hence, as such there is no any disadvantage but how to get maximum benefit from the Koha software depends upon the devotion and availability of technical manpower in libraries as well as commercial service providers in Koha. As far as users of Koha is concern they are spread all over the globe, and many libraries have implemented it successfully like public, special, academic, etc. Apart from these many institutions, many governments like Kerala state in India has made it mandatory and declare it as official software related to library management. Some of the important are shown in the below table:

Table 5.1. Some libraries adopted Koha for Automation

Name	**Type**	**Website**
Antioch University	Academic	*http://library.afognak.org/*
IIM Ahmedabad	Academic	*http://vslopac.iimahd.ernet.in/*
Childcare Resource and Research Unit – University of Toronto	Academic	*http://circonline.ca*
Delhi Public Library	Public	*http://delhipubliclibrary.in/*
National Institute of Technology Rourkela	Academic	*http://opac.nitrkl.ac.in/*
Horowhenua Library Trust	Public	*http://www.library.org.nz/*
List of other Library Users	All type of Libraries	*http://wiki.koha-community.org/wiki/Koha_Users_Worldwide*
NIT Rourkela	Academic library	*http://opac.nitrkl.ac.in/*
MGAHV, India	Academic Library	*http://www.hindivishwa.org/contentdtl.aspx?category=13&cgid=34*

There are so many commercial software's available in the market today, but Koha almost has all features and capability to handle various types and size of libraries as compared to propriety solutions. Koha provides all state of the are features in latest versions and developing others in the short span of time in next releases. Some of the features compared with other ILMS are indicated in below table:

Table 5.2. Comparison of Koha with other software

S. No	***Modules***	***VTLS***	***New Genlib***	***Soul***	***Libsys***	***Koha***
1.	System setup and configurations	Yes	Yes	Yes	Yes	Yes
2.	Acquisition Management	Yes	Yes	Yes	Yes	Yes
3.	Cataloguing	Yes	Yes	Yes	Yes	Yes
4.	Circulation Management	Yes	Yes	Yes	Yes	Yes
5.	Serial Management	Yes	Yes	Yes	Yes	Yes
6.	Web OPAC	Yes	Yes	Yes	Yes	Yes
7.	Data Import/ Export/ bar-code	Yes	Yes	Yes	Yes	Yes
8.	Standards like MARC21/z39.5	Yes	Yes	Yes	Yes	Yes
9.	Reporting and budgeting	Yes	Yes	Yes	Yes	Yes

5.1. BASIC MODULES OF KOHA AND ITS FEATURES

As discussed earlier Koha has many features which will be described in coming sections in detail with a lot of examples. Koha provides all modules which are very well integrated with each others in such a way that duplicate work and the relationship between them is well established. Library and Users feel very comfortable in using and exploring its features. Graphical user interface and staff interface are friendly and functioning smooth, Bootstrap feature of Koha provide flexibility to smart mobile users for accessioning it without any compatibility issues. The Main modules of the Koha are shown in home page of Koha staff client (Fig.5.1) and discussed below:

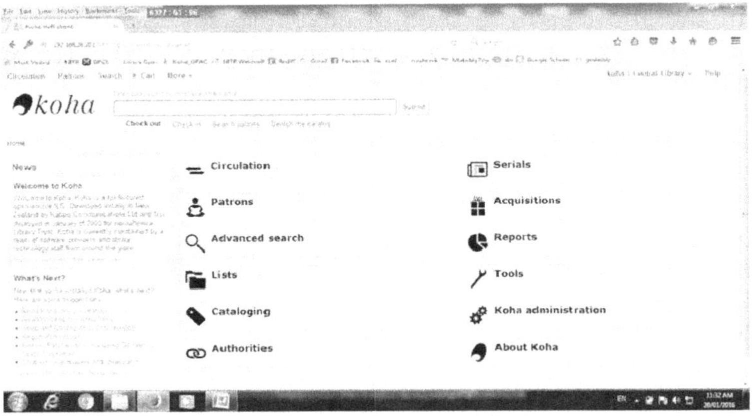

Fig. 5.1. Koha staff interface home page displaying various modules

Basic Koha OPAC Feature

- Koha provides a full-functioned Online Public Access Catalog (OPAC).
- OPAC users can carry out searches starting from ten fields (Keyword, Subject, Title, Class, Barcode, author, publisher, etc.). As in the librarian interface, they can order the results according to several criteria.
- OPAC users who are logged-in members can place reservations on library items.
- Bibilio basket: Logged-in members can select records from an OPAC search and retrieve them by e-mail, either in human-readable form or an ISO2709-format file. An ISO2709 file can be processed using bibliographic software like EndNote.
- OPAC users can submit suggestions for acquisition. Koha automatically informs the OPAC user (by e-mail) of the action taken on each suggestion.

Koha delegation of authority to library staffs

Super-librarian : access to all functions.

Circulation : carry out circulation tasks.

Catalogue : search the catalogue.

Parameters : administer the system parameters.

Borrowers : manage the public users (addition, modification, restriction, etc.).

Permissions : administer staff access to functions.

Reserves for others : place reserves on items for any borrower.

Reserves for oneself : place reserves for oneself

Loan : loan items to borrowers.

Cataloguing : manage the catalogue.

Charges : manage the fines and fees levied against members.

Koha Circulation module features

- Borrowing a book from any branch in case of multiple branch/department library (not just the branch where the borrower first registered)
- Returning an item at any branch
- Reserving an item for at any branch.
- Circulation rules can be defined very finely by the library: for each member category, item category, and holding a branch of the item, the duration of the loan and the maximum number of books loan able can be defined.
- Returning items ("checking-in") is extremely easy: Simply scan the barcodes of the items being returned.

Koha cataloguing features

MARC Management : The cataloguing module is one of the principal strong points of Koha. Several "frameworks" can be defined to do different cataloguing for monographs, electronic resources, periodicals, etc.

Export/Import : Importing records in MARC and through Z39.50 (client) for fast cataloguing.

Copy records : One or more copy records can be attached to each bibliographic record.

Fast cataloguing : To accelerate cataloguing, Koha provides, Management of a MARC record reservoir, A Z39.50 client that can access several Z39.50 servers

MARC view and simple view : Catalogue data can be displayed in MARC format, in simplified form.

Searching : searches can be performed on any MARC field. Advanced functions, search on one word, the beginning of the field, greater than, less than, etc. are also available.

Koha serial features

- It is possible to register subscriptions with reviews and to track the arrival of periodicals.
- Koha manages late issues, skipped issues, and claims with the suppliers.
- Koha manages complex classifications, allowing the librarian to work with eleven different publication periods (from daily newspapers to annual publications), with delayed publications, and with publications out of sequence.
- A state of the collection can be defined which will synthesize the missing publications, received publications, etc.
- The state of the collection can be displayed differently in the OPAC and the librarian interface.

Koha Acquisition features

Simple Acquisitions: The simple acquisitions module makes it possible to acquire materials and add them directly to the catalogue. It does not manage budgetary matters, the orders placed with the suppliers, etc.

Full Acquisitions: The full acquisitions module makes it possible to manage: Budgets and book funds: Budget available, Committed, Spent Suppliers. Orders, via 'shopping baskets'.

5.2. KOHA INSTALLATION AND HARDWARE/SOFTWARE REQUIREMENTS

To learn the system we have to first install some operating system, it is the basic first step where technical work starts and library professionals face a lot of difficulty in doing so. There are many misconceptions about the Koha platforms especially operating system on which it can be installed. Koha supports all the Linux-based operating system, but Debian based Linux is recommended by the developers which provide many easy installation methods also like online package installation. Windows operating system never supported Koha but version 2.2.9 can be installed on it, however, many features does not supports as it require to run cron jobs like fine management. The author has high experience on installation of Koha on Ubuntu operating system (both server edition and desktop edition) which is successfully running on many universities/institutes for many years without any disturbances. Hence, the current book will cover all the methods and technical issues applicable to Ubuntu operating system.

Installation of Ubuntu Operating system

At the time of writing this book, Ubuntu 14.04 Long-term support (LTS) version was available on the website and installation of which is very easy as described in the bellow screenshots. Please note that the same installation method is also applicable for Koha Live DVD. As discussed above Ubuntu is having two editions Desktop and Server.

A desktop system is typically used for personal computing tasks and has a graphical user interface (GUI) while a server system typically has a command-line interface (CLI). Ubuntu is officially compatible with three very common processor architectures - x86 (aka i386), AMD64 (aka x86_64) and PowerPC. The minimum recommended system requirement for Ubuntu both the versions are shown in below table.

Table 5.3. Minimum System requirement for Ubuntu installation

Ubuntu Desktop Edition	*Ubuntu Server (CLI) Installation*
• 700 MHz processor (about Intel Celeron or better)	• 300 MHz x86 processor
• 512 MiB RAM (system memory)	• 192 MiB of system memory (RAM)
• 5 GB of hard-drive space (or USB stick, memory card or external drive but see Live CD for an alternative approach)	• 1 GB of disk space
• VGA capable of 1024x768 screen resolution	• Graphics card and monitor capable of 640x480
• Either a CD/DVD drive or a USB port for the installer media	• CD drive

Ubuntu can be installed along with other operating system already installed on the computer machine i.e. dual boot mode where Ubuntu and Windows both will be available on single machine and any one can be used at a time. This type of installation is basically used for learning purpose or where machine is lacking. There are various methods by which it can be installed but first we need to download the iso file of Ubuntu which is available at *http://www.ubuntu.com/download/desktop* . There are two versions 64 bit and 32 bit (for machines less than 2 GB of Random access memory (RAM). In this book we will take the installation of Ubuntu desktop edition but server installation is also almost same.

After downloading the file we need to make bootable

DVD or USB with any iso burner tool like Nero, ISO image, MagicISO, YUMI etc. Once the iso image is burned on the DVD insert it into the DVD drive of computer and restart it, on restarting the computer keep pressing F12 key from Keyboard (please note the key may be different in different machine) to get the boot menu and then select the option boot from CD/DVD to get the series of 6/7 screen for further instructions which is shown below and described for each screen. Please note sometime you need not to press any key like f12 etc. and system automatically detects the DVD and start reading data from there.

Table 5.4. Ubuntu 14.04 Installation Screenshots and description

---

This is the first screen which you will get just after booting the system. Through this window, you can select whether to install the Ubuntu permanently on the system or just want to try hence accordingly you can select the option. Please note that if you select "Try Ubuntu" it will not write anything on your computer, but it will allow testing every feature of Ubuntu through. Once you remove the DVD from the drive, everything will disappear without affecting the system. Here I have selected option "Install Ubuntu".

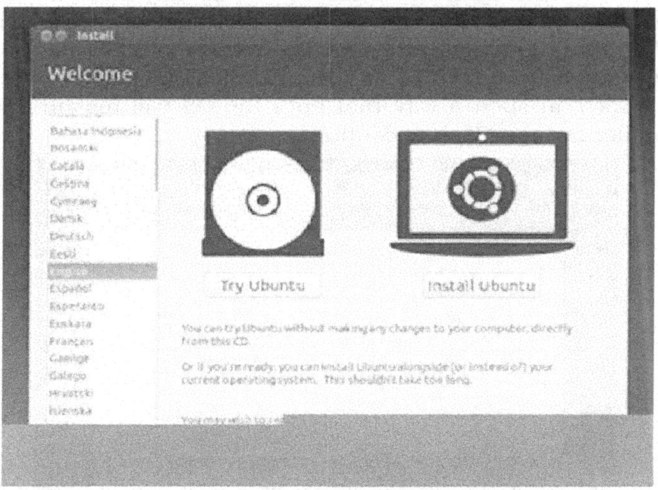

Screen Shot

During this step be insure to connect computer/Laptop with the power source and The Internet so it may download the updates and power should not go down as the complete process of installation may take much time. Minimum space on the hard disk also needs to be ensured as per your requirements. Usually, downloading updates during installation may take too much time, so I did not recommend selecting that option. However after installation, same can be done easily. Click to continue.

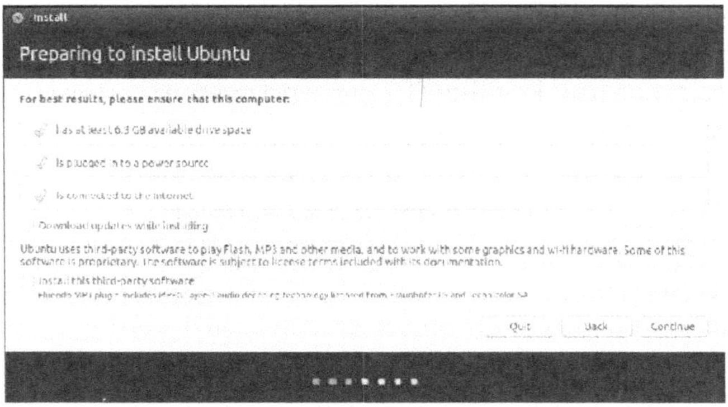

Screen Shot

In the screenshot you can see three options by default first is selected which indicates Windows 7 is already installed on the computer. However advance users may select the option "Something else" so that they can do the installation is specified drives or free space. If we select the default, Ubuntu will be installed along side Windows 7 in such a way that both the OS will remain on the computer for use. Click to continue.

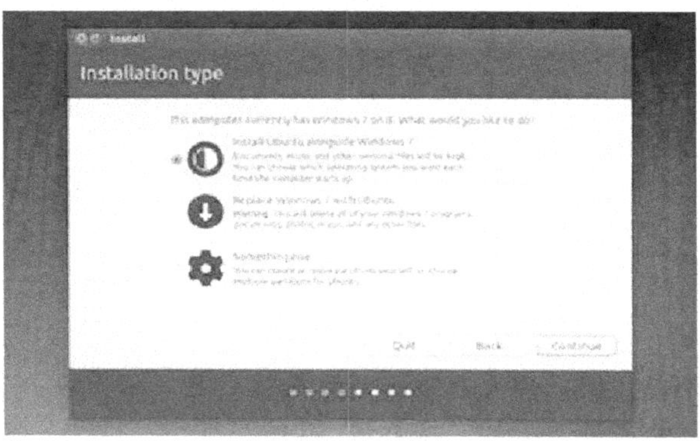

Screen Shot

Depending upon the option selected on the previous screen we will get the screen which displays the OS and the size allocated. Ubuntu needs 4.8 Gb so you should provide some more space than this. Now click the option "Install Now" which will take you to the next screen.

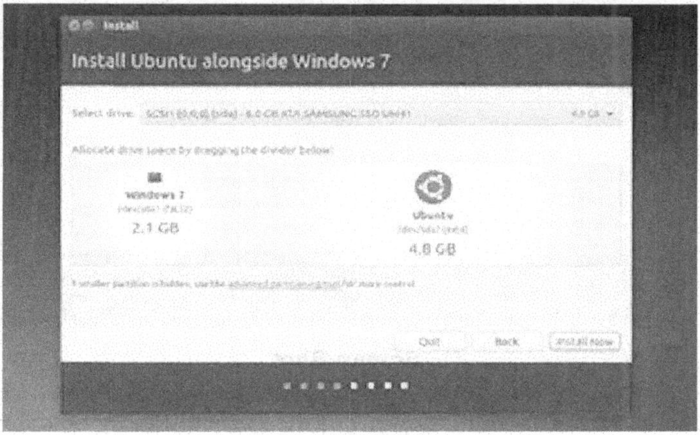

Screen Shot

If you are connected to the internet than automatically, you can see green highlighted area in your country on the world map. If not than you can click the mouse within you country region until not display the name of the country in specified field. This is just to ensure the location of the computer on the globe. Click on Continue.

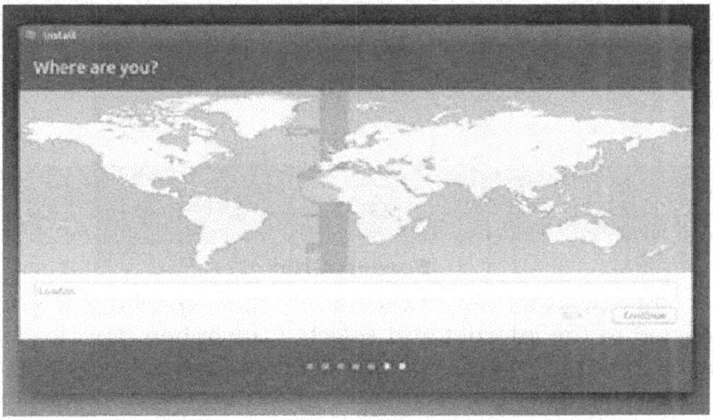

Screen Shot

Click on the language option you need. If you're not sure, click the **"Detect Keyboard Layout"** button for help.

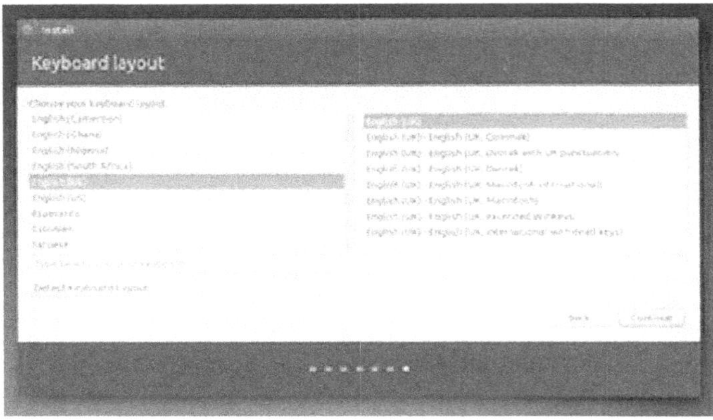

Screen Shot

This is the screen which allows you to create the administrative ID and Password of the system. Kindly note down the entered credential details future use. Click to continue.

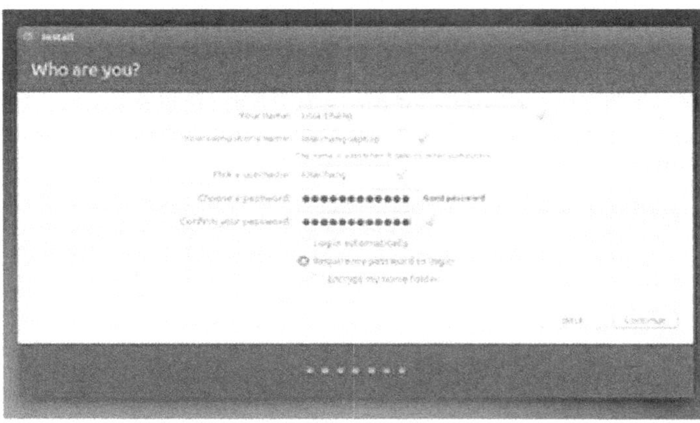

Screen Shot

This process may take much time specially if you are connected to the internet and selected the option download files/ updates in the previous step. Hence, keep patience as the system is copying the files from your DVD to computer. And wait for the next screen to appear for restarting the computer.

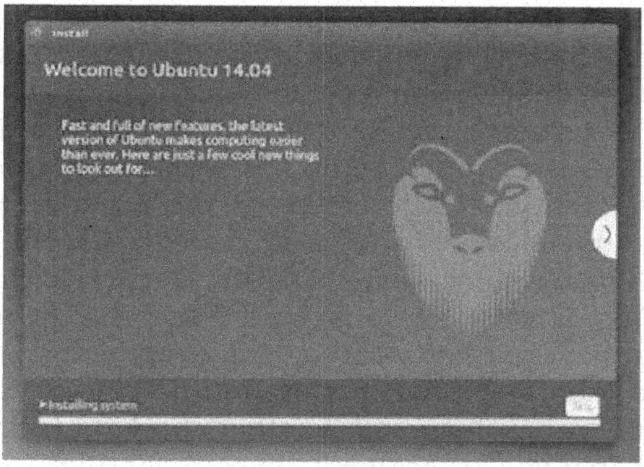

Screen Shot

Now ultimately this screen will appear and ask you to restart the system, and you can see your fresh installed Ubuntu 14.04.

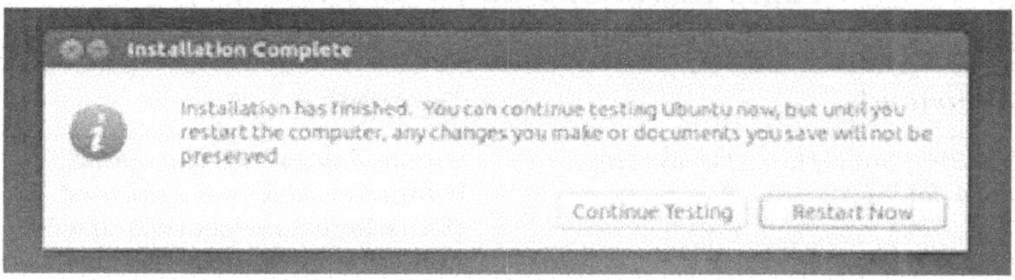

Screen Shot

Basic Ubuntu Commands

Ubuntu is having graphical user interface (GUI) and now a day's all Linux based OS provide for the same through which one can create, delete, copy, paste, move the files and folders, but GUI features are very different in all the Linux OS, but command line operations is almost similar in Linux all the flavors hence many advance users find it easy to work with the commands. Further, the logged in user is not having permission to do any kind of modifications in system files and folders hence he/she needs to be good enough to use the command line operations for maximum exploitation of Ubuntu.

Some of the basic Ubuntu commands which need

to know for all beginners and useful for handling Koha library management software is mentioned below along with their descriptions. First you need to open the Terminal for using the command which can be done by using the 'search' function on the dash. Or you can click on the 'More Apps' button, click on the 'See more results' by the installed section, and find it in that list of applications. A third way, available after you click on the 'More Apps' button, is to go to the search bar, and see that the far right end of it says 'All Applications'. Then click on that, and you'll see the full list, after that go to Accessories then Terminal. Another short cut key to open the terminal is: Ctrl + Alt + T. In command line or Linux based OS are very case sensitive hence it should be used accordingly.

Table 5.5. Useful basic commands of Ubuntu and their description

Command	***Description***
mkdir /home/koha/Desktop/new_folder	Create Folder: "mkdir" is the command and rest indicated the path where directory (folder) will be created.
rm -rf /home/joe/useless_Parent_folder	This command is perfectly fine for deleting a dir and all its sub-dirs.
rm /home/koha/file_to_be_deleted	The rm (remove) command is used to remove anything from a CLI environment.
cp /home/koha/file /home/koha/vkm	This will copy the '/home/koha/file ' to the '/home/koha/vkm '.
cp -r /directory/to/be/copied/ /where/to/copy/to/	To backup one directory to another, use *cp -r* (recursive) option.
ip addr	To see the status of your network connection, use this command
Pwd	You will see the directory that you are currently working in (*pwd* stands for 'print working directory').
Ls	The ls command will show you

	('list') the files in your current directory.
cd	The cd command will allow you to change directories. When you open a terminal, you will be in your home directory. To move around the file system you will use cd. Examples: to navigate into the root directory, use "cd/"
Mv	The mv command will move a file to a different location or will rename a file.
Man	The man command is used to show you the manual of other commands
sudo	The sudo command is used to perform file operations on files that the Root User would only be allowed to change
./filename.extension	Run a file using the command-line.
df	The df command displays filesystem disk space usage for all mounted partitions. "df -h" is probably the most useful - it uses megabytes (M) and gigabytes (G) instead of blocks to report. (-h means "human-readable")
uname –a	The uname command with the –a option prints all system information, including machine name, kernel name & version, and a few other details. Most useful for checking which kernel you're using.
adduser newuser	This command will create a new general user called "newuser" on your system, and to assign a password for the newuser account use "passwd newuser".

Koha Package Installation and preparation of system

Koha can be installed by direct package installation method with internet connectivity or by downloading individual required software. Apart from this there are many LiveDVD which is very easy to use and its detail will be discussed later in some other chapter. To install Koha minimum and recommended hardware software are tabulated below:

Table 5.6. Hardware-software requirement of Koha

Hardware	***Software***
• Pentium-4, 2.6 GHz or higher	• A Linux server – Debian recommended
• RAM 2 GB	• Apache
• HDD 40 GB (depends on size of database)	• MySQL
• DVD/USB Drive	• Perl
	• Root access to the server
	• A better than average level of skill with the command line, Apache, and MySQL tools

The following detail method of Koha (Version 3.22.01) package installation has been tested on Ubuntu 14.04 which seems to be work perfectly without any issue. Once Ubuntu has been installed in the computer as per the instruction is given on above section please ensure to connect the computer with some good internet speed connectivity as the package installation require fetching of a lot of files from the Koha repository. The detail installation steps are described below:

Ubuntu Locale setting

Setting locale UTF-8 is very important for a UNICODE compliant system, so when you run the locale commands in the terminal it will show something like this:

```
$ locale
LANG=en_PH.UTF-8
LANGUAGE=
LC_CTYPE="en_PH.UTF-8"
LC_NUMERIC="en_PH.UTF-8"
```

If it ends with UTF-8 means you need not do anything but if not than use the following command:

$ sudo update-locale LANG=en_US.UTF-8

Note : In place of US you can inter your country code like for India it is IN. Log out and log back in to see the locale change reflected when you use the locale command and the locale should end with UTF-8.

Adding Koha community repository on Ubuntu

Use the following commands to record the repository on your installed Ubuntu file, it is nothing but instruct the computer to fetch the listed links data inside the computer for an update or new installation purpose.

echo deb http://debian.koha-community.org/koha stable main | sudo tee /etc/apt/sources.list.d/koha.list

(latest stable release most people use)

OR

echo deb http://debian.koha-community.org/koha oldstable main | sudo tee /etc/apt/sources.list.d koha.list

(this is oldstable release)

OR

echo deb http://debian.koha-community.org/koha unstable main | sudo tee /etc/apt/sources.list.d/koha.list

(current unstable under development stage)

wget -O- http://debian.koha-community.org/koha/gpg.asc | sudo apt-key add - (This command is to add the key in gpg.asc to your APT trusted keys to avoid warning messages on installation)

Update Ubuntu

The following commands will update and upgrade the Ubuntu operating system to the latest version and fix any issues. Kindly keep patience as Upgrade step may take a lot of time depending upon the speed of internet and computer hardware.

sudo apt-get update

sudo apt-get upgrade

sudo apt-get clean

Installation of the latest stable Koha release

sudo apt-get install koha-common

(If you face any error like message below)

Errors were encountered while processing:

libapache2-mpm-itk

apache2-mpm-itk

koha-common

E: Sub-process /usr/bin/dpkg returned an error code (1)

Apply following commands else skip the following section.

sudo a2dismod mpm_event

sudo a2enmod mpm_prefork

sudo service apache2 restart

sudo apt-get install –f

Initial configuration for IP based Installation

Koha is having two interfaces (Staff and OPAC) and both run on different ports hence we need to instruct in the file koha-sites.conf about the ports on which it will run.

sudo nano /etc./koha/koha-sites.conf (it will open a file as shown below)

Apache virtual hosts creation variables

DOMAIN=".myDNSname.org"

INTRAPORT="8080"

INTRAPREFIX=""

INTRASUFFIX=""

80 may have "It Works!" problems.

default site could be used by other applications

OPACPORT="80"

OPACPREFIX=""

OPACSUFFIX=""

SQL file to load into new instances

DEFAULTSQL=""

Zebra global configuration variables

ZEBRA_MARC_FORMAT="marc21"

ZEBRA_LANGUAGE="en"

BIBLIOS_INDEXING_MODE="dom"

AUTHORITIES_INDEXING_MODE="dom"

Memcached global configuration variables

USE_MEMCACHED="no"

MEMCACHED_SERVERS="127.0.0.1:11211"

MEMCACHED_PREFIX="koha_"

This means that the OPAC client with being at *http://ipaddress:80/* and the staff client will be at *http://ipaddress:8080/* . Further, if you wish to open your Koha on public IP/Domain than please contact to your network administration for help.

MySQL installation and Instance creation (database)

sudo apt-get install MySQL-server (Please enter a strong password when it ask during installation)

sudo a2enmod rewrite

sudo a2enmod cgi

sudo service apache2 restart

sudo koha-create —create-db library (Please note library is the name of database)

Ubuntu MySQL Security Tweak

In Ubuntu default setup there are some security related issues which may be known to all hence to overcome this situation we have to remove such risks by using the below command.

sudo MySQL_secure_installation

While entering the above commands, it will start asking many questions and proceed after your reply N or Y, i.e., So the first answer will be "n" as the password has been already set at the time of installation of MySQL and rest will be "Y".

Set default Ports in Apache

sudo nano /etc/apache2/ports.conf

(It will open a file then write Listen 8080 below the line Listen 80)

Enable modules and sites

The following commands enable koha configurations and restart apache

sudo a2enmod deflate

sudo a2ensite library

sudo service apache2 restart

If you are getting any error message like (AH00558: apache2: Could not reliably determine the server's fully qualified domain name, using 127.0.1.1. Set the 'ServerName' directive globally to suppress this message) then run the following command:

echo "ServerName localhost" | sudo tee /etc/apache2/conf-available/fqdn.conf

sudo ln -s /etc/apache2/conf-available/fqdn.conf /etc/apache2/conf-enabled/fqdn.conf

Web installation

Now try to visit the Koha staff home page *http://ipaddress:8080/* you will get a screen indicating web installation where we have to provide the user name which is now (koha_library) and the password. We may get the password by entering following command:

sudo xmlstarlet sel -t -v 'yazgfs/config/pass' /etc/koha/sites/library/koha-conf.xml

Once you enter with the id and password, it will ask some questions and setup of some default data you may select or not select these. So ultimately Koha will be configured, and it will jump to staff client page in which you can enter by entering the same id/password as of web installer.

Now base install finish and you can login to staff and opac interface at:

http://ipaddress:8080 (Intranet staff interface)

http://ipaddress:80 (OPAC interface)

Upgrade Instructions

To upgrade the Koha after release of new version following commands need to be executed:

sudo apt-get update

sudo apt-get upgrade

This should generally upgrade your koha-common. However, if the dependencies for Koha have increased, you may have to:

$ sudo apt-get install koha-common

If you are upgrading from a version older than Koha 3.4.x, run the following command which may take a long time to complete for large databases: koha-upgrade-to-3.4

It is always safest to run a full reindex after an upgrade, where {instance} is the name of your instance:

koha-rebuild-zebra -v -f {instance}

On your librarians, clients consider clear browser cache after upgrading.

Uninstall Instructions

The package installation method is unique in that a removal command is already provided. Determine what instances you have:

$ koha-list

And then for each instance:

$ sudo koha-remove {instance}

If you encounter any problems, please request help from the mailing list, author or IRC channel.

$ sudo apt-get remove koha-common

Encoding and Character Sets in Koha

In MySQL please make sure you have the following lines in the [MySQLd] section of your /etc/MySQL/my.cnf:

init-connect = 'SET NAMES utf8'

character-set-server=utf8

collation-server=utf8_general_ci

character_set_client=utf8

Then restart MySQL with: /etc/init.d/MySQL restart

In Apache please make sure you have following lines in your /etc/apache2/httpd.conf (or for Ubuntu in /etc/apache2/conf.d/charset):

AddCharset UTF-8 .utf8

AddDefaultCharset utf-8

Zebra configuration for regional language searching

To enhance the search results in regional languages following method has been adopted and found it is more helpful provides much accuracy and filter the search results in regional languages. Open the following file:

sudo su

nano /etc/koha/zebradb/etc/default.idx

Find the line similar to "charmap word-phrase-utf.chr" and comment it by inserting a # symbol. The same lines appear in next paragraph too hence comments it also. Then Add following line below the commented lines:

icuchain words-icu.xml

Rebuild zebra

sudo koha-rebuild-zebra -v -f library

5.3. SYSTEM SETUP AND OTHER PARAMETERS OF KOHA

System setup and parameters can be defined as almost same thing as we do some manual work/planning at the time of starting any new library. The planning may involve nomenclature of the library, type of reading materials, type of users, holiday's calendar, book transaction limits, fine policy, a currency for acquisitions, etc. There are so many rules we defined in the library depending on the type and services of the library before we begin; Koha provides a lot of flexibility to configure the system as per the local library requirements. Hence, some of the options we need to setup before using the system, however, many we can change/alter as and when to require. Each module has many options to be configured under the system preferences option. All the basic options will be discussed in detail in below section. Please note that to login into the Koha staff client it is strongly recommended to use the Mozilla Firefox. On choosing the option Koha administration from the staff interface, it will display the options out of which some are very essential and common for all type of libraries hence it has to be configured in the system before using it.

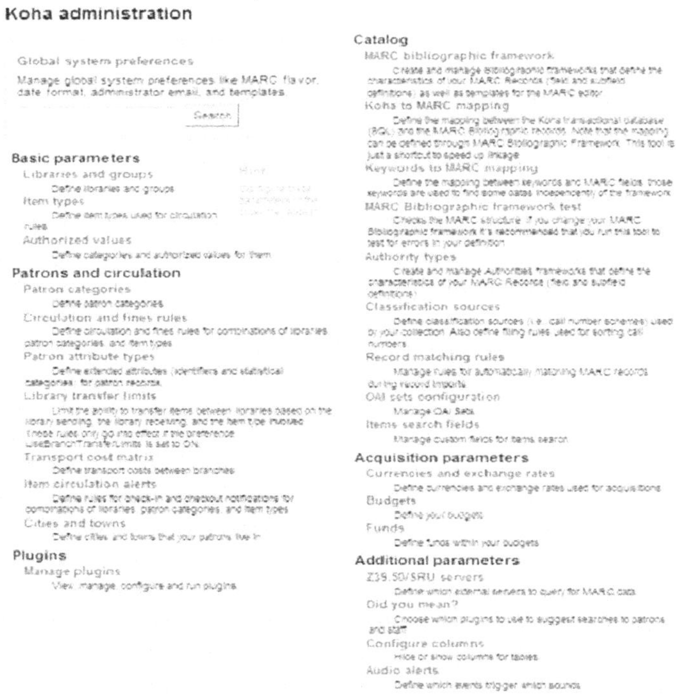

Fig. 5.2. Koha administration options

Basic Parameters

As an instruction is given in the above screenshot Fig. 5.2 that these parameters should be followed as per the order, it appears on the screen. Therefore, each option should be checked and configured as per the library requirements. In this book, the author has attempted to cover all the parameters which may be needed for many libraries in general.

Libraries and Groups

This is the parameter where we need to configure the detail of the library these details will be reflected on each module and require while generating various reports as well as automated email generations/reply etc. To add a library click on Administration > Basic Parameters > Libraries and Groups > New library. On top of the screen library code needs to be entered along with its name. Please note that whenever code is asked to enter in the entire Koha system always enter the small code (less than 10 characters) having mnemonic value and description of code can be used in full in other field. For example if your library name is Biju Patnaik Central Library than you can enter BPCL as its code, further the code is used in the database which can't be altered later and the code is also used during generation of barcode and various reports which help in identification of the library if there are more than one library exist in the system.

Similarly you can select the group or search domain if you wish and your library belongs to any specific group like academic library, public library, and special library etc., search domain helps in searching the particular type of libraries in an OPAC in a group rather than single library. All the detail address like city, state, contact number, email for reply etc. need to be filled as these are used for communicating with the vendors and users of the library. IP address helps you in increasing the security and restricts the access of staff client on particular IP or range of IP's. Some of the options are self explanatory as reflected by their headings. Once the entire detail has been filled you can save it but remember you can alter everything except the code and entire library can't be deleted if any patron and items available it that.

Item type

In Koha just like other ILMS you can organize your entire library collection by item type as well as collection. In general item type is nothing but material of a library like reference books, DVD, Maps, Paintings, Manuscripts etc. To add new item select the option Administration > Basic Parameters > Item Types > New item type. As discussed earlier item code and its detail need to be entered which is mandatory and thumb rule should be followed as in the case of creating new library. Once item code and description is defined it can be grouped in a specific search category like in case of library, for example Manuscript category and Palm leaves can be searched together if you have defined that under the authorized value. Image can be selected against the item which reflects in the OPAC and help in identification of type of material too.

Similarly if reference books or any materials can't be issued than not for loan option can be checked and there are other options which is very well defined against each option like hiding an item to be searched from OPAC, message alert on return of items, etc. Please note that item type is one of the most important parameter as circulation rule is also depends on that hence libraries must first plan their transaction rules and privileges. Symbols, special characters and spaces should be avoided while defining the codes. Similar to library you can't delete the item type if any record exists against it but the details/ description can be altered except the code.

Authorized value

Authorized value gives much flexibility and freedom to Koha users in various modules like generation of statistical reports, defining locations of items, items status etc. Koha provides many default values on installation. The various options and their description are provided in below table.

Table 5.7. Authorized value and their description

Authorized Value	***Description***
Asort1 Asort2	The value is to use it for acquisition related statistical purpose
Bor_notes	Data/ Message can be enter here to display in patrons OPAC page

Bsort1	Data/Message that can be entered to fill in the patron's sort 1 field
Bsort2	Data/Message that can be entered to fill in the patron's sort 2 field
Cart	It is the shelving location of a book
Ccode	It is collection codes like children's book, manuscripts etc
Damaged	Generally number is enter to indicate the Damage book at the time of editing the data or entering the data in item field 952.
Department	This is used if you would like to activate course reserves
Hings_as	General holdings and reflect the acquisition status
Hings_c	General Holdings with Completeness Designator
Hings_pf	Physical form designators
Hings_rd	General Holdings: Retention Designator :: This data element specifies the retention policy for theUnit at the time of the holdings report.
Hings_ut	Type of Unit Designator
Loc	Shelving location like general section, reference section etc.
Lost	Descriptions for the items marked as lost
Manual_inv	Description for manual invoicing types
Not_loan	Reasons to specify why a title is not for loan
Order_cancellation_reason	Reasons to specify why an order might have been cancelled
Proc	The default location to be used for adding new items to the collection
Report_group Report_subgroup	Various reports script can be categorized in groups like circulation, cataloguing etc and further sub grouping to ease in generating reports.
Restricted	To display restricted status of an item
Roadtype	Some fixed road types value to be used in patron addresses
Sip_media_type	SIP related assignment when using for sorting etc.
Suggest	List of patron suggestion reject or accept
Withdrawn	Description of a withdrawn item
Yes_no	A generic authorized value field that can be used anywhere in Koha system.

Apart from above, new authorized value category can also be created, and description can be defined after which at least one authorized value against above should be created. The description which you would like to display in OPAC can be altered, and it can also be made activated for any particular library among many.

Patrons and Circulation

Section of this administration described the patrons and their circulation rules like transactions etc. almost similar to the philosophy of item types which are explained above.

Patron category

As we have created item type in the previous section, in the same way, we need to create patron/user category of a library, find the option at Administration, > Patrons & Circulation > Patron Categories.

Fig. 5.3. Patron category

To create new patron you have to click on new category tab, the Red highlighted heading would be mandatory to fill, and rest is optional. You can enter Category code like UG for undergraduate students, FACU for faculty, etc. The expiry period of a category may be defined either by a specific date by choosing the calendar, or it may be defined in the month also which will be applicable from the time of creating member. Overdue notice may be clicked as yes if the library is intended to send email for book renewals, reservation, etc.

Category type is mandatory in Koha, and it is also limited to six only where an adult is used for the general patron, and staff professionals are used under the guardianship of organization. Patrons can be blocked on the expiration of membership, and their privacy history can also be altered. A lot of messages preferences have been provided in Koha to choose for a specific category of users as given in below screenshot out of which all can be checked, or few may be ignored. Please note that some of the options like expiry, notices preferences will appear same during creation of new membership this has been done in order to save the time of data entry operator and to maintain the uniformity.

Default messaging preferences for this patron category

	Days in advance	Email	Digests only	Do not notify
Advance notice	0	☐	☐	☐
Item checkout	-	☐	-	☐
Hold filled	-	☐	-	☐
Item due	-	☐	☐	☐
Item check-in	-	☐	-	☐

Fig. 5.4. Message preferences

Circulation and Fine Rule

Every library is having their own defined circulation and fine rules in addition to many other privileges to users like online renewals, reservations, etc. Koha provides much flexibility and many options to configure the system as per various library rules and policy. The circulation rules are applicable from most specific to less specific, in the following order.

- Same library, same patron type, same item type
- Same library, same patron type, all item type
- Same library, all patron types, same item type
- Same library, all patron types, all item types
- Default (all libraries), same patron type, same item type
- Default (all libraries), same patron type, all item types

- Default (all libraries), all patron types, same item type
- Default (all libraries), all patron types, all item types

Please note that at least a default circulation rule needs to be configured. This rule should be set for all item types, all libraries and all patron categories. If you do not set, this default rule patrons may face problems in placing holds. Koha generally check that which rule is applicable to users if it is not default. Further, rule should be also configured for items which is not supposed to be issues to particular category for example if category A patron is not allowed to issue Item type B then it should be configured as Zero under the limit, so that Koha can understand that this book can't be issued to the A category member.

To set up a circulation rule, you need to select a library from the drop-down menu in case you have multiple libraries or select all libraries if the rule is common for all. In case, only single library exist than that particular library needs to be selected before configuring the fine and circulation rules. Each important option and their description are provided in below table.

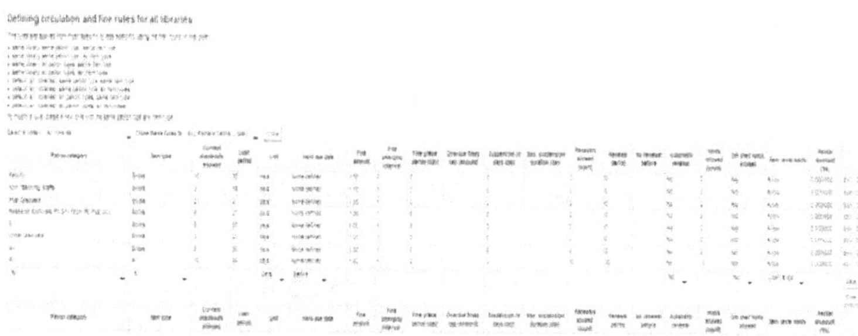

Fig. 5.5. Screenshot of Circulation and fine rules

Table 5.8. Circulation Options and their descriptions

Circulation rules option	***Description***
Patron category	First patron category needs to be configured else it will apply to the entire available category in Koha system.
Item Type	It is the type of the issues on which you are going to apply the rule you may select all if by default you wish to issue a total number of book limit irrespective of the particular item.
Current checkouts allowed	The total number of the particular item you wish to issue to the particular category of member.
Loan period	The total number of days for which particular item will be issued.
Unit	Koha may calculate the Loan period in days as well as hours because some libraries issue books in hours to be consulted within the library.
Hard due date	This is applicable when the library is willing to issue any item up to any particular date like Book Bank collection is issued to students for the entire semester. Please note that loan period still needs to be defined which must be more than length of hard due date from the date of issue. For example, if 31st December is the last due date to be fixed and the book will be issued from July first than Loan period must be say 200 as Koha will catch/ identify the minimum days fixed.
Fine amount	The amount which needs to be charged in case of overdue book, please note that symbols of currency need not to be defined here.
Fine charging interval	This may be every day or every two days and so on.
Fine grace period (day)	This is the time in days given to start calculating fine once the item reached their overdue date.
Overdue fines cap (amount)	Maximum limit of fine which can be fixed on members i.e. once the fine reached the limit system will stop calculating more.
Suspension in days (day)	You can fix the number of days for which member fine can be suspended if the book is overdue.
Max. Suspension duration (day)	Members can also be suspended if books are overdue in defined number of days.
Renewals allowed (count)	If library wished to allow renewal of books than it can be set here the number of times, particular

	issued items could be renewed.
Renewal period	If allowing to renew then you can decide if a member renews the books than for how many days he/she can
No renewal before	The days before the due date of issued books during which member can renew the book.
Automatic renewal	This allows the system to automatically renew the books on reaching the due date, provided there is no hold on that.
Holds allowed (count)	How many items can be put on Hold/Reserve by members of this category?
On shelf holds allowed	You can set if you wish to allow reserve/hold on items available on the shelf.
Item level holds	This will allow the patron to choose the specific items for placing it on holds for example if the book is multivolume than they can place the hold on that particular volume else system will place hold on next available volume which may not be require.
Rental discount (%)	If library charges fee for the issue than discount % can be fixed here if member renews it next time.

When finished configuring each option, click 'Add' to save your changes. To modify a rule, simply click the 'Edit' link to the right of the rule and edit the values that appear filled in at the bottom of the form. You can delete the rules with option "Delete" at right corner.

Under the option "Default checkout limit by patron category" you can specify the maximum number of loans that a patron of a given category can make, regardless of the item type. If the total amount loanable for a given patron category is left blank, no limit applies, except possibly for a limit you define for a specific item type. "Default holds policy by item type" option gives flexibility to edit rules for given item types, regardless of the patron's category. Currently, this means hold policies. The various policies have the following effects:

- From any library: Patrons from any library may put this item on hold. (default if none is defined)

- From the home library: Only patrons from the item's home library may put this book on hold.
- No holds allowed: No patron may put this book on hold.

Note that if the system preference Allow Hold Policy Override is enabled, these policies can be overridden by your circulation staff. Also, these policies are based on the patron's home library, not the library where the hold is being placed.

Patron attributes type

This option can be used to define patron custom fields to associate with patron records for example if you wish to display book barcode of issued book in patron detail on OPAC than SHOW_BCODE needs to be configured as shown in the below screenshot.

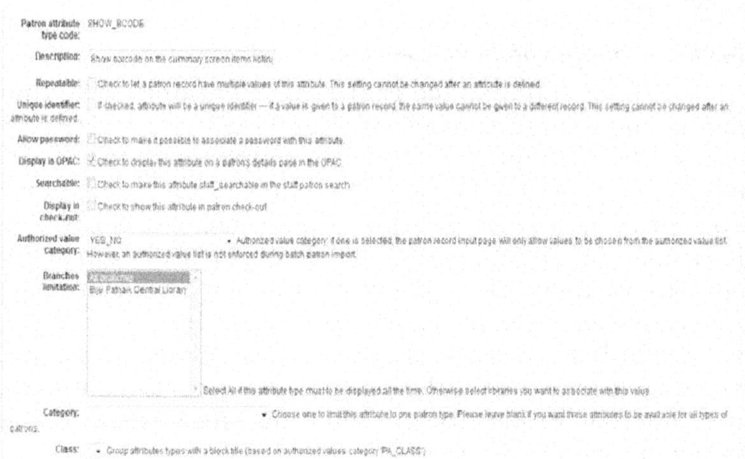

Fig. 5.6. Options to create Patrons attribute

The description of each option is given in the screenshot which is self-explanatory for example if you wish to display the attribute to patterns detail page on OPAC than you can choose option "Display in OPAC".

There are many other options which fall under the patrons and circulation rule like "library transfer limits" which is meant for restricting the transfer items between libraries based on the library sending, the library receiving, and the collection code involved."Transfer cost matrix" used to define the charges involve in transferring the book from one library to another these can be defined in decimal and figures without the symbol of currency, To enter transport costs simply click in the cell you would like to alter, uncheck the 'Disable' box and enter your 'cost'. "Item circulation alert" is set to display alert depending on the library and item type at the time of transactions which may be in green/red etc. colour. "Cities and Town" are useful for creating the pre-configured value which helps in maintain the uniformity and promptness in data entry of users.

Catalogue

MARC bibliographic framework

Create and manage Bibliographic frameworks that define the characteristics of your MARC Records (field and subfield definitions) as well as templates for the MARC editor. This option helps in creating library and items specific templates for data entry worksheet like for books, journals, CD/DVD, maps, etc. Each MARC framework can be edited and created at any time as well as activating and deactivating of any particular tags can also be done, but Default framework should not be deleted or altered because it may create the problem for records. However, it is advised to plan before creating any framework for items as per the standards.

If you wish to edit any of the above shown MARC frameworks than click the MARC option structure which will open a window having all the MARC tags, the search option is also given to find the particular tag for ease in editing/adding new tags in the already defined framework or the new one. For example, if a library wishes to activate the 952$v subfield in already existing "Books, Booklets, Workbooks" framework than he has to select MARC structure > tag 952 location and item information (Koha) subfields > than click the edit option under the "v" subfield which will display the below screen.

+ New framework

MARC frameworks

Framework name, then go to MARC biblio to set MARC editor parameters

Code	Description		Edit	Delete	Export	Import
	Default framework	MARC structure			Export	Import
ACQ	Acquisition	MARC structure	Edit	Delete	Export	Import
BKS	Books, Booklets, Workbooks	MARC structure	Edit	Delete	Export	Import
SER	Bound Volumes/Journals/Serials/Magazines	MARC structure	Edit	Delete	Export	Import
CF	CD-ROMs, DVD-ROMs	MARC structure	Edit	Delete	Export	Import
EB	E-Books	MARC structure	Edit	Delete	Export	Import
FA	Fast Add Framework	MARC structure	Edit	Delete	Export	Import
THE	Thesis/Dessertation/Project	MARC structure	Edit	Delete	Export	Import
VC	Videocassette	MARC structure	Edit	Delete	Export	Import

Fig. 5.7. Defined MARC frameworks

Fig. 5.8. Editing/Adding subfield in framework

Text for librarian is meant for display of tag details in librarian/staff interface, while Text for OPAC is for any user accessing the OPAC. The repeatable option allows the cataloguer to add same multiple tags and enters the data as it happens in 650$a subject MARC field. Mandatory can be selected if cataloger is forced to enter some data like 245$a is mandatory which is title. Managed in tab is one of the most important and care must be taken while choosing it, because all subfields of a given MARC tag must be in same tab else system may show error while testing Marc framework.

Advanced constraints allow for default text entry in the sub fields at the time of cataloguing which saves time; maximum length can also be controlled, visibility option allows selecting whether it should be displayed on OPAC or not, collapse in framework, etc. If URL option is checked system is URL address of any web page hence will allow you to click that text to jump on web page. Other options like Authorized value help in setting the option to select the data from the pre-defined drop down value and cataloguer need not to enter the data. One of the most significant option in Koha which is hardly find in any ILMS is import/export of bibliographic frameworks i.e. if a library wishes to have a standard data entry framework for CD/DVD than they can create the framework and instead of making their own lengthy tags format they can request any library to provide framework in csv format if they already use such framework for entry of CD/DVD. Once the file is received they can use the import option and the job is done which saves a lot of time and maintains uniformity among the library and helps in resource sharing too.

Koha to MARC mapping

Define the mapping between the Koha transactional database (SQL) and the MARC Bibliographic records. Note that the mapping can be defined through MARC

Bibliographic Framework. This tool is just a shortcut to speed up linkage.

Keywords to MARC mapping

Define the mapping between keywords and MARC fields; those keywords are used to find some data's independently of the framework. Presently the only keyword in use is the subtitle, and this tool affects the only sites which do not use XSLT style.

MARC Bibliographic Framework test

Check the MARC structure. If you change your MARC Bibliographic Framework, it's recommended that you run this tool to test for errors in your definition. This is the very important tool always to check the errors when we created any new framework as well. The below screen indicates the well defined bibliographic framework.

MARC bibliographic framework test

Test	Result
OK	itemnum : the field itemnumber is mapped to a field in tab -1
OK	All item fields are in the same tag and in item tab
OK	Only 1 MARC tag mapped to items
OK	biblioitems.itemtype defined
OK	homebranch defined
OK	holdingbranch defined
OK	at least 1 item type defined
OK	at least 1 library defined
OK	biblionumber and biblioitemnumber mapped correctly
OK	no NULL value in frameworkcode
OK	all subfields for each tag are in the same tab (or ignored)
OK	all authority types used in the frameworks are defined
OK	items.permanent_location is not mapped on the frameworks

Configuration OK, you don't have errors in your MARC parameters table

Fig. 5.9. MARC bibliographic framework test result

Authority types

Create and manage Authorities frameworks that define the characteristics of your MARC Records (field and subfield definitions). It is almost similar to creating the framework for bibliographic records.

Classification sources

Define classification sources (i.e., call number schemes) used by your collection. Also, define filing rules used for sorting call numbers. You can also add your own source of classification by using the New Classification Source button.

Record matching rules

Manage rules for automatically matching MARC records during record imports. This tool is very helpful especially when you are importing the external records to already available catalogue but you do not wish to add the already available title in Koha. This option facilitates to create the match points say match with 245$a title hence at the time of importing the records you can choose the match rule as Title (245$a) and Koha will give the results for the number of records matched with existing records which can be either added to catalogue or ignored also. If you are importing the MARC records of multiple copies of same books but not combined as one record in MARC this option helps you to combine all as one record with some techniques which will be discussed in another section.

OAI sets configuration

Manage OAI Sets. Fill the mandatory fields 'setSpec' and 'setName'. Then you can add descriptions for this set. Select 'Add Description' and fill the newly created text box, than you can add as many descriptions as you want. The created sets can be modified and delete. Once all sets have been configured then you need to build the sets which can be done by running the script misc/

migration_tools/build_oai_sets.pl. Please note that these are helpful in harvesting the Metadata from your Koha by another through OAI-PMH.

Items search fields

Manage custom fields for items search in staff client interface only. It gives a lot of flexibility to staff for quick services and reporting.

Acquisition parameters

Acquisition module of Koha helps in purchasing of the library materials and management of orders, budgets, invoices, etc. So before using the acquisition module some parameters needs to be defined in this section which is as follows.

Currencies and exchange rates

Library may be subscribing journals and purchasing books from various countries and their currency as well as exchange rate is always different, so we have to define here the currency and their conversion rates applicable in the country of the library. We may make many as per the requirements out of which we need to make one active currency.

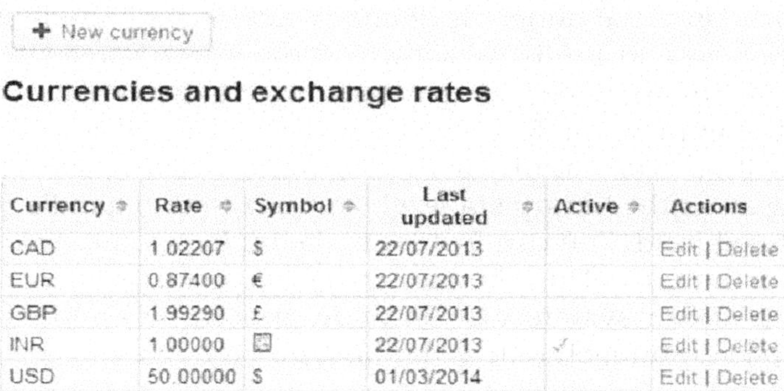

+ New currency

Currencies and exchange rates

Currency	Rate	Symbol	Last updated	Active	Actions
CAD	1.02207	$	22/07/2013		Edit | Delete
EUR	0.87400	€	22/07/2013		Edit | Delete
GBP	1.99290	£	22/07/2013		Edit | Delete
INR	1.00000	[illegible]	22/07/2013	✓	Edit | Delete
USD	50.00000	$	01/03/2014		Edit | Delete

Fig. 5.10. Currency and their exchange rates

Budget and funds

This section concern with defining the budgets of the library, for example, the total budget of the library is if 1000/- then it can be further subdivided into the funds which may be library periodicals, books, etc.

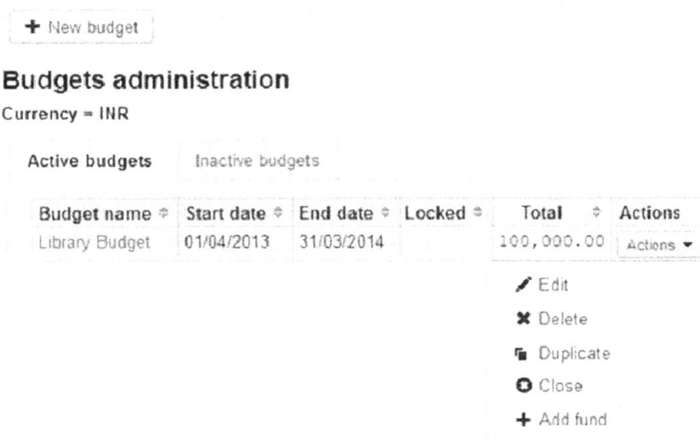

Fig. 5.11. Defining budget and funds

While defining the budget, we need to select the start date as well as end date too and the total amounts which will be spent during the defined period (Budget year). Once the budget is defined system will provide the option to add funds as shown in the above screenshot. Many funds can be added by bi-furcating the total budget of the library; the fund creation screen will allow you to add fund code and their descriptions, warning amount, as well as the library staffs who are allowed to handle the defined fund. You can further make budget active or lock it at the end of the budget year/ financial year. Apart from above system also provide options to create the duplicate budget, delete the budget, etc.

Addition parameters

Z39.50/SRU servers are the option which allows

configuring as much as possible the external server from where cataloguer wishes to fetch the bibliographic records and authority records at the time of cataloguing, for example, Library of Congress server, Columbia University etc. Before configuring the new server, one has to know the hostname, port number and database. Did you mean option provide configuration which works at the time of searching the OPAC. The column setting will help to hide or display columns on fixed tables throughout the staff client only.

Koha global system preferences

Global system preferences control the entire Koha how it works and how a library wishes to get work from the Koha, therefore, before doing anything in Koha, it is strongly recommended to configure the options given under these settings. This is a big list of various options related to almost each module of the Koha hence to search a specific option Koha has provided very strong searching option inside the global system preference. Therefore any library staff can search the required option with keywords/string. After changing any options, it will be saved only by clicking the "Save all enhanced system preferences" then you can see a popup screen indicating which changed options has been successfully saved. The system global preferences have been divided into various sub-sections as shown in Fig. 5.12.

At the left-hand side various main modules are given and in right, options available and their description has been explained. Whatever a library requires as per their policy like acquisition, cataloguing, OPAC, circulation etc. that needs to be configured for using the Koha. Here I will try to explain common option for each module which is almost requiring by any library. Each section of preferences can be sorted alphabetically by clicking the small down arrow to the right of the word 'Preference' in the header column.

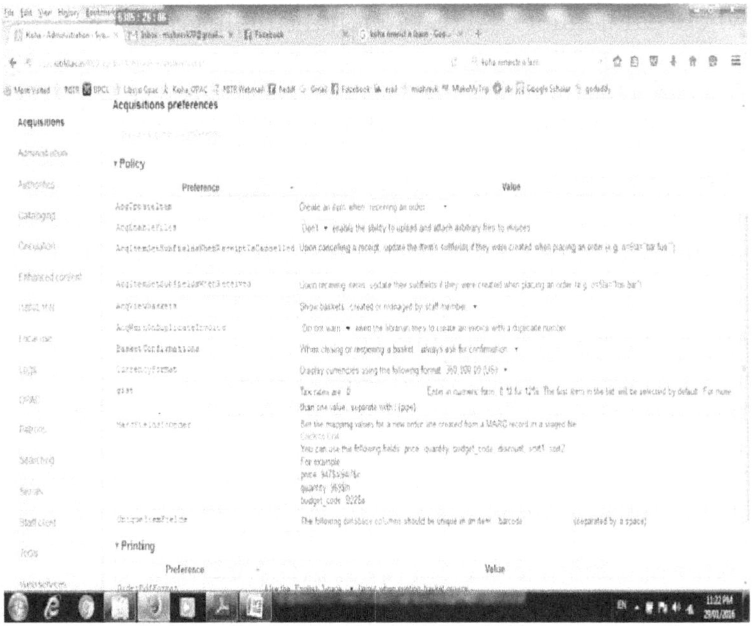

Fig. 5.12. Global system preferences screen

Table 5.9. Koha System preferences and their description

Acquisition Preferences	
Preference	***Description/Value***
AcqCreateItem	This option helps to configure when a library wishes to create Item record in the Koha i.e. at the time of placing order/receiving an order/cataloguing a record. Hence, the library can select accordingly, and the item will start displaying in the OPAC.
AcqEnableFiles	If a library wishes to attach scan copy of invoice they can by activating the option at the time of invoicing in the acquisition.
AcqViewBaskets	This option gives flexibility as well as restrictions also to see the order baskets created by the staff itself or any member of

	the library staffs so that all can manage the baskets created by others or only those created by concern staff.
AcqWarnOnDuplicate Invoice	This option helps in setting the system in such a way that if any duplicate invoice is entered a warning will be displayed.
BasketConfirmations	Option to give you the warning at the time of opening and closing of baskets.
Gist	Default goods and service rates configurations
MarcFieldsToOrder	Koha provides flexibility to use the stage file upload for ordering, and you can select which fields should be used to order the title like title, author, ISBN, etc.
UniqueItemFields	To decide which will be the Unique identifier number for an item created in the system like barcode/accession number.
OrderPdfFormat	Option to select the layout for order printing.
Administration preferences	
casAuthentication	Central authentication system (CAS) is a technique by which people used to login on multiple websites with single ID/Password. You may leave it or contact the Institute computer center for the same configurations who manage the CAS.
DebugLevel	This option help in getting the quantity of error message in case of any bug or system errors, the detailed messages helps in identifying the problems and getting their solutions easy.
Delimiter	These options provide flexibility in changing the symbol for separating the various data in csv file at the time of generating the reports.
KohaAdminEmailAddress	A common email needs to be configuring here as all the reminders of books, and other things will be replied on this email for further action by the library.
noItemTypeImages	Set if you wish to display the icon of item type in OPAC/Staff Client.
ReplytoDefault	If the library wishes to get the reply to email on another email than they can configure here.
ReturnpathDefault	Email address where the bounce emails will be delivered.
Virtual shelves	This option gives facility to allow staff/patrons to create List of books/items and save to display in OPAC and staff client.

Login options	Under this section, various options are given to set the security/ block member if IP address of remote server changes, Restrict access by IP ranges defined at the time of library creation, MySQL session timeout, restricting staff to modify the records of other branch libraries etc.
Persona	Mozilla Persona is an OpenID-like service that lets you log in to multiple websites with your Mozilla credentials. If you allow Persona log in for Koha, then your patrons can log in to the OPAC using their Mozilla Persona.
Share anonymous usage statistics	This section allows Koha system to access your Koha records, country, Library URL, Library type, etc. by Koha community website so that statistics of Koha users can be viewed globally.

Authorities preferences

AuthDisplayHierarchy	Display authorities in hierarchies if entered in 5XX MARC fields
AutoCreateAuthorities	It allows creating automatic authorities if already does not exist in the system.
BiblioAddsAuthorities	While editing record allows creating authorities
Done merge	If any authority record is edited, it will update all the records also associated with it if the option is set to Do.
UseAuthoritiesForTracings	This option if set to Don't Use then it will not search the records associated/linked with subject/author on clicking instead it will perform a keyword search and display the possible results.
Linker	These preferences will describe how Koha links bibliographic records to authority records. All bibliographic records added to Koha after these preferences are set will link automatically to authority records, for records added before these preferences are set there is a script (misc/link_bibs_to_authorities.pl) that need to be run to link the records together.

Cataloging preferences

AcquisitionDetails	It will allow the staff to see the acquisition detail in staff client under the bibliographic detail page of a record, which will further link to acquisition module.

AuthoritySeparator	It allows assigning the symbol for separating various authorities in a record like —
hide_marc	This option allows or not allows displaying MARC tag numbers, subfield codes and indicators in MARC views.
IntranetBiblioDefaultView	There are four formats given to display while viewing the detail of a record, so it allow choosing one.
ISBD	You can define your ISBD template
LabelMARCView	Collapse repeated tags of the same type into one tag entry on the staff and OPAC, which avoids scrolling the long page.
NotesBlacklist	Allow hiding the Notes MARC field from staff client and OPAC
OpacSuppression OpacSuppressionBy IPRange OpacSuppression RedirectOpacSuppression Message	You can hide the items to display in the OPAC as well as restrict to display by IP range or it will redirect to some defined message page.
SeparateHoldings SeparateHoldingsBranch	You can set to display holding information on multiple tabs in a bibliographic detail page.
URLLinkText	You can set the URL link text here to be click to jump on linked page.
AggressiveMatchOnISBN	When matching on ISBN with the record import tool (don't/do), attempt to match aggressively by trying all variations of the ISBNs in the imported record as a phrase in the ISBN fields of already cataloged records. Note that this preference has no effect if UseQueryParser is on.
advancedMARCeditor	It allows to display or not the description of fields and subfields in the MARC editor.
DefaultClassificationSource	Allows to select the default classification source
EasyAnalyticalRecords	Display or not the easy ways to create analytical record relationships. It is a way of linking articles/book chapters etc.
AlternateHoldingsField AlternateHoldingsSeparator	If holding information is given in some other field apart from 952 than library can configure to display it on OPAC
autoBarcode	Different format of Barcode/Accession number is given to choose as well as to create automatically or enter barcode manually.
DefaultLanguageField008	Allows to display default language code in 008 field

item-level_itypes	Item type Koha usages will be an attribute of Bibliographic records or Item record; it determines the icon display on OPAC.
Itemcallnumber	We enter the Class number and book number in 082 and the same need to be enter in call number (952$o) so it helps to map 082 on required field to avoid the duplicate work and save the time.
Marcflavour	Allows choosing one out of three MARC flavor in Koha system.
MARCOrgCode	It allows displaying/store the code of marc cataloguing organization/agency.
NewItemsDefaultLocation	It allows displaying the default location of items at the time of creation say for new books it may be new display location.
PrefillItem	This is good option to avoid repetitive entry of an item record
SubfieldsToAllowForRestrictedBatchmod	Define a list of subfields for which editing is authorized when items_batchmod_restricted permission is enabled, separated by spaces.
SubfieldsToAllowForRestrictedEditing	Define a list of subfields for which editing is authorized when edit_items_restricted permission is enabled, separated by spaces.
SubfieldsToUseWhenPrefill	Define a list of subfields to use when prefilling items (separated by space)
SpineLabelAutoPrint	When using the quick spine label printer, (do/don't) automatically pop up a print dialog.
SpineLabelFormat	Allows to define the formats to be printed on spine level
Circulation preferences	
BlockReturnOfWithdrawnItems	Sometimes users attempt to return the items which have been withdrawn from the collection after issuing, so it allows stopping such process from system to validate the reason.
CalculateFinesOnReturn	Do/Don't calculate the overdue fine of a book on return of books and update the total fine
UpdateNotForLoanStatusOnCheckin	This is a list of value pairs. When an item is checked in, if the not for loan value on the left matches the items, not for loan value it will be updated to the right-hand value. E.g. '-1: 0' will cause an item that was set to 'Ordered' to now be available for loan. Each pair of values should be on a separate line.

AgeRestrictionMarker	Restricting patrons circulation on age basis
AgeRestrictionOverride	It allows or don't allows checkout of patrons with the age restriction.
AllFinesNeedOverride	Option for Staff to manually override all fines, even fines less than noissuescharge.
AllowFineOverride	It restricts the staff not to over the right fine amount.
AllowItemsOnHoldCheckout	It restricts the staffs to check-out those books which are on hold/reserve
AllowMultipleIssuesOnA Biblio	Patrons to check out multiple items from the same record. (NOTE: This will only affect records without a subscription attached.)
AllowNotForLoanOverride	Staff to override and check out items that are marked as not for loan.
AllowRenewalLimitOverride	staff to manually override renewal blocks and renew a checkout when it would go over the renewal limit or be premature on the "No renewal before" setting in the circulation policy or has been scheduled for automatic renewal.
AllowReturnToBranch	Restricts the return of items to which branch in case the Koha handles many branch libraries
AllowTooManyOverride	Staff to override and check out items when the patron has reached the maximum number of allowed checkouts.
AutomaticItemReturn	Automatically return the items to their home branch when it return to the Koha system
AutoRemoveOverdues Restrictions	allow OVERDUE restrictions triggered by sent notices to be cleared automatically when all overdue items are returned by a patron.
CircControl	It allows imposing fine rules to be applied to books by branch libraries/issuing library
DefaultLongOverdue ChargeValue	Set amount if long overdue/lost book reached the limit; patron will be fined.
DefaultLongOverdueLost Value DefaultLongOverdue Days	Default lost value of item and the period in days to be considered as lost
HomeOrHoldingBranch	Check out/in and fine rules applicability will depend on issuing/returning library/item belonged library etc.
HomeOrHoldingBranch Return	On check-in route the returned item to home branch or returned branch etc.

InProcessingToShelvingCart	Directs the items PROC location to CART when they are checked in before returning to their actual shelving location.
IssueLostItem	Sometimes library marked some items as lost, but users found it and attempt to issue hence this options control transaction of such items.
IssuingInProcess	Control Patrons from checking out an item whose rental charge would take them to the limit.
ManInvInNoissuesCharge	MANUAL_INV charges when summing up charges for noissuescharge.
Maxoutstanding	Restrict patrons to holding items if some amount is dues
Noissuescharge	Prevent members to issue a book if having some defined fine
OnSiteCheckouts	Provide an option to check out not for loan items so that statistics can be drawn to see who check outs such books.
OnSiteCheckoutsForce	This preference lets the staff override any restrictions a patron might have and check out items for use within the library. The OnSiteCheckouts preference must first be set to 'Enable' for this preference to be considered.
OverdueNoticeBcc	Allow to set email address to get all messages
OverdueNoticeCalendar	when working out the period for overdue notices
OverduesBlockCirc	Allows to block checkout if member has overdue books
RenewalPeriodBase	When renewing a book the new due date will be based on renewal date or last due date
RenewalSendNotice	Allows to control sending renewal notices
RentalFeesCheckout Confirmation	When checking out an item with rental fees (do/don't) ask, for confirmation.
ReturnBeforeExpiry	Restricts patrons to return books before their accounts expire (by restricting due dates to before the patron's expiration date).
ReturnToShelvingCart	Control All items to the location CART when they are checked in
useDaysMode	Control the due date should fall by calendar if due date falls on closed date it may configure to fall due date on next opening date
UseCourseReserves	A special feature to use if the collection of books to be reserved for some specific courses during semesters etc.

finesCalendar	This option gives the flexibility to choose whether the fine should be calculated including the days library is closed or not.
FinesIncludeGracePeriod	Grace period should be included during calculation of fine or not which is defined during circulation rules
finesMode	Fine should be calculated and send to admin only or calculate and display or not to calculate when (misc/cronjobs/fines.pl is being run)
RefundLostItemFeeOn Return	Refund or not if Lost item fees charged to a borrower when the lost item is returned
WhenLostCharge ReplacementFee	Charge or not to charge if a patron loses items
WhenLostForgiveFine	Fine should be charged or not is item is lost
AllowHoldDateInFuture	This option provide flexibility to choose the date from which hold will be applicable to item
AllowHoldPolicyOverride	Privilege to staff for override hold policies
AllowHoldsOnDamaged Items	Hold is allowed or not on items which are marked as damaged
AllowHoldsOnPatrons Possessions	Allow or not to place a hold on a record where the patron already has one or more items attached to that record checked out.
AllowRenewalIfOtherItems Available	Through this option system can allow renewing the books which are on hold if another same item is available
AutoResumeSuspended Holds	Allow or not suspended holds to be automatically resumed by a set date
Canreservefromother branches	Patron should be allowed to place hold on items belong to other libraries exist in Koha system
DisplayMultiPlaceHold	Enable/disable the ability to place holds on multiple biblio from the search results
emailLibrarianWhenHoldIs Placed	Email will be sent if hold is placed on items to Koha administrator
ExpireReservesMaxPick UpDelay	Allow or not holds to expire automatically if they have not been picked by within the period specified in ReservesMaxPickUpDelay
Maxreserves	How many maximum holds can be placed on items
OPACAllowHoldDateIn Future	Allow or not patrons to place hold that doesn't enter the waiting list on a certain future date. (AllowHoldDateInFuture must also be enabled

OPACAllowUserToChoose Branch	Allow or not a user to choose the library to pick up a hold from
ReservesMaxPickUpDelay	For how many days Koha system should wait after placing the hold on items before hold expires
ReservesNeedReturns	Don't automatically/automatically mark a hold as found and waiting when a hold is placed on a specific item and that item is already checked in
SuspendHoldsIntranet	Suspend the holds from intranet
SuspendHoldsOpac	Suspend the holds from OPAC
AllowAllMessageDeletion	It gives privileges to staff for deletion of messages added to other libraries
AllowOfflineCirculation	Koha provides excellent feature of offline circulation i.e. if there is disconnection with Koha server to client than staff can issue/ return the books and upload to the main server once connection is made
CircAutocompl	It gives excellent feature of guessing the patron i.e. when staff enters first three character of Patrons name system starts searching and display the probable match (maximum 10 at a time)
DisplayClearScreenButton	A option to clear the patrons detail from the staff interface once the transaction is over against the patron
ExportRemoveFields	Unnecessary fields can be removed from displaying the patron check out history in csv format
FineNotifyAtCheckin	If there is fine on items return by patrons system, send the email notification
itemBarcodeFallbackSearch	Option to issue a book by searching with Keyword in place of barcode in the concern box
numReturnedItemsToShow	Configure how many items can be displayed on the return screen of staff client
Soundon	Koha system produces a sound on check in or check out of items
SpecifyDueDate	Gives freedom to staff for altering the due date at the time of checkout contradictory to loan days defined in circulation and fine rules
SpecifyReturnDate	Similar to SpecifyDueDate but it applicable on retuning of books
UpdateTotalIssuesOnCirc	Do or don't update a bibliographic record's

	total issues count whenever an item is issued (WARNING! it increases server load significantly; if performance is a concern, use the update_totalissues.pl cron job to update the total issues count).
AllowSelfCheckReturns	Koha provides excellent option of self-check out and In of books by the patrons so here you can enable or disable the feature
AutoSelfCheckAllowed AutoSelfCheckID AutoSelfCheckPass	Option to login on the self-check out and check in screen by the defined ID and Password
SelfCheckoutByLogin	How patrons should login the self-check out and check in system for the transaction i.e. with user id and password or simply with barcode/patron id
SelfCheckTimeout	Setting the time after which self-check out screen will disappear when patron logged in and left as it is
WebBasedSelfCheck	Enabling the web-based self-checkout system. (available at: /cgi-bin/koha/sco/sco-main.pl)
Enhanced Content preferences	
Amazon, Babelthèque, Baker and Taylor, Coce Cover images cache, Google, Local Cover Images, Library Thing, Open Library, OverDrive	These are the options provides provisions to display the cover image of a book and their contents. You can select one or more out of the given and Koha will display images from all sources. Please note Google are very popular and free of cost without any limitations but others may charge for the same having lot of limitations too.
HTML5 Media	Display a tab with html5 media player for files catalogue in 856 tag
UseKohaPlugins	Enable or disable of using Koha plugins option
Syndetics	Syndetics is a pay service. You must first contact Syndetics directly for pricing and subscription information
Tagging	Koha provides the option to tag on the items on the OPAC or through staff client. Through various options you can enable/disable, moderate, total number of tags to display at a time, tagging on search items, etc. can be enabled and configured as per library choice
I18N/L10N	
AddressFormat	Controls how postal address of patrons enters in the system display

Alphabet	You can select the letters of English alphabet which will be browsable
CalendarFirstDayOfWeek	Which day library wished to select as the first day of week
Dateformat	Choosing date format
Language	Language option to display on staff interface
Opaclanguages	Language option to display on OPAC interface
Opaclanguagesdisplay	It allows the user to select the language to display on OPAC
TimeFormat	Time format 24 hours or 12 hours
	Local Use
printcirculationslips	Configure to print circulation slips
Version	Shows the latest version of Koha installed. Apart from above these contain other preferences which are new to Koha or obsolete so one can ignore all.
	Logging preferences
AuthoritiesLog, BorrowersLog, CataloguingLog etc.	As the preference itself indicates it is system logs which can be generated for specific activities.
	OPAC preferences
OpacAdvSearchMore Options	Provide option to select various fields for searching on the OPAC by item type, language, etc.
OpacAdvSearchOptions	Options to display on the OPAC
AuthorisedValueImages	You can select images for authorized value to display on the OPAC or not
BiblioDefaultView	By default to display biblio detail record in various formats like MARC, ISBD, etc.
COinSinOPACResults	Include or not the COinS / OpenURL / Z39.88 in OPAC search results
DisplayOPACiconsXSLT	The format, audience, and material type icons in XSLT MARC21 results and detail pages in the OPAC
GoogleIndicTransliteration	Show or not the Google indic translation on OPAC
Hidelostitems	You can show and hide the lost items from OPAC
LibraryName	You can configure here name of your library to display in OPAC
NoLoginInstructions	If a patron is not logged in you can show the customized message on the OPAC

OpacAddMastheadLibrary Pulldown	Option to show drop down menu to select on OPAC while searching the items
OPACBaseURL	Base URL configuration which may be used for sharing items on social media etc.
Opaccredits	The customization field to display in OPAC credit area
OpacExportOptions	You can choose various options to display on OPAC for exporting the records
OPACFallback	Theme to display on OPAC
Opacheader	Fields to customized header section of OPAC with HTML
OpacHighlightedWords NotHighlightedWords	This option allows configuring highlight the searched words and not the stop words
OpacKohaUrl	Powered by Koha' text on OPAC footer. Will suggest not to disable this from OPAC
Opaclayoutstylesheet	It gives the option to select which layout should be displayed on the OPAC. You can make your own and link here
OpacLocationBranchTo Display	Display the Items belonging libraries if there is more than one library
OpacMaintenance	Enable here message to display if any error appears on the OPAC or you can use when Koha is under maintenance
OpacMainUserBlock	You can customize here main (Central part) of the OPAC with HTML
OpacMaxItemsToDisplay	While searching how many items should be displayed on the OPAC on a single page
OPACMySummaryNote	You can write any message for patrons to display when they logged into the Koha OPAC
OpacNav	Koha left top corner navigation links customization field
OpacNavBottom	Koha left bottom navigation links customization
OpacNavRight	Koha right navigation links customization with HTML
OPACNoResultsFound	Which message to display on OPAC when no item is found after searching
OpacPublic	You can make OPAC private or public in case of private users need to log in before searching
OPACShowBarcode	You can display or hide the accession number/barcode to display on OPAC
OPACShowCheckoutName	Enable or disable the name of patron who has checked out the document

OPACShowHoldQueue Details	Hold queue details can be displayed on OPAC
OpacShowRecent Comments	Comments to display on OPAC made by others
OpacStarRatings	Star rating on items to display
OpacSuggestion ManagedBy	It allows to show the name of staff manages the suggestion on OPAC
OPACURLOpenInNew Window	URL can be opened in new windows when clicked from OPAC
OPACUserCSS	Field to write CSS code to display on all pages
Opacuserjs	Javascript to display on all pages
OPACXSLTDetailsDisplay and OPACXSLTResults Display	Various style sheets to display on OPAC be default in result page and detail page
numSearchRSSResults	How many results to display in RSS
OPACAcquisitionDetails	You can display the acquisition details on OPAC
OpacAuthorities	You can allow or disallow the patron to search the authority records
Opacbookbag	Activate the temporary cart for storing the items on OPAC
OpacBrowser	patrons to browse subject authorities on OPAC (run misc/cronjobs/build_browser_and_cloud.pl to create the browser list)
OpacBrowseResults	browsing and paging search results from the OPAC detail page
OPACFinesTab	Activate to access fine on patron account on OPAC
OpacItemLocation	Allows to display call number on search results
OpacPasswordChange	Allows patron to change their passwords
OPACPatronDetails	Allows patron to change their contact details from OPAC
OPACpatronimages	You can show the patron image on patron account
OpacTopissue	Allows to display most issued items on the OPAC
Opacuserlogin	Allows user to log into their account
QuoteOfTheDay	Display quote of the day to display on OPAC home page
RequestOnOpac	Allows patron to place hold from OPAC
Reviewson	Enable patron to make comment on the items

ShowReviewer	Show the full name of the commentator/ reviewer
ShowReviewerPhoto	Display reviewer picture on OPAC
SocialNetworks	Allows to display social network links on OPAC item detail pages
Suggestion	Allows or not to make purchase suggestion from OPAC
BlockExpiredPatronOpac Actions	You can block the patrons to place hold/ renew if expired
OpacAllowPublicList Creation and OpacAllow SharingPrivateLists	Allows creating public list to store their items and display on account/OPAC. List can be shared also
OPACFineNoRenewals	You can fix the fine amount above which patron can't make renewal of books
OpacHiddenItems	Define custom rules to hide specific items from search and view on the OPAC. How to write these rules is documented on the Koha wiki
OpacRenewalAllowed	Allow or not to renew the books via OPAC
OPACViewOthers Suggestions	Allow to view the purchase suggestion made by others
singleBranchMode	Allows patrons to select their branch on the OPAC or show branch names with callnumbers
EnableOpacSearchHistory	Set to save OPAC search history
OPACPrivacy	Option to choose their own privacy settings for their reading history. This requires opacreadinghistory and AnonymousPatron
Opacreadinghistory	Allows patron to save reading history in their account
TrackClicks	Allows to track the links patron click on
PatronSelfRegistration	You can enable for new patron self-registration
OPACShelfBrowser	Shelf browser on item details pages, allowing patrons to see what's near that item on the shelf. Note that this uses up a fairly large amount of resources on your server, and should be avoided if your collection has a large number of items
ShelfBrowserUsesCcode, ShelfBrowserUsesLocation	Location and collection code to chose when finding items on the self-browse
Patrons preferences	
AutoEmailOpacUser	Allows to send email to newly created members

AutoEmailPrimaryAddress	Use first valid email to send notification
autoMemberNum	Card number to fill automatically or manually
BorrowerMandatoryField	Option to make mandatory fields of patron
BorrowerRenewalPeriod Base	When renewing member the base period selection
BorrowersTitles	The setting of borrower titles likes Dr. Mr. etc.
BorrowerUnwantedField	Disable the unwanted fields of patron data entry
CardnumberLength	Length of member card number
EnableBorrowerFiles	Enable the ability to upload and attach arbitrary files to a borrower record
EnhancedMessaging Preferences	Patrons to choose which notices they receive and when they receive them. Note that this only applies to certain kinds of notices
Intranetreadinghistory	Allows staff to check borrower history
MaxFine	Fix the maximum fine beyond which system will not calculate
minPasswordLength	Define the minimum password length for patrons
NotifyBorrowerDeparture	Fix the number of days before the expiry to send email
Patronimages	Allows to upload and display patron image on staff client
PatronsPerPage	Number of patrons to display per page
useDischarge	Librarian can discharge member and member can request for discharge
	Searching preferences
EnableSearchHistory	Keep or not to keep patron search history in staff client
QueryAutoTruncate	Perform wildcard searching (where, for example, *Har* would match *Harry* and *harp*
QueryFuzzy	Match similarly spelled words in a search (for example, a search for *flang* would also match *flange* and *fang*; REQUIRES ZEBRA)
QueryWeightFields	Ranking of search results by relevance (REQUIRES ZEBRA)
TraceCompleteSubfields	Force or don't force subject tracings in the OPAC and Staff Client to search only for complete-subfield matches
defaultSortField default SortOrder	Options to select the sorting order of the search results
displayFacetCount	Show not to show facet counts. The relevance

	of these numbers highly depends on the value of the maxRecordsForFacets preference. Applies to OPAC and staff interface
DisplayLibraryFacets	Show facets for holding or other branch libraries
FacetLabelTruncation Length	Facets length truncate limit on staff client and OPAC
FacetMaxCount	Number of facets settings for each category
maxItemsInSearchResults	Maximum item to display in search result
maxRecordsForFacets	Facets will be built on how many search results
numSearchResults	Setting for how many results display in staff client
AdvancedSearchLanguages	You can limit the language list in advance search
AdvancedSearchTypes	You can limit the search by item type in staff and OPAC
expandedSearchOption	By default shows the more/fewer options of search on OPAC
Serials preferences	
opacSerialDefaultTab	Which tab to display default tab in OPAC for serials
OPACSerialIssueDisplay Count	How many serial issue to display by default
RoutingListAddReserves	You can place serial on hold if it is on routing list
RoutingSerials	Use not to use the routing list feature in serial
StaffSerialIssueDisplay Count	How many loose issues to display in staff client
SubscriptionHistory	Allows to display brief of full subscription history of serials
Staff Client preferences	
DisplayIconsXSLT	Show the audience, item type in the staff client
IntranetmainUserblock	You can customize the message to display in intranet staff client with the help of HTML
IntranetNav	As above navigation can be customized with HTML coding
Intranetstylesheet	You can customize and link the intranet display i.e. look and feel with the help of CSS
IntranetUserCSS and intranetuserjs	CSS and Java script to display on all staff client pages
HidePatronName	Show or hide the patron name having books check out and hold

viewISBD	Allows the staff to view the ISBD
viewLabeledMARC	Staff to view records in labeled MARC form on the staff client
viewMARC	Staff to view records in plain MARC form on the staff client
	Tools and Web services Preferences
MaxItemsForBatch	Maximum items selection for modifications and deletions
OAI-PMH	This is open archives initiatives protocol for metadata harvesting once it is enabled and properly configured another person on the globe can harvest your Koha metadata records

5.4. ACQUISITION MANAGEMENT IN KOHA

Acquisition section of the library looks after the process of budget management, receiving the book purchase request, selecting the vendor, deciding the various terms and condition of supply of books like discount rate, conversion rates, supply durations etc., invoicing, receipt of shipment/order, accessioning of books and many other processes involve in procurement of books.

Koha library management system provides a complete solution for acquisition management through its module. In brief, the entire process involves in the procurement of books and procession though Koha module is described in below flow chart.

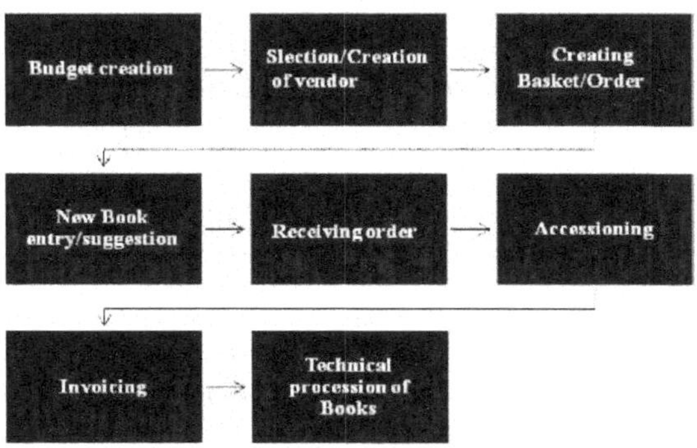

Fig. 5.13. Flow chart of Acquisition in Koha

Manage Order

The first step in Koha to start ordering the Book is to select the vendor for which search option is provided. If the budget is not defined by the Koha admin module, it will alert for the same as shown in the below screen. The budget and new vendor can also be created from this screen if it is not available in the Koha for further processing.

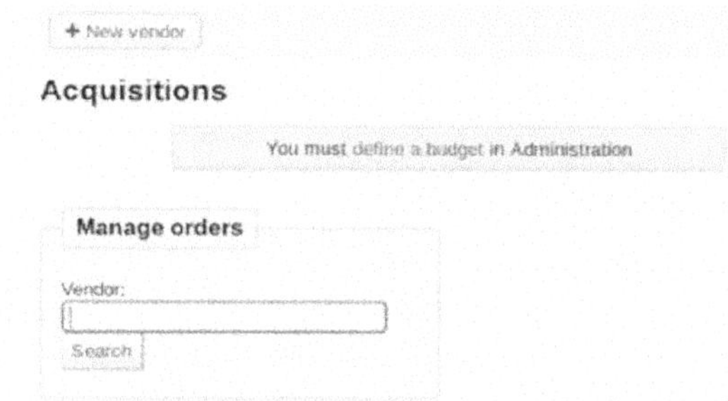

Fig. 5.14. Manage order screen

Adding Budget

Adding the budget to the Koha system is very first requirement to start using the acquisition module as without budget there is no meaning of using the concerned module. Koha provides a lot of flexibility in defining the budget and further bi-furcating it in many funds, the budget can be calculated in monthly/item wise, etc.

The budget duration may vary from library to library, but it is a financial year, after putting the total budget of the library it can be made it active. The total budget of the library can be further bi-furcated (Funds for the defined budget), and the funds can be further divided into the child funds. There is good administrative control over the library staff about funds utilization and use i.e. administrator can define who is the owner and the users supposed to place an order of books from the defined funds. Much flexibility has been provided in editing/ deleting/creating the defined budget and funds in Koha system at any point in time.

Fig. 5.15. Formats for Budget Configuration

Adding new Vendor

New vendor data entry worksheet in Koha is divided into three sections out of which the first represents the very basic information about the Vendor; the second is the contact detail of their office including email, phone, etc. and the last third is for billing purposes which indicate its status like active/inactive, list/invoice price currency, tax rate, discount percent, delivery time, note, etc. All the three screens are displayed below:

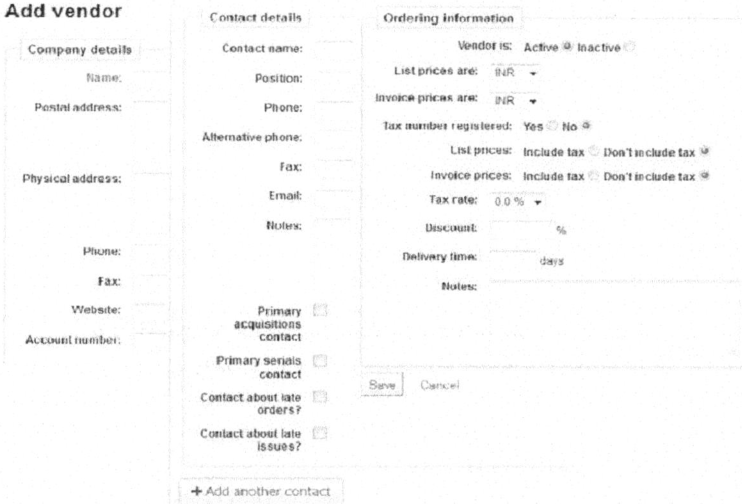

Fig. 5.16. Vendor details data entry form

The vendor details can be edited further by searching for any part of vendor name on the home screen of acquisition. The detail vendor page will display edit, new and delete vendor options but if there is basket/ order exist with the currently selected vendor then in place of delete screen system will show receive shipment option in the right corner.

Placing order to Vendor

In order to start acquisition module for placing the order of books the first requirement is to select the vendor to whom library is intended to place the order for a book to do this you can search the vendor with key words or any of the alphabet within the name of vendor (it facilities keyword as well as string search). If the searched keyword matches with many vendors of the data base, then you will see all the vendor out of which you can select the desired one if there is only one vendor exist then the system will display the below screen.

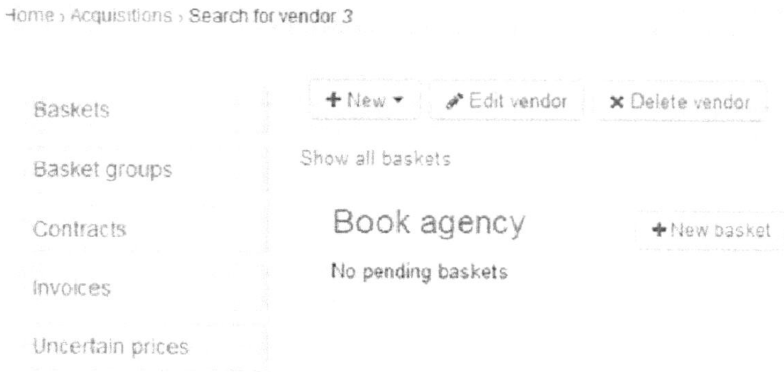

Fig. 5.17. Display vendor detail in acquisition

To create the order you need to click on new basket option, some basic data need to be fill like basket name (order number) and internal/vendor note rest of the data is already displayed like vendor/library name etc. on saving the created basket the screen to add items/titles to the basket and provide some options to edit/change like Add user, Edit basket etc. We will discuss each six options given for adding the titles in the basket one by one.

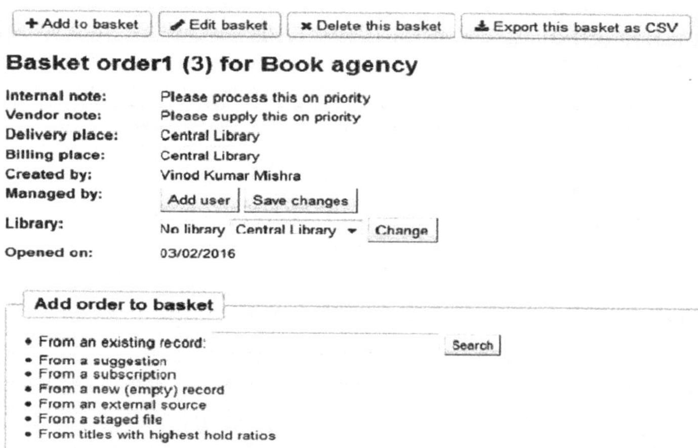

Fig. 5.18. Adding Title to Basket

Adding order to basket

There are six methods given to add order/title to the basket which is as follows:

From and existing record

This is the option used by the library if multiple copies of the same item/title are required in the library. The search box provides facility to search the title which is required for purchasing then on selection of titles it will display the accounting and other details which need to be fill up as discussed in next sections.

From a suggestion

This is the main option which is used when we are creating the records through new purchase suggestion from staff client or if any of the patrons is placing a request from his/her account via OPAC. On selection of this option system will direct to the page and display if there is any approved/accepted title is pending for placing the order/ to be included in the new basket as displayed in below screen.

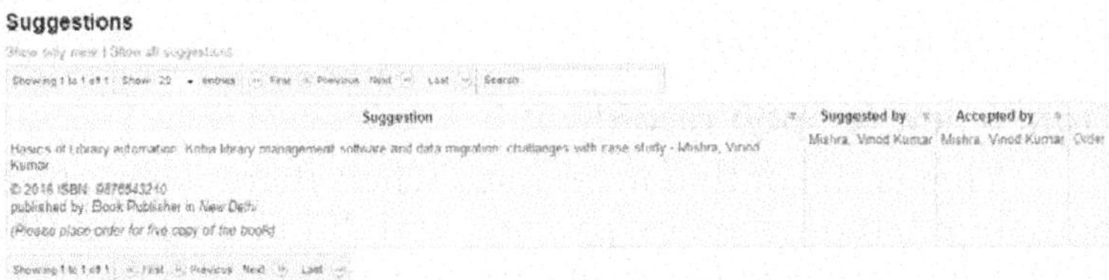

Fig. 5.19. Adding Title to Basket from Suggestion in Koha

Now you have to select the highlighted/linked option "Order" to include this title in the basket/order but before this system will present a detail form with description about Basket details, patrons to add for notification on arrival, catalogue details, suggestions detail and accounting detail. You are required to complete all the details which is mandatory and as shown in the below screen then finally save the details, now on saving the title has been added to the basket. Please note uncertain price is if you are not aware of the price at the time of placing the order and system will automatically calculate the prices once you enter the Quantity and vendor price.

Fig. 5.20. New order form

From a subscription

This is meant for placing the order/basket when we are subscribing the journals hence will be discussed in detail in the serial module.

From a new (empty) record

This is the option to be used when there is new title demanded/requested by patrons and did not exist in the database. On selection of this option you will be presented with forms to complete which is similar to form displayed under purchase from suggestion section (Fig. 5.18). After addition of all the titles system will display the detail of all the titles as shown in the screen below which can be further modified, transferred, deleted, add vendor notes if require etc. Therefore, after review of all the tiles added the basket needs to be closed (Close this basket) for further processing.

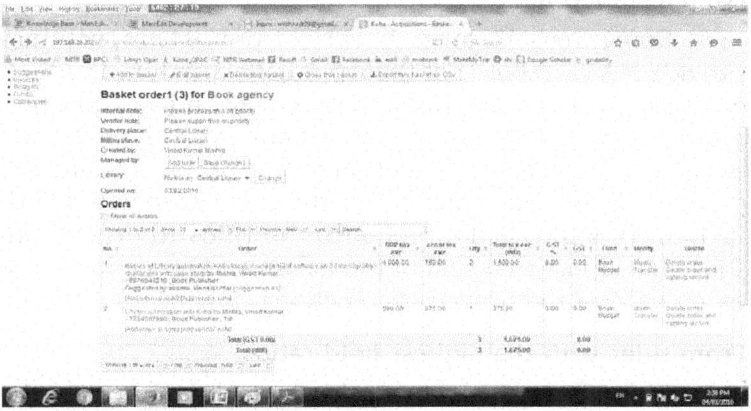

Fig. 5.21. Detail of the titles added in basket/order

From an external source

Placing the order/Title by selecting/importing the bibliographic detail of the document from an external source like Library of Congress, Columbia University, etc. with the help of Z35.50 protocol is known as placing the order from an external source. However, rest of the forms and other editing/deleting, etc. options are similar to above methods.

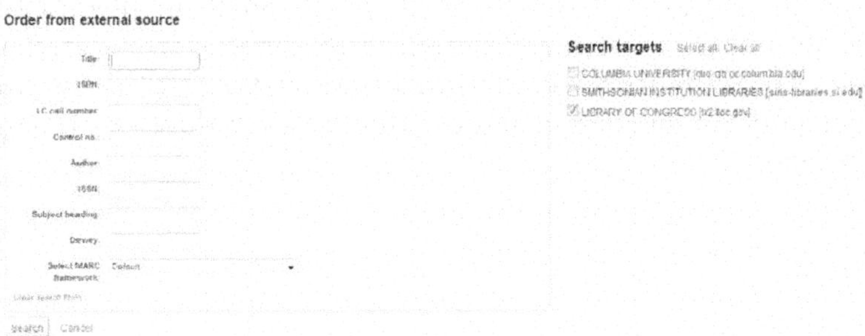

Fig. 5.22. Placing the order from external source (Z39.50 server)

From a staged file

Sometimes in large libraries, publishers/vendors provide MARC records of their published materials which can be imported to the Koha temporarily and as and when require library staff can select the book from these records called (staged file). On selection of this option system will display all the files staged and the titles associated with it. Library staff needs to choose the titles to order from these lists after that rest of the forms and procedures are same as described in above sections.

From titles with the highest hold ratios

This option has been added recently to order the books from the list which is frequently placed on hold/ reserve. Hence, it gives flexibility to librarians to purchase the additional copy of highly demanded books for the patrons. The other procedures and forms are same after choosing the titles from the highest holds ratios list.

Receiving Procedure of shipment/Order

Once all the order has been placed to the vendor the next procedure is to receive the same. Libraries used to give some time to vendor for delivery of orders if it is not sent on time reminders is generated for the same which will be discussed in next sections. On receipt of order library staff needs to search the vendor whose order is in hand with some keyword and system will show all the pending order against the displayed vendor as shown below.

Fig. 5.23. Pending order against the particular vendor

Invoicing of shipment

In case there is more than one order pending against the vendor staff need first to verify with an order number which order/shipment he/she received in hand then click the "Receive shipment" option for invoicing process. Fill the desired information like invoice number, fund, etc. as shown in the below-invoicing detail form and proceed to next.

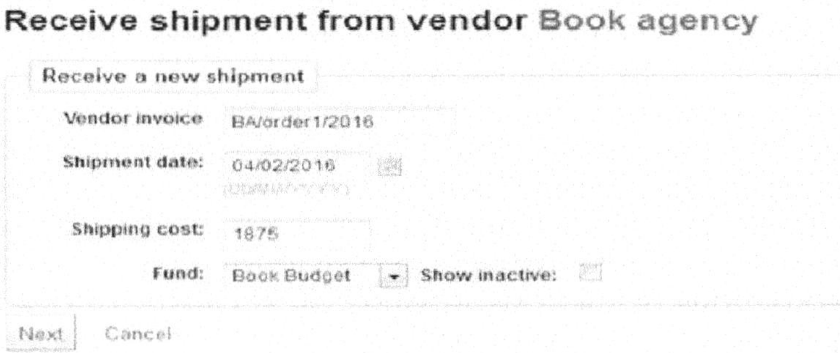

Fig. 5.24. Invoicing Form

Receiving/Viewing of order detail after invoicing

After invoicing of the received shipment, the detail of the titles available in the order will be presented along with various details like order summary, basket detail, fund, order cost unit cost, etc. The system provides flexibility for deleting the order, editing the title, etc. at this stage also.

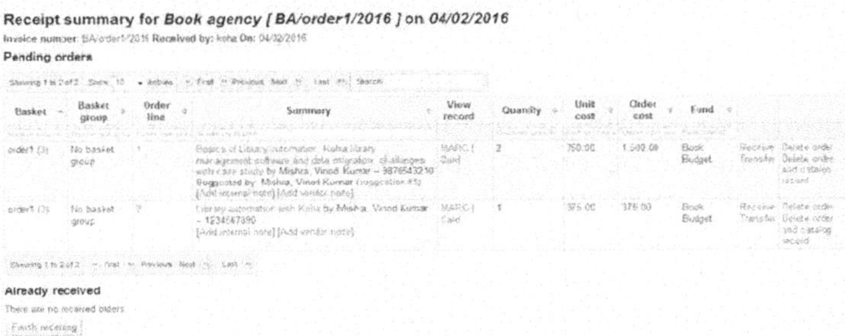

Fig. 5.25. Detail of the Receipt/Order Summary

Accessioning of Titles/Items

There is an option in second last column to receive the items as shown in the above screen (Fig. 5.23) and on the selection of above Koha will present a detailed screen for receiving items against the particular ordered title. The screen is divided into two parts (Right and left). In left screen system displays the catalogue detail, Suggestion by an item details to be filled, but the right screen is generally none editable and it display the accounting details like how many items ordered and how many received/pending, etc.

We have to complete the item detail form by putting desired information about the items received like its location, date of received, etc. out of which Barcode number/Accession number and item type must be required. On adding the item system will update all the accounting detail at right hand side like items received, pending etc. and again displayed the item detail page at left side, these process will continue to be repeated until all the items is accessioned/received. However if suppose some of the item is not yet received you can leave as part receive of the ordered item which can be received later by repeating the above procedure but once all item is received system will not display the item detail screen more hence you have to save now the item received the screen.

On saving the received items against the ordered title system will update the receipt/order summary page as shown in above screen and display the detail of items received and pending along with accounting details as shown below. Now to receive pending items you have to repeat the same procedure. Koha gives the flexibility to cancel the receipts if require; once all the ordered title has been received you can see there are no pending title details hence you have to click the "Finish receiving" to complete the process. On the display of invoice detail and account details, you can close the account and save it which can be reopened later for any modifications if desired.

Fig. 5.26. Items receiving form

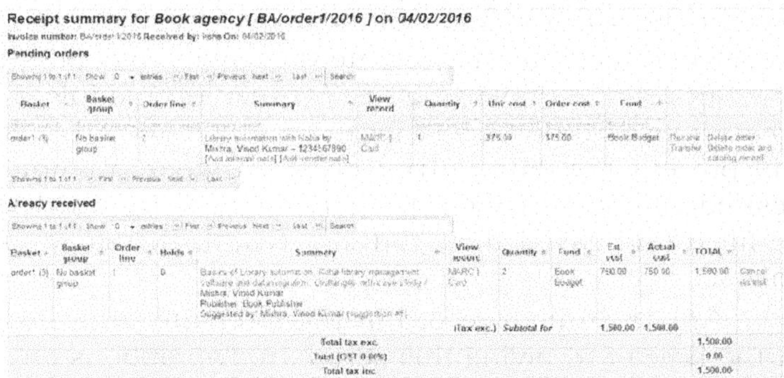

Fig. 5.27. Update Receipt summaries after part receipt

5.5. SERIAL MANAGEMENT IN KOHA

Serials module can be accessed by going to the more menu at the top of staff screen and choosing serials or by clicking serials on the main Koha staff client page. The Serials module in Koha is used for keeping track of journals, newspapers and other items that come on a regular or irregular schedule. As with all modules, make sure you go through the related system settings before using the Serials module.

We will start with the purchase of the new serials, the process of serial purchase needs to be done through the acquisition module similar to book purchase procedures except we have first to create a new subscription through serial module then we will go to acquisition for rest of the purchase procedure like ordering, invoicing, etc.

New subscription

We have to first create the subscription detail of serials to be procured for the library; this can be started with serial home page "New subscription" option. There are various fields which are mandatory, and some are not. First you have to select by searching the vendor to whom this serial will be placed the order similarly title needs to be selected if any of the above does not exist in the system than you may create the same. To create the new vendor you have to go to acquisition module and create a new vendor record for titles, create record option will present the data entry worksheet where minimum desired information about the serial to be subscribed can be filled and saved then you can search the same and choose.

Create an item record or not to create item record at the time of receiving this serial are two options out of which one need to be selected as per the policy of the library, if you select to create the record than on receiving it will ask for item details else will not. When there are irregular issues, you may select to keep issue number or skip the issue number. The grace period is the period given to vendor after which automated reminders will be generated in case a serial missed the scheduled arrival date i.e. if a serial date of arrival is 10 of each month but if it does not arrived up to 20 (if given ten days grace period) than reminder will be initiated. You can choose how many current issues to display in staff client and OPAC for users. There are several other details like a library, location, notes etc. need to be selected as per suitability and requirements.

Fig. 5.28. New subscription form 1

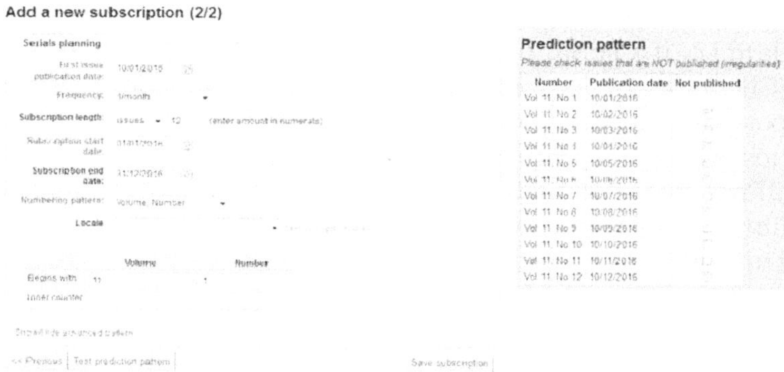

Fig. 5.29. New subscription form 2

The above new subscription form 2 will provide the fields especially about the serial subscription length, numbering pattern, etc. As shown in the above form fill the specific data related to the new serial than hit the "Test prediction pattern", this will display the correct pattern/schedule at the right-hand side, after verification of the pattern and all the data you may save the subscription details. Koha gives you facility to create/modify the subscription pattern with the option "Show/Hide advanced pattern" for example if you wish to create a new pattern having numbered and issues only which are not available like (No.2, issue 1) then you may create new and save it permanently to be used in future.

Ordering of New subscription

To order the serial, you need to select the acquisition module and start the process as you have done for the purchase of books and described in the acquisition module. At the time of adding order to basket you have to select the option "From Subscription," it will land on the journal search page as shown below from where you can select/order the require serial. Next page will display to add accounting details, quantity, etc. same as Book then save the details and close the basket.

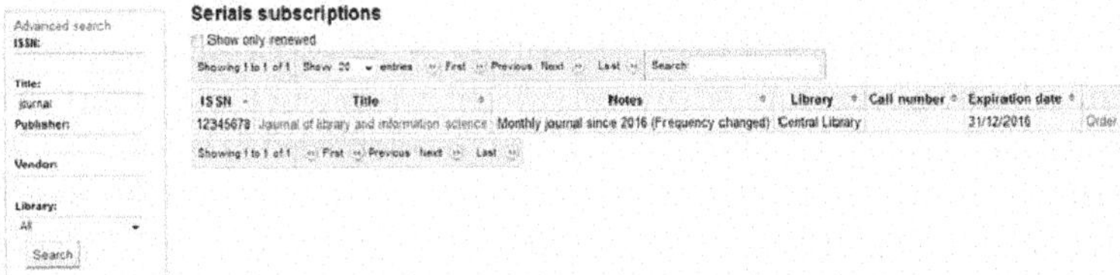

Fig. 5.30. Selection of serial for ordering from subscription

Receiving of Shipment/New subscription

On receipt of shipment for the ordered Serial we need to enter the invoice details as we have done in the books, but here we may not get the Item detail page like books as we have selected "no items should be created at the time of receiving the serial" during the new subscription creation for this title because this practice is more prevalent in libraries. Generally, libraries place the order and pay the amount in advance then throughout the year libraries receive the loose issues of serials and get it bound, after bounding the loose issues of journal accessioning is done directly through the catalogue module i.e. library can add the item barcode number/ accession number and other details against the subscribed title. Therefore, on the display of below screen simply save and then close the receiving of order for completing the accounting details and other processes.

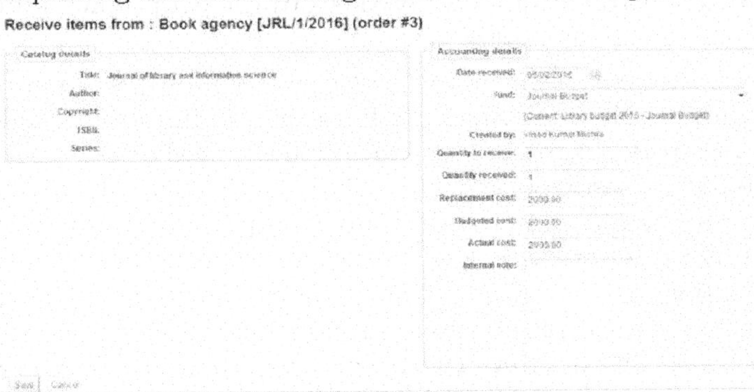

Fig. 5.31. Receiving screen for Serials

Receiving of loose issues

We have processed the order and receiving for new serial subscription "Journal of library and information science" as discussed and demonstrated above. Now library will start receiving of loose issues of serial from the vendor/publisher therefore once the concern serial arrived in the library it will be first searched in the Koha serial module either with ISSN number or title key words.

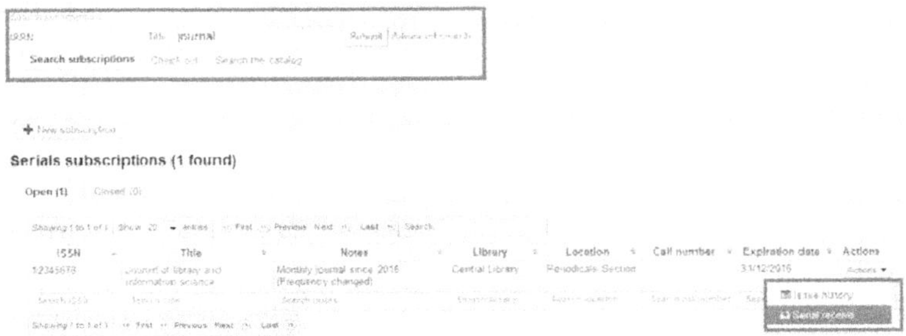

Fig. 5.32. Serial selection and search option

On selection of "Serial receive" option under the "Action" heading of a serial in hand, Koha will present the detail of the serial along with number, date of publications, etc. Under the Status heading lot of status related option is presented by the Koha out of which one has to select as per the status for example if Vol. 11, No.1 of the journal has been received than library staff will select the option "Arrived" from the drop down menu as shown in the below screen.

In case if there are any notes and supplementary issues received against the loose issue that can be filled in the appropriate box. If you have decided at the time of creating subscription detail to have an item record created for each issue an item add form will appear after choosing 'Arrived' where all details can be filled with barcode number, call number, shelving location, etc. If you are receiving multiple issues at once or have marked an issue as 'Late' or 'Missing' there you can click the 'Generate Next' button to appear the next issues for an update.

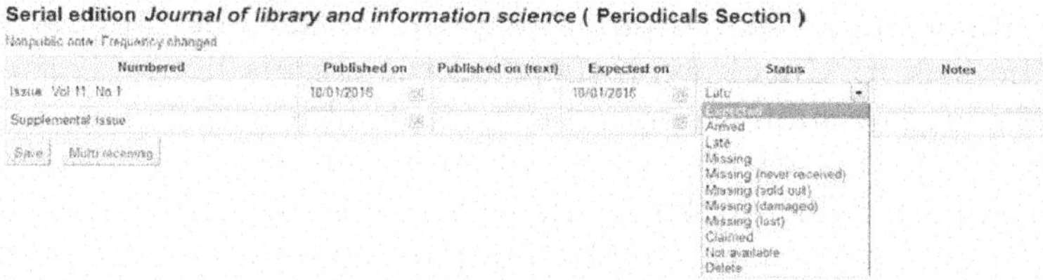

Fig. 5.33. Receiving of serial

Claim late issues

The serial claim is nothing but sending a reminder to the vendor/publisher from whom library has subscribed the journal, generation of claims is a routine and most important process for any library for proper management of loose issues of serials and their binding without missing of loose issues. Koha can generate the automatic email reminder for the late marked loose issues, to send the reminder go to the serial home page and click the Claims option and choose the vendor to whom library wishes to send the reminder for late issues.

Fig. 5.34. Missing issues screen

On selection of vendor Koha will display all the journals against which loose issues are late along with many details like Title, ISSN, Claim counts, etc. Library can generate and download the CSV/Excel file of late issues, or directly they can send the email notification as shown in the above screen.

Other options for serial module

The serial module provides other options like check expiration tool from which you can see when your subscriptions are about to expire. To use the tool click the link to 'Check expiration' on the serials home menu. Manage frequency option provides flexibility to define new serial frequency if it is not already defined in the Koha, similarly, you can define the new numbering pattern with the option Manage numbering pattern Apart from above there are many other options available which can be customized and configured as per the library requirements.

5.6. CATALOGUING IN KOHA

Koha is one of the best ILMS, which provides a lot of flexibility and ease in the cataloguing of the library materials. To start cataloguing / data entry of any library materials, it is a basic requirement to setup the cataloging system preferences and design the various mark frameworks as per the standards applicable for library materials like Thesis, CD/DVD, map, books, serials, etc. Koha has divided there data entry procedure in two parts i.e. Bibliographic record and Item record. In the bibliographic record, the detail about the library material is filled like the author, title, edition, pages, etc. and in the item record local details like barcode/accession number, the location of book, call number, etc.

Cataloguing of new record

There are two methods to make entry of any new bibliographic record of a library material (direct entry in the selected framework or through the z39.50/SRU methods in a specific framework).

On selection of new record system presents the list of frameworks configured in the system, similarly if cataloguer is wished to enter the record via Z39.50/SRU methods than accordingly the option can be selected and the system will pop up the search screen to fetch the data from various Z39.50 servers if it is available. In case any record is available on remote servers it will display the result with the option to Import the record in the selected framework which can be further modified as per requirements.

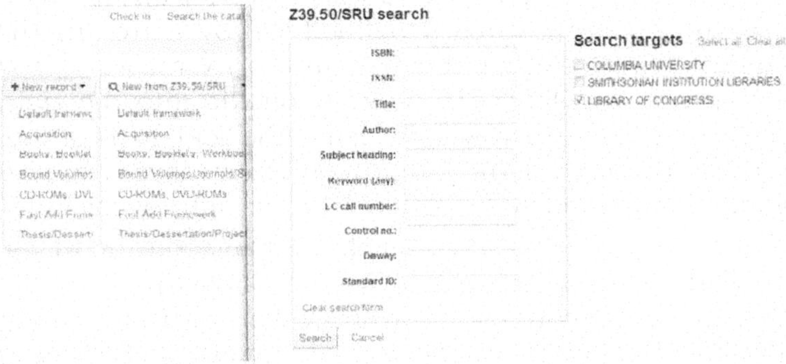

Fig. 5.35. Framework selection screen for data entry and Z39.50

Cataloguing of Bibliographic records in Marc framework

Marc framework customization has been discussed in Koha admin as it is required to be done before using of Koha system. Koha default framework is too much lengthy and has been divided into ten tags from 0-9 hence cataloguer need to go through the tags for data input in the concern MARC fields. Bibliographic Mark framework option provides flexibility to design short framework in a single tag having less number of MARC fields i.e. as per the requirement of the library which saves lot of time of a cataloguer and provides error free bibliographic entry of records. On selection of framework for data entry, some of the MARC fields are marked with a red asterisk which indicates the mandatory fields and some data needs to be entering before saving the record. There are some small icons which are highlighted in the below screen and used for addition additional field if it is repeatable (like subject 650) or it will pop up a new screen (like fixed field 008).

Some fields may not be editable because the value

in BiblioAddsAuthorities system preference is set not to allow catalogers to type in fields controlled by authorities so you may see a lock symbol to the left of the field (like in 100), hence in such case you need to click on the small icon and select the already defined text by searching the database or you can enter new authority record if it is not already available. To move subfields into the right order, click the up arrow to the left of the field, to duplicate a subfield click on the clone icon (to remove a copied field, click the delete clone icon) to the right of the field.

Once you've finished, click the 'Save' button at the top and choose whether you want to save and view the bibliographic record you have created or continue to add/edit items attached to the record. Choosing 'Save and view record' will bring you right to the record you just cataloged. Choosing 'Save and edit items' will bring you to the add/edit item form after saving the bibliographic record so that you can attach holdings. Choosing 'Save and continue editing' will allow you to save your work so far and keep you in the editor to continue working. If you are about to add a duplicate record to the system, you will be warned before saving

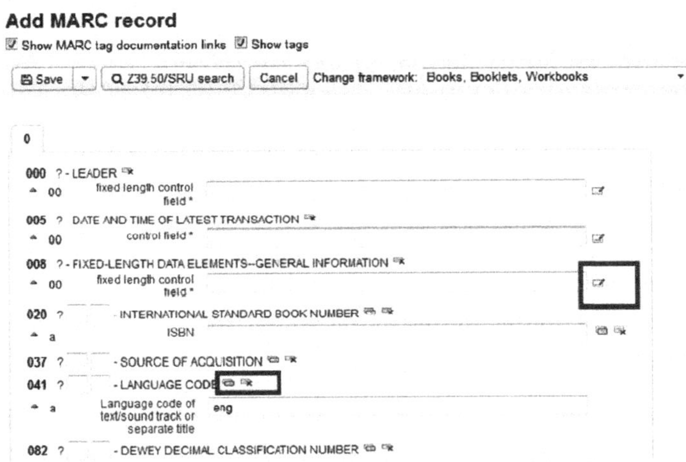

Fig. 5.36. Customized MARC Framework

Advance editor Cataloguing

Advance cataloguing/editor is a new feature which gives great flexibility to cataloguer for data entry in a minimum time. To use the advanced cataloging editor, you need to enable the EnableAdvancedCatalogingEditor preference. In the advanced editor once you've opened a blank framework or imported a record via Z39.50 you will be presented with the form to continue cataloging and you can do the modification or entry of data as per bibliographic details of the items in hand. In the bottom of editor you can see reference from the library of congress for concern MARC field and in case, your MARC tag is invalid it will alert with red highlight. There are many shortcut keyboards which can be used to fasten the work of cataloguing as shown in the below screenshot. The features also provided with options of Import ISO records, many settings, etc.

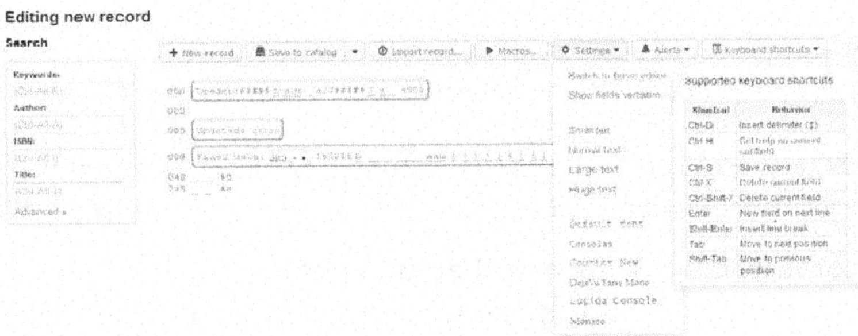

Fig. 5.37. Advance new MARC record editing screen

Cataloguing of Item records in MARC framework

As we have seen how to enter and save the bibliographic data in defined marc framework in above section, so the next step is to add the item detail like barcode/accession number, call number, copy number, etc. On saving of bibliographic record, the system presents the screen as shown below which is meant for filling local detail of item/material already catalogued. If a book has multiple copies than it can be added simultaneously by adding multiple items options rather than one by one to do this you have to add the barcode/accession number of first accessioned book in the concerned field than total number of copies in the concerned field, on saving the item record system will automatically add the copies with consecutive accession numbers.

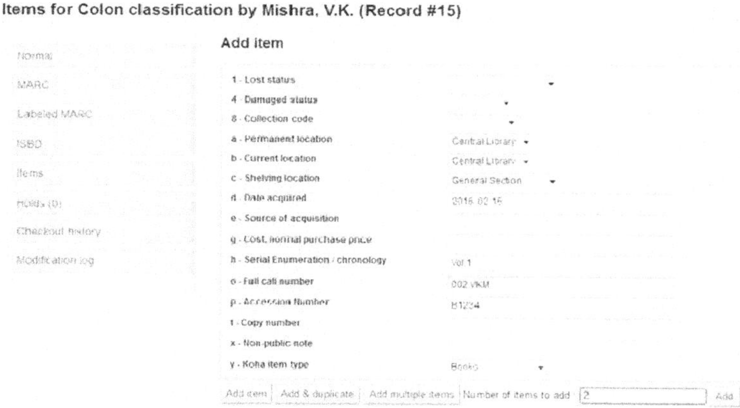

Fig. 5.38. Item details data entry screen

In the left side of the screen, there are options to view the record in MARC, labeled MARC, items detail, total checkout history, etc.

Local fields in Koha and their description

Almost Every ILMS software has some local fields which are used for entry of call number, accession number, type of material, the location of materials, etc. similarly Koha has so many local fields which are defined in tag 952. The description of each such field is given in the below table. Please note that same tags must be used while converting and migrating the data from one system to another.

Table 5.10. Detail of Koha MARC local fields

Tag/ subfield	Data element	Description	Notes
952$0	Withdrawn status	Status of the item connects with the authorized values list 'WITHDRAWN.'	The defaults values of the list are: 0 = "" [Not withdrawn]; 1 = 'Withdrawn'
952$1	Lost status	Status of the item connects with the authorised values list 'LOST.'	The defaults values of the list are: 0 = "" [Not Lost]; 1 = 'Lost'; 2= 'Long Overdue (Lost)'; 3 = 'Lost and Paid For'; 4 = 'Missing'
952$2	Source of classification or shelving scheme	A classification scheme that defines filing rules used for sorting call numbers.	If no classification scheme is entered, the system will use the value entered in the Cataloging preference "DefaultClassificationSource".
952$3	Materials specified (bound volume or another part)	Specific issues of serials or multi-part items.	Copy/volume data is stored in 952$h and $t for display in Normal views. $3 isn't displayed anywhere except the MARC view.
952$4	Damaged status	Status of the item connects with the authorized values list 'DAMAGED.'	The defaults values of the list are: 0 = "" [Not damaged]; 1 = 'Damaged'
952$5	Use restrictions	Status of the item connects with the authorized values list 'RESTRICTED.'	The defaults values of the list are: 0 = "" [Not restricted]; 1 = 'Restricted'
952$6	Koha normalized classification for sorting		
952$7	Not for loan	Status of the item connects with the authorised values list 'NOT_LOAN.'	The defaults values of the list are: -1 = Ordered; 0 = "" [Available for loans]; 1 = Not for Loan; 2 = Staff Collection

952$8	Collection code	Status of the item connects with the authorised values list 'CCODE'	The collection code provides another means for breaking down the library collection into categories (Example: Fiction, Mysteries, etc.) for reports. It is also used for cataloging and circulation statistics.
952$9	Koha itemnumber (autogenerated)		System-generated item number. Does not display in the item record
952$a	Branchcode	owning library	Code must be defined in System Administration '! Libraries, Branches and Groups
952$b	Branchcode	holding library (usu. the same as 952$a)	Same note of the previous subfield
952$c	Shelving location code	Coded value, matching the authorized value list 'LOC'	
952$d	Date acquired	YYYY-MM-DD	The date the item was purchased or acquired.
952$e	Source of acquisition	coded value or vendor string	Name or abbreviation of the publisher, distributor, or vendor. This may also be the vendor code from the acquisitions module, but there is little functionality currently that uses this field.
952$f	Coded location qualifier	A three-character code that identifies the specific issues of the item that are located apart from the main holdings of the same item.	This has no function in Koha.
952$g	Purchase price	Original purchase price or list price	a decimal number, no currency symbol
952$h	Serial enumeration caption	Volume and issue information for serial items.	

952$i	Inventory number	The inventory number.	It is not repeatable and not mandatory. Added with 3.4.0
952$j	Shelving control number	The stack number of the item, inventory code.	
952$l	Total Checkouts	A total number of checkouts. Display only field.	
952$m	Total Renewals	The total number of renewals. Display only field.	This is the cumulative total. The total number of renewals is not reset to 0 when the item is checked in.
952$n	Total Holds	The total number of holds. Display only field.	
952$o	Koha full call number		
952$p	*barcode* *	max 20 characters	
952$q	Due date	Due date of a checked out item. YYYY-MM-DD.	When the item needs to return from a loan. NULL if it's not issued.
952$r	Date last seen	The date that the item was last seen in the library (checked in / checked out / inventoried).	
952$s	Date last checked out	The last checkout dates of the item. Display only field.	
952$t	Copy number	Copy number for items that have the same location and call number.	
952$u	Uniform Resource Identifier	A URL or URN, which provides access electronic data in a standard syntax.	

952$v	Replacement price	The decimal number, no currency symbol	If an item is marked lost, this value is charged to the patron.
952$w	Price effective from	YYYY-MM-DD	This date relates to 'normal purchase price'.
952$x	Non-public note	Internal staff note.	
952$y	*Koha item type* *	coded value required field for circulation	Coded value, must be defined in System Administration '! Item types and Circulation Codes
952$z	Public note		

Adding analytic records

In libraries particularly in special libraries, many times they create bibliographic records for each of the chapters of book, article of journals, etc. so that patrons can find their specific interested articles from the host documents like Books, Journals, CDs etc. The Koha analytic tool help in cataloguing of such articles and attaching it to host items, therefore, the separate bibliographic record is created for such articles, but it is not physically separated with the host attached item.

After creating of analytic records choose the option edit>Link to host item as shown in the Fig. 5.37 then it will ask for an item barcode/accession number to which you wish to attach it i.e. the source of article catalogued followed by a confirmation message. To view all of the items attached to the host record, you have to search for the record then click the Analytics tab on the left side and the analytics attached to each barcode will be shown under the "Used in" column tab.

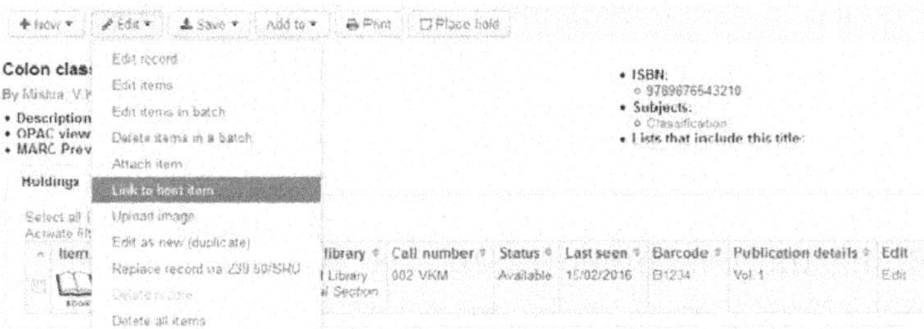

Fig. 5.39. Creating analytic record

Editing bibliographic records and item record

Edition, deletion, addition, etc. is a general feature of any software and almost routine works of any library to keep updated holding details of a library. Koha provides various options for the same. In order to edit the records library staff first needs to search the record in the catalogue and select the option "edit record/edit item" which is given by each search result as shown in the below screenshot Fig. 5.38, on selection of options system will display the bibliographic details framework/item details framework of concern item which can be modified. If library wished to add more new items in the same record than the same method is applied, and they can use the edit items option for adding more copies of the item already available in the library. Optionally you can also select the title to get more option for editing, delete, etc. as shown in the screenshot of "creating analytic record" above.

Fig. 5.40. Edit record/items screen

Authorities control in Koha

Authorities control is one of the major activities in libraries to find consistency and error-free in the result retrieval during a search. Authority records will provide better control over the subject headings, personal names and places, etc. as shown in the screenshot below (Fig. 5.39). Authority records can be created or searched from z39.50 servers; the entire process is almost similar to adding the new bibliographic records as discussed in previous sections of cataloguing. Please note that the same records are displayed/used at the time of new data entry in fields MARC fields 100, 650, etc. There are many other options like editing, the merging of same records similar, etc. to the cataloguing module.

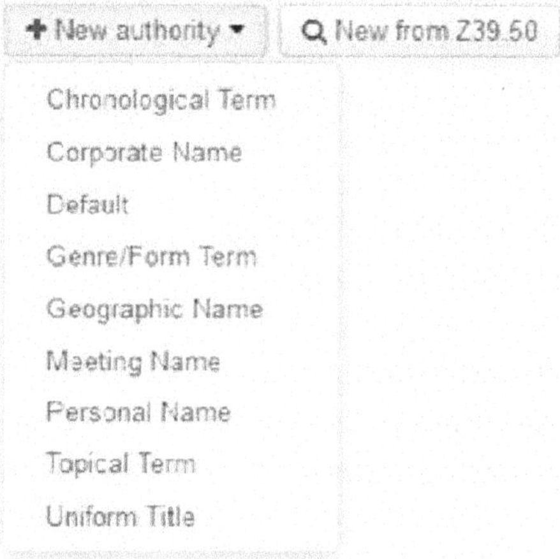

Fig. 5.41. Adding new authority records

5.7. PATRON MANAGEMENT IN KOHA

Patron management in Koha has many features which help in proper control on users of any libraries like Public/Academic/Special. To start with patron management/creation, it is necessary to configure the type of patrons and setup the system preferences.

Adding patron

To enter new patron click the Circulation option in staff client home page and select the appropriate category of a member which you wish to create from the available drop down list as shown below.

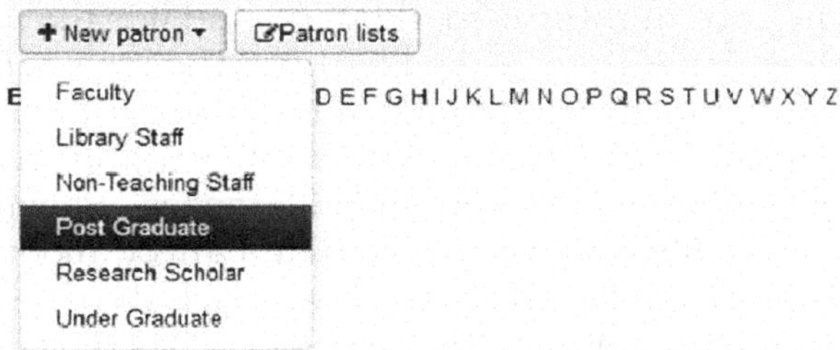

Fig. 5.42. Creation of new member

The Koha system will present a detailed format for entry of member details out of which red highlighted are mandatory, and rest are optional. The entire format is divided into several sub-sections which are as follows:

- Patron identity
- Guarantor information
- Main address
- Contact
- Alternate address
- Alternate contact
- Library management
- Library set-up
- OPAC/Staff login
- Additional attributes and identifiers
- Patron messaging preferences

Some of the features can be configured in system preferences to appear/disappear in this format like salutation. Koha has given the flexibility to enter as much as possible alternative contacts which may be required in many public libraries. Address fields can be used as member departments, office, etc. if they are not from the public library system. While entering the data library staffs must take many precautions and adopt a proper policy to fill minimum data of a member so that they can be contacted as and when require like its home address, phone number, email, etc.

The card number is mandatory, and it is the number through which Koha mainly identifies the member at the time of automates circulation via barcode/RFID etc.; this can be auto generated or manual depending upon the settings configured in system preferences. Registration date is auto filled while expiry date can be modified as per requirement else on saving it will pick the expiry date from the selected member category. Username and password can be assigned to members so that they can access their account through OPAC; further minimum password length can be restricted via system preferences, and it can be changed at any time by editing the same if a member forgets the username and password. Patron messaging preferences allows activating or deactivating the type of messages alerts like item due, items check-in, check-out, etc. On saving the record member system will provide the option to upload the image of member in proper recommended formats like jpg, gif, etc. with the image size restrictions.

Adding staff patron

Staff patrons are those members who are having the privilege to access the staff client of the Koha ILMS. It is suggested to create one separate group/category of staff to whom library wishes to give Koha access rights.

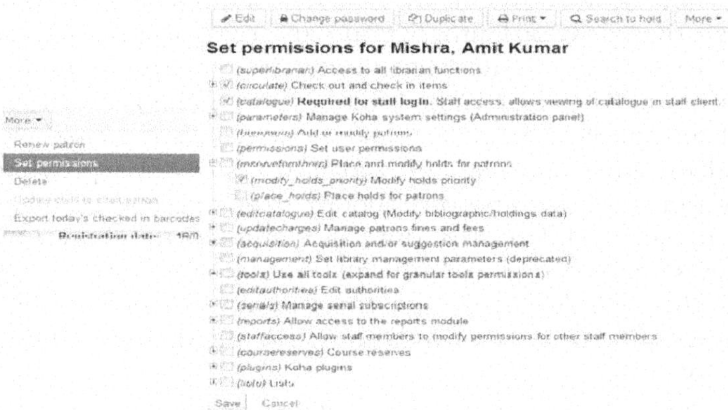

Fig. 5.43. Adding staff patron

The process of adding new staff patron is similar to adding library patrons as discussed above only the difference is we have to assign the access rights with the option available in right corner of the screen (More) which we get after saving the member records and as shown in the above screenshot. Set permission option under the more menus presents a list of options as shown above which library administrator needs to assign as per the policy. For example, if library has decided to assign staff "Amit" only the privilege of circulation and modify hold priority than accordingly he/she can check/tick the box given against each option. Please note that "catalogue required for staff login. Staff access allows viewing of catalogue in staff client" option mandatorily needs to be given to all staff.

Editing patron and other details

Sometimes library may wish to edit the patron details or change anything like their address, forgotten password, put the restrictions, etc. To do this you need to search the patron in the same way as you are searching for check-out then click the option "Edit" which will take you to the original form of patron creation/edit where staff can do any modifications, for example if a patron forgot the password simply you can create the password and inform the user. Sometime due to any reasons patrons need to be blocked like if there is long overdue, and he/she is not returning the book, in such case we used to block the member and to do this Koha provide good option of "Restriction" under patron detail page, once the reason is filled, and date has entered as shown in below screen patron account will be automatically blocked and they can't check-out the book from next time. However, it can be remove later as per the decision of the library.

The left side of the patron details page as shown in above screen is various options through which staff can check the Circulation history, Fines, Notices, Purchase suggestions, etc. of a particular member.

Fig. 5.44. Restricting patron account and other details

5.8. CIRCULATION MANAGEMENT IN KOHA

Circulation management of a library is one of the major works which applies to all type of libraries since circulation functions need to be frequently used by the staffs, so Koha provides flexibility to access these features in various ways. On the main page of the staff client, it can be accessed from the center of the page; top left corner, top drop down menu and the search box is given on the home page. To access complete list of circulation functions you can visit the circulation page which is linked from the top left of every page. Some of the major features of circulation are described in the below sections.

Check-out and Check-in

Check-out option in Koha can be accessed from quick search bar on circulation page, from the patron record and the top of the main staff client home page. To check an item to patron first you need to search the patron either by their barcode or part of the name which will land on the main circulation page of a patron as shown below.

Fig. 5.45. Check-out screen

On the top of the screen, you will see a box where barcode needs to be scan or typed manually then on clicking the check-out option system will display the detail of the book issued to its title, check-out date, due date, etc. as shown in above screen. Further, Koha provides option to check the automatic renewal/specify the customized due date, i.e., not the default due date as defined in the system for that particular category of member. In case barcode is not found system will present an option "fast cataloguing" through which you can enter the data of book on the spot and check-out the book.

To check-in/return the book almost same method needs to be followed as in check-out but instead of user barcode here simply barcode of a book needs to be scanned as shown in the below screen (Fig. 5.44) and system will display the details of the book returned to its barcode number, title, patron, etc.

If you are returning items which were put in the book drop while the library was closed you can check the 'Book drop mode' box before scanning items. This will effectively roll back the returned date to the last date the library was open. Further, you can also choose to forgive all overdue charges for items you are checking in by checking the 'Forgive overdue charges' box before scanning items.

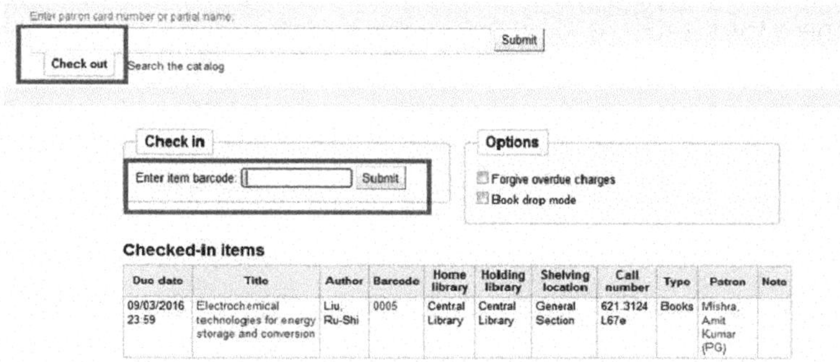

Fig. 5.46. Check-in screen

Holds/Reservation and Renewal of Books

Koha allows the patron to place the Hold/Reserve the books either through OPAC or staff client; there are several methods given to place the hold like from patron detail page, search result, etc. Most frequently used is from the bibliographic record for a book which is supposed to be put up on hold, to do this you have to search the books which are needed to be reserved for member then system will ask you the barcode of the member as shown in the below screen. Holds can also be altered and cancelled from the holds tab found on the left of the bibliographic records.

If items that are on hold/reserve are checked in/ out the Koha will alert the circulation staff that the item is on hold and display options for managing the hold. If the hold item is check in the system will ask you to either confirm or transfer the item. Clicking the Confirm button will mark the item as on hold for the patron, transferred the item will also be marked as in transit to the proper branch and clicking 'Ignore' will retain the hold, but allow you to check the item out to another patron. Choosing to confirm and print will present you with a printable page that you can slip into the book with the necessary hold and transfer information. Once confirmed the hold will show on the patron record and the checkout screen under the 'Hold' tab.

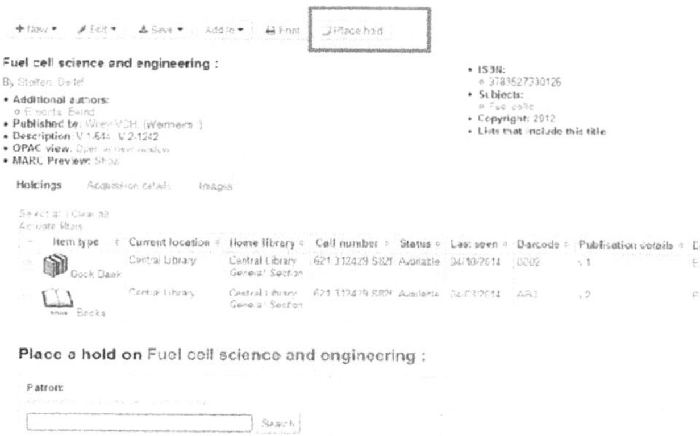

Fig. 5.47. Placing hold on an Item

To renew the books, you can log in to the members detail page and select the books shown in the check-out which is supposed to be renewed and click the option "Renew or check-in selected item". The new due date will be displayed, and renewal allowed count will decrease by one.

Other features of circulation module

Apart from above major basic features of circulation of Koha, it provides many other options as briefly described below and shown in the below screenshot of circulation home page.

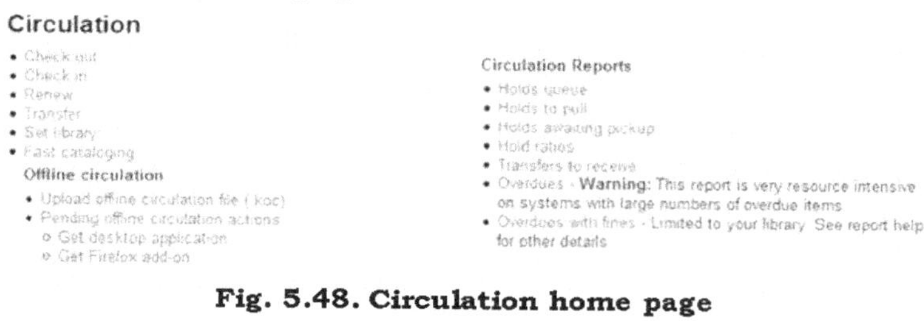

Fig. 5.48. Circulation home page

5.9. REPORTING AND STATISTICS IN KOHA

Report is one of the required major components of any ILMS; any system in general life must have reporting feature strong. Reporting facility provide output from the system in which we input the data, reports are the fundamental requirement to get the statistics and forecast about the future development. Koha is having brilliant feature of reporting and drawing statistics about the library since it uses the unlocked MySQL database so any person having knowledge of generating MySQL query can make end number of reports as per requirements. There are many MySQL reports queries are shared by Koha developers and users at wiki page of the Koha community some reports and statistics of Koha are discussed in below section.

SQL reports in Koha

Since Koha is open source and there is no restriction and locking so, any individual can see the various table made in the Koha ILMS through which a person having basic knowledge of MySQL can make report query as per the demands without any limitations. You can select and save the reports written by Koha users which are available at *https://wiki.koha-community.org/wiki/SQL_Reports_Library* . To make new report click the link to New Reports > Create from SQL and fill in the detail form presented as below.

Fig. 5.49. Form to save SQL report

In the above form red colored highlighted fields are mandatory, you have to assign one name to the report in the first field then choose the group and subgroups. Groups can be created through authorized value or in the form itself similarly, the sub-group of groups may also be created, these groups and sub-groups help in organizing various reports to filter at the time of generation because sometime in case of many reports in the Koha it will be difficult to find and run.

If you want to make reports public than select yes else leave to the default of 'No' in most cases. A report can be made public if you intend to allow access to it through the JSON web service interface. This is a system that can be used by developers to make custom presentations of the data from the report. A public report is accessible via a URL that looks like *http://MYOPAC/cgi-bin/koha/svc/report?id=REPORTID*. In SQL field, you can enter the SQL query and save the report to run it once it is saved, you can use it as and when require. Some of the most useful common SQL reports and there description are mentioned in the table below.

Table 5.11. General SQL reports

<table>
<tr><th>Description</th><th>SQL query</th></tr>
<tr><td></td><td>Holds/Reserve</td></tr>
<tr><td>List of all patrons at branch with holds awaiting pickup</td><td>SELECT p.surname, p.firstname, p.email, p.cardnumber,h.waitingdate AS 'hold date', i.barcode, b.title FROM reserves h
LEFT JOIN borrowers p USING (borrowernumber)
LEFT JOIN items i USING (itemnumber)
LEFT JOIN biblio b ON (i.biblionumber= b.biblio number)
WHERE h.waitingdate IS NOT NULL AND h.branchcode=<<Waiting at|branches>></td></tr>
<tr><td>This report will give you a list of holds titles on loan in a specific user card (you will enter the</td><td>SELECT
biblio.title,
biblio.author,
issues.date_due,
CONCAT(bi.firstname, ' ', bi.surname, '</td></tr>
</table>

cardnumber you're interested in).

```
    (',bi.cardnumber, ')') AS
'Prêté à',
    reserves.reservedate,
    CONCAT(br.firstname, ' ', br.surname, '
    (',br.cardnumber, ')') AS
'Réservé pour'
FROM issues
    LEFT JOIN items USING(itemnumber)
    LEFT JOIN reserves USING(biblionumber)
    LEFT JOIN biblio ON items.biblionumber=
    biblio.biblionumber
    LEFT JOIN borrowers AS bi ON
issues. borrowernumber=bi.borrowernumber
    LEFT JOIN borrowers AS br ON
reserves.borrowernumber=br.borrowernumber
WHERE bi.cardnumber=<<Numéro de carte>>
    AND reserves.biblionumber IS NOT NULL
```

This will ask you to enter the date range twice, use the same range both times. It will show you with a count of holds placed in that time period

```
SELECT sum(count) AS holds
    FROM (
    SELECT count(*) AS count
    FROM reserves
    WHERE date(reservedate) BETWEEN <<Hold
    Placed BETWEEN
    (yyyy-mm-dd)|date>> AND <<and
    (yyyy-mm-dd)|date>>
    UNION ALL
    SELECT count(*) AS count
    FROM old_reservesWHERE date(reservedate)
    BETWEEN <<Repeat Hold Placed BETWEEN
    (yyyy-mm-dd)|date>> AND<<and (yyyy-mm-
    dd)|date>>) AS myholds
```

A list of items that are overdue that have holds on them. A report to help you know who to call with overdues to tell them others are waiting for their items

```
SELECT p.cardnumber, p.surname, p.firstname,
    p.phone, p.address, p.city, p.zipcode,
    c.date_due, (TO_DAYS(curdate())-
    TO_DAYS( date_due)) AS 'days overdue',
    i.itype, b.title, b.author, i.itemcallnumber,
    i.barcode, COUNT(h.biblionumber) AS 'holds'
    FROM borrowers pLEFT JOIN issues c USING
    (borrowernumber) LEFT JOIN items i USING
    (itemnumber) LEFT JOIN biblio b ON
    (i.biblionumber=b.biblionumber) LEFT JOIN
    reserves h ON (b.biblionumber=h.
    biblionumber) WHERE c.branchcode =
    <<Branch Code|branches>> AND c.date_due
    < curdate()GROUP BY h.biblionumber
    HAVING COUNT(h.biblionumber) > 0 ORDER
    BY p.surname ASC, c.date_due ASC
```

List items that are on hold, not checked out and not waiting on the holds shelf

```
SELECT b.title, i.itemcallnumber, date(r.timestamp) AS "hold date" FROM reserves r LEFT JOIN biblio b ON (r.biblionumber=b.biblionumber) LEFT JOIN items i ON (i.biblionumber=b.biblionumber) WHERE i.itemnumber NOT IN (SELECT issues.itemnumber FROM issues) AND r.waitingdate IS NULL ORDER BY r.timestamp ASC
```

This report asks for you to enter a year (twice) and then shows you hold counts for all months that year.

```
SELECT month, sum(count) AS holdsFROM (SELECT MONTHNAME(reservedate) AS month, count(*) AS countFROM reservesWHERE YEAR(reservedate) = <<Hold Year (yyyy)>>GROUP BY monthUNION ALLSELECT MONTHNAME(reservedate) AS month, count(*) AS countFROM old_reservesWHERE YEAR(reservedate) = <<Repeat Hold Year (yyyy)>>GROUP BY month) AS myholdsGROUP BY monthORDER BY month ASC
```

Patron Reports

List of patrons/staff with their permission levels

```
SELECT borrowernumber, firstname, surname, categorycode, description, flags FROM borrowers JOIN user_permissions USING (borrowernumber) JOIN permissions USING (code) UNION ( SELECT borrowernumber, firstname, surname, categorycode, 'module-level permissions; 1 is superlibrarian' AS description, flags FROM borrowers WHERE flags > 0) ORDER BY borrowernumber ASC
```

New patrons added by category in a date range (even if they have been deleted since)

```
SELECT categorycode, COUNT(borrowernumber) AS 'new patrons'FROM (SELECT borrowernumber, categorycode, dateenrolled FROM borrowers UNION ALLSELECT borrowernumber, categorycode, dateenrolled FROM deletedborrowers) AS patrons WHERE dateenrolled BETWEEN <<Added BETWEEN (yyyy-mm-dd)|date>> AND <<and (yyyy-mm-dd)|date>> GROUP BY categorycode
```

List patrons expired in a specific year who do not currently have any checkouts

```
SELECT surname, firstname, borrowernumber FROM borrowers WHERE borrowernumber NOT IN (SELECT borrowernumber FROM issues) AND YEAR(dateexpiry) = <<Year>>
```

List of items checked out to patrons

```
SELECT issues, biblio.title, author, surname, firstname, borrowers.sort1, items.itemcall number, items.barcode, issues.issuedate, issues.lastreneweddate FROM issues LEFT
```

JOIN borrowers ON borrowers.borrower number =issues.borrowernumber LEFT JOIN items ON issues.itemnumber=items. item number LEFT JOIN biblio ON items. biblionumber=biblio.biblionumber WHERE issues.branchcode=<<Checked out at|branches>> ORDER BY issues.branchcode, borrowers.sort1, borrowers.surname, issues. issuedate, biblio.title

Count of patrons added between two dates at a branch

SELECT COUNT(borrowernumber) AS 'New Patrons' FROM borrowers WHERE dateenrolled BETWEEN <<Added BETWEEN (yyyy-mm-dd)|date>> AND <<and (yyyy-mm-dd)|date>> AND branchcode=<<Branch|branches>>

Count of patrons who's cards have expired before today

SELECT COUNT(cardnumber) AS countFROM borrowers WHERE dateexpiry < <<Today's Date (yyyy-mm-dd)|date>>

List of patrons who have been marked as restricted

SELECT cardnumber, surname, firstname, debarred, debarredcomment FROM borrowers WHERE branchcode=<<Select your branch|branches>> AND debarred IS NOT NULLORDER BY surname ASC, firstname ASC

Circulation Reports

To generate date wise list of checked in books

SELECT old_issues.returndate,items.barcode, biblio.title,biblio.author,borrowers. firstname, borrowers. surname,borrowers. cardnumber, borrowers.categorycode FROM old_issues LEFT JOIN borrowers ON borrowers. borrowernumber =old_issues.borrower number LEFT JOIN items ON old_issues. itemnumber=items.itemnumberLEFT JOIN biblio ON items.biblionumber=biblio. biblionumber WHERE old_issues.returndate BETWEEN <<Between Date (yyyy-mm-dd)|date>> AND <<and (yyyy-mm-dd)|date>> ORDER BY old_issues.returndate DESC

To generate date wise list of checked out books (based on Nicole's "All Checked Out Books" report)

SELECT DATE_FORMAT(c.issuedate, "%d %b %Y %h:%i %p") AS Issue_Date, DATE_FORMAT (c.date_due, "%d %b %Y") AS Due_Date, i.barcode AS Barcode,b.title AS Title,b.author AS Author, p.cardnumber AS Card_No,p. firstname AS First_Name, p.surname AS Last_Name FROM issues c LEFT JOIN items i ON (c.itemnumber=i.itemnumber) LEFT JOIN borrowers p ON (c.borrowernumber=p.

```
borrowernumber) LEFT JOIN biblio b ON (i.biblionumber=b.biblionumber) WHERE c.issuedate BETWEEN <<Between Date (yyyy-mm-dd)|date>> AND <<and (yyyy-mm-dd)|date>> ORDER BY c.issuedate DESC
```

A report to show you all items that are currently checked out and who they're checked out to

```
SELECT c.date_due, p.surname, p.firstname, p.phone, p.email, b.title, b.author, i.itemcallnumber, i.barcode, i.location FROM issues cLEFT JOIN items i ON (c.itemnumber= i.itemnumber) LEFT JOIN borrowers p ON (c.borrowernumber=p.borrowernumber) LEFT JOIN biblio b ON (i.biblionumber=b.biblionumber) ORDER BY c.date_due ASC
```

A report that shows items overdue more than a specific number of days for contacting the patrons

```
SELECT p.cardnumber, p.surname, p.firstname, p.phone, p.email, c.date_due, (TO_DAYS (curdate())-TO_DAYS( date_due)) AS 'days overdue', b.title, b.author, i.itemcallnumber, i.barcodeFROM borrowers pLEFT JOIN issues c ON (p.borrowernumber=c.borrowernumber) LEFT JOIN items i ON (c.itemnumber= i.itemnumber) LEFT JOIN biblio b ON (i.biblionumber=b.biblionumber) WHERE c.branchcode = <<Branch|branches>> AND (TO_DAYS(curdate())-TO_DAYS(date_due)) >= <<Days overdue>>ORDER BY p.surname ASC, p.firstname ASC, c.date_due ASC
```

Previous Month Checkouts/Renews by Patron Category

```
SELECT borrowers.categorycode AS PatronType, COUNT( statistics.itemnumber ) AS Count FROM statistics LEFT JOIN borrowers ON (statistics.borrowernumber = borrowers.borrowernumber) WHERE (statistics.datetime LIKE concat(date_format(LAST_DAY(now() - interval 1 month),'%Y-%m-%'))) AND statistics.type IN ('issue','renew') GROUP BY borrowers.categorycode
```

Give you stats for all circ actions on a specific date

```
SELECT type AS action, COUNT(datetime) AS count FROM statistics WHERE DATE(datetime)=<<Date (yyyy-mm-dd)|date>>GROUP BY type;
```

Asks for date range and shows you the checkouts and renewals

```
SELECT type, count(datetime) AS count FROM statistics WHERE datetime BETWEEN <<Checked out BETWEEN (yyyy-mm-dd)|date>> AND <<and (yyyy-mm-dd)|date>> AND type IN ('issue','renew') GROUP BY type
```

List items that have not circulated in X Years

```
SELECT b.title, b.author, b.copyrightdate,
i.itemcallnumber, i.barcode, i.datelastborrowed, i.issues AS totalcheckouts,
```

	i.dateaccessionedFROM items iLEFT JOIN issuesUSING (itemnumber)LEFT JOIN biblio bUSING (biblionumber)WHERE i.itemnumber NOT IN (SELECT issues.itemnumber FROM issues) AND YEAR(NOW())-YEAR(i.date lastborrowed) > <<Years NOT circulated>> UNION SELECT b.title, b.author, b.copyright date, i.itemcallnumber, i.barcode, i.datelast borrowed, i.issues AS totalcheckouts, i.dateaccessionedFROM items iLEFT JOIN issuesUSING (itemnumber)LEFT JOIN biblio bUSING (biblionumber)WHERE i.itemnumber NOT IN (SELECT old_issues.itemnumber FROM old_issues) AND YEAR(NOW())-YEAR(i.datelastborrowed) > <<Years NOT circulated (again)>>
Top 10 circulating books for the last 6 months	SELECT count(s.datetime) AS circs, b.title, b.author, i.ccode FROM statistics sJOIN items i ON (i.itemnumber=s.itemnumber) LEFT JOIN biblio b ON (b.biblionumber= i.biblionumber) WHERE DATE(s.datetime) > DATE_SUB(CURRENT_DATE(),INTERVAL 6 MONTH) AND DATE(s.datetime)<=CURRENT_ DATE() AND s.itemnumber IS NOT NULL AND s.type IN ('issue','renew')GROUP BY b.biblionumber ORDER BY circs DESC LIMIT 10
A count of checkouts by shelving location at a specific branch in a specific timeframe	SELECT i.location, count(s.datetime) AS count FROM items iLEFT JOIN statistics s USING (itemnumber) WHERE date(s.datetime) BETWEEN <<Date BETWEEN (yyyy-mm-dd)|date>> AND <<and (yyyy-mm-dd)|date>> AND s.type='issue' AND s.branch=<<Pick your branch|branches>> GROUP BY i.location ORDER BY i.location ASC
Find the circulation numbers for specific staff logins. Often used to track the checkouts at self check machine. Replace BORROWER NUMBER-# with the borrowernumber for the self check machine (add as many as you have separated by commas).	SELECT p.cardnumber, count(l.timestamp) AS circs FROM action_logs l LEFT JOIN borrowers p ON (p.borrowernumber=l.user) WHERE l.module='CIRCULATION' AND l.action='ISSUE' AND l.user IN (BORROWER NUMBER-1, BORROWERNUMBER-2) AND l.timestamp BETWEEN <<Between (yyyy-mmd-dd)|date>> AND <<and (yyyy-mm-dd)|date>> GROUP BY p.cardnumber

Catalog/Bibliographic Reports

Records without ISBN

```
SELECT itemcallnumber, isbn, concat('<a href=/cgi-bin/koha/catalogue/detail.pl?biblionumber=', biblio.biblionumber,'>', biblio.title,'</a>') AS TitleFROM biblioitems, biblio,itemsWHERE biblio.biblionumber=biblioitems.biblionumberAND items.biblionumber=biblio.biblionumberAND (isbn IS NULL OR isbn ='')GROUP BY biblio.biblionumber
```

To create an Accession Register Sorted by Barcode Number Report

```
SELECT CONCAT('<a href=\"/cgi-bin/koha/catalogue/detail.pl?biblionumber=', biblio.biblionumber,'\">', biblio.biblionumber,'</a>') AS biblionumbers, items.barcode, items.dateaccessioned, items.itemcallnumber, biblioitems.isbn, biblio.author, biblio.title, biblioitems.pages, biblioitems.publishercode, biblioitems.place, biblio.copyrightdate FROM items LEFT JOIN biblioitems ON (items.biblioitemnumber=biblioitems.biblioitemnumber) LEFT JOIN biblio ON (biblioitems.biblionumber=biblio.biblionumber) WHERE items.homebranch =<<Branch|branches>> ORDER BY LPAD(items.barcode,40,' ') ASC
```

Count of items by branch, then by item type

```
SELECT homebranch, itype AS 'Item Type', COUNT( barcode ) AS CountFROM itemsWHERE barcode <> '' AND barcode IS NOT NULL GROUP BY homebranch, itypeORDER BY homebranch, itype ASC
```

List new bibs in specific time frame

```
SELECT monthname(datecreated) AS month, year(datecreated) AS year, count (biblionumber) AS count FROM biblio WHERE datecreated BETWEEN <<Between (yyyy-mm-dd)|date>> AND <<and (yyyy-mm-dd)|date>> GROUP BY year(datecreated), month (datecreated)
```

Count of items added by collection in a specific date range

```
SELECT count(ccode), ccode AS collectionFROM (SELECT ccode, dateaccessioned FROM itemsUNION ALLSELECT ccode, dateaccessioned FROM deleteditems)AS itemsaddedWHERE date(dateaccessioned) BETWEEN<<Added BETWEEN (yyyy-mm-dd)|date>> AND <<and (yyyy-mm-dd)|date>>GROUP BY ccode
```

Damaged Items with Title

```
SELECT items.damaged, items.itemcallnumber, items.barcode, biblio.title, biblio.author FROM items INNER JOIN biblio ON
```

<table>
<tr><td></td><td>items.biblionumber = biblio.biblionumber WHERE items.damaged = True ORDER BY biblio.title ASC</td></tr>
<tr><td>Items added in a time period (will ask for date range twice)</td><td>SELECT sum(count) AS addedFROM (SELECT count(*) AS count FROM items WHERE date (dateaccessioned) BETWEEN <<Added BETWEEN (yyyy-mm-dd)|date>> AND <<and (yyyy-mm-dd)|date>>UNION ALLSELECT count(*) AS count FROM deleteditems WHERE date(dateaccessioned) BETWEEN<<Added BETWEEN (yyyy-mm-dd)|date>> AND <<and (yyyy-mm-dd)|date>>) AS items</td></tr>
<tr><td>Withdrawn Items</td><td>SELECT biblio.title,biblio.author,items. itemcallnumber,items.barcode,items. datelastborrowed, items.withdrawn FROM items LEFT JOIN biblioitems ON (items. biblioitem number =biblioitems.biblioitem number) LEFT JOIN biblio ON (biblioitems. biblionumber=biblio.biblionumber) WHERE items.withdrawn != 0 ORDER BY biblio.title ASC</td></tr>
<tr><td>Show records with duplicate ISBNs; download for full list (doesn't paginate)</td><td>SELECT GROUP_CONCAT(biblionumber SEPARATOR ', ') AS biblionumbers, isbn FROM biblioitems GROUP BY isbn HAVING COUNT(isbn)>1</td></tr>
<tr><td>This report shows all bib records with a subject that contains a specific keyword in the 650a</td><td>SELECT CONCAT('<a href=\"/cgi-bin/koha/catalogue/detail.pl?biblionumber=', biblio number,'\">', biblionumber,'</a>')AS bibnumber, lcsh FROM (SELECT biblio number, ExtractValue(marcxml,'//datafield [@tag="650"]/subfield[@code>="a"]')AS lcsh FROM biblioitems) AS subjects WHERE lcsh LIKE <<Enter keyword surrounded BY %>></td></tr>
<tr><td>Finds all items that are marked as lost in some way</td><td>SELECT i.itemnumber, b.title, b.author, i.itemcallnumber, i.barcode, v.lib FROM items iLEFT JOIN biblio b ON (i.biblionumber= b.biblionumber) LEFT JOIN authorised_ values v ON (i.itemlost=v.authorised_value) WHERE i.itemlost != 0 AND v.category='LOST'</td></tr>
<tr><td>Asks for librarian's borrower number and shows them with a count of items they've added. [Requires CataloguingLog to be on]</td><td>SELECT count(timestamp) AS 'items added' FROM action_logs WHERE module=' CATALOGUING' AND user=<<Borrower number>> AND info='item' AND action='ADD'</td></tr>
<tr><td>Get biblionumber of biblio records without</td><td>SELECT CONCAT('<a href="http://', (SELECT value FROM systempreferences WHERE</td></tr>
</table>

items

```
variable='staffClientBaseURL'), '/cgi-bin/
koha/catalogue/detail.pl?biblionumber=',
biblionumber, '">', biblionumber, '</a>') AS
'biblionumber', titleFROM biblioWHERE
biblionumber NOT IN (SELECT biblionumber
FROM items)
```

Accounting Reports (Fines/Credits/Etc)

List of unpaid fines with patron and item information

```
SELECT b.surname, b.firstname, b.email,
bib.title, i.barcode, a.amountoutstanding,
ni.issuedate, ni.date_due, IF ( ni.returndate
IS NULL , " ", ni.returndate ) AS returndate
FROM accountlines a LEFT JOIN borrowers
b ON ( b.borrowernumber = a.borrower
number ) LEFT JOIN items i ON ( a.item
number = i.itemnumber ) LEFT JOIN biblio
bib ON ( i.biblionumber = bib.biblionumber )
LEFT JOIN ( SELECT * FROM issues UNION
SELECT * FROM old_issues ) ni ON (
ni.itemnumber = i.itemnumber AND
ni.borrowernumber = a.borrowernumber )
WHERE a.amount outstanding > 0 GROUP
BY a.description ORDER BY b.surname,
b.firstname, ni.timestamp DESC
```

List of unpaid fines with patron and item information, with an incremental charge: $1 per day the first fortnight overdue, $2 for the next, $5 daily after that; it can be tailored by patron category.

```
SELECT borrowers.cardnumber,borrowers.
categorycode, borrowers.surname,issues.
date_due, (TO_DAYS(curdate())-TO_DAYS(
date_due)) AS daysoverdue, items.barcode AS
'Accession Number', biblio.title,biblio.author,
IF((TO_DAYS(curdate())-TO_DAYS( date_due))
<=15,(TO_DAYS(curdate())-TO_DAYS(
date_due)),IF((TO_DAYS(curdate())-TO_DAYS(
date_due))<=30,2*(TO_DAYS(curdate())-
TO_DAYS( date_due))-15,5*(TO_DAYS
(curdate())-TO_DAYS( date_due))-105)) AS fine
FROM borrowers LEFT JOIN issues ON
(borrowers.borrowernumber=issues.borrower
number) LEFT JOIN items ON (issues.item
number=items.itemnumber) LEFT JOIN biblio
ON (items.biblionumber=biblio.biblionumber)
WHERE (borrowers.categorycode=<<Patron
Category|categorycode>>) AND
(TO_DAYS(curdate())-TO_DAYS(date_due)) >
'0' ORDER BY borrowers.cardnumber ASC
```

Payment (Date range wise) with patron details (entire system)

```
SELECT borrowers.borrowernumber, borrowers.
cardnumber, accountlines.amount, account
lines.dateFROM accountlines, borrowers
WHERE borrowers.borrowernumber =
```

```
accountlines.borrowernumber AND account type = 'pay' AND date BETWEEN <<Between (YYYY)
```

Asks you to enter the date range for which you would like to see all of the money collected at all branches

```
SELECT FORMAT(abs(sum(amount)),2) AS 'Total Collected' FROM accountlines WHERE (accounttype='C' OR accounttype='PAY') AND timestamp BETWEEN <<Between (yyyy-mm-dd)|date>> AND <<and (yyyy-mm-dd)|date>>
```

Acquisition and Serial Reports

Show order information for a specific date period

```
SELECT v.name AS vendor, b.title AS 'book title', format(o.listprice,2) AS 'list price', format(o.unitprice,2) AS 'actual price', ba.basketname, o.notes FROM aqorders o LEFT JOIN aqbasket ba USING (basketno) LEFT JOIN aqbooksellers v ON (v.id = ba.booksellerid) LEFT JOIN biblio b USING (biblionumber) WHERE o.entrydate BETWEEN <<Ordered BETWEEN (yyyy-mm-dd)|date>> AND <<and (yyyy-mm-dd)|date>>
```

Show the number of items ordered vs. received for a given vendor

```
SELECT aqbasket.basketno, aqbasket.basket name, aqbasket.creationdate, aqbasket. closedate, sum(aqorders.quantity) AS 'Items ordered', sum(aqorders.quantityreceived) AS 'Items received', sum(aqorders.quantity) - sum(aqorders.quantityreceived) AS difference FROM aqbooksellers INNER JOIN aqbasket ON (aqbooksellers.id = aqbasket.booksellerid) INNER JOIN aqorders USING (basketno) WHERE aqbooksellers.id = 91 AND aqbasket.creationdate BETWEEN <<Ordered BETWEEN|date>> AND <<and|date>>GROUP BY basketnoORDER BY aqbasket.creationdate
```

Show's a ledger of all items ordered

```
SELECT b.name AS vendor, i.itype, p.budget_branchcode AS branch, k.basketno, o.entrydate AS 'order date', format(o.listprice, 2) AS 'list price', format(o.unitprice,2) AS 'unit price', o.quantity, format(o.totalamount,2) AS 'total amount', o.datereceived AS 'date received' FROM aqbasket k LEFT JOIN aqbooksellers b ON (k.booksellerid=b.id) LEFT JOIN aqorders o USING (basketno)LEFT JOIN items i USING (biblionumber)LEFT JOIN aqbudgets p USING (budget_id)
```

Total spent against each budget

```
SELECT b.budget_name, format(sum(b.budget_amount),2) AS 'amount budgeted', format (sum(o.listprice*o.quantity),2) AS 'amount
```

	spent’ FROM aqorders o LEFT JOIN aqbudgets b USING (budget_id)WHERE o.datereceived IS NOT NULL GROUP BY b.budget_name
Shows the total serials received with Title, Frequency, latest issue detail	SELECT serial.subscriptionid,serial. biblio number, serial.serialid,biblio.title, serial. serialseq, serial. planneddate,serial. publisheddate,IF(LOCATE(‘<datafield tag=”310"’, biblioitems.marcxml) = 0 OR LOCATE(‘<subfield code=”a”>’, biblioitems. marcxml,LOCATE(‘<datafield tag=”310"’, biblioitems.marcxml)) = 0 OR LOCATE (‘<subfield code=”a”>’, biblioitems.marcxml, LOCATE(‘<datafield tag=”310"’, biblioitems. marcxml)) > LOCATE(‘</datafield>’, biblioitems.marcxml, LOCATE(‘<datafield tag=”310"’, biblioitems.marcxml)), ‘’,SUBSTRING(biblioitems. marcxml, LOCATE(‘<subfield code=”a”>’, biblioitems. marcxml, LOCATE(‘<datafield tag=”310"’, biblioitems.marcxml)) + 19,LOCATE(‘</ subfield>’, biblioitems.marcxml, LOCATE (‘<subfield code=”a”>’, biblioitems.marcxml, LOCATE(‘<datafield tag=”310"’, biblioitems. marcxml)) + 19) -(LOCATE(‘<subfield code=”a”>’, biblioitems.marcxml, LOCATE (‘<datafield tag=”310"’, biblioitems.marcxml)) + 19)))AS FREQUENCY FROM serial, biblio,biblioitemsWHERE serial.biblionumber = biblio.biblionumber AND serial. biblionumber =biblioitems.biblionumber AND MONTH(planneddate) = 03 AND YEAR (planneddate)= 2011 AND (STATUS)=2ORDER BY serial.subscriptionid ASC
A list of items that should have arrived by now	SELECT b.title, s.serialseq, s.planneddate FROM serial s LEFT JOIN biblio b USING (biblionumber) WHERE s.planneddate < CURDATE() AND s.STATUS NOT IN (‘1’,’2’)

Guided reports wizard in Koha

Guided report wizard will help in generating the report in six user friendly steps as shown below rather than knowing about the SQL query.

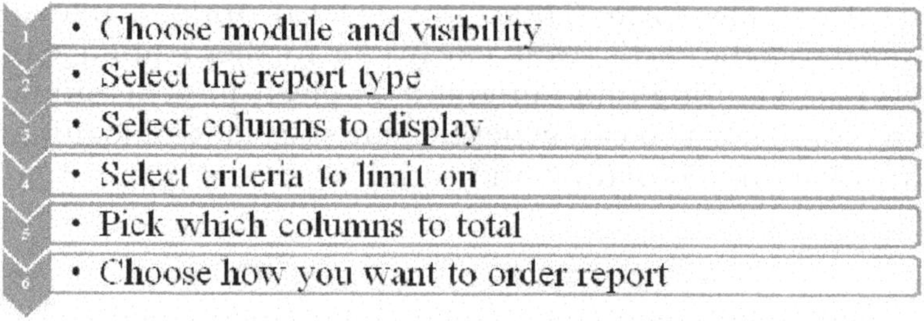

Fig. 5.50. Steps for creating Guided reports

When you finished the above six process system will ask you to save the report in the same way as you saved the SQL query report in previous section which can be run and edited at any time.

Statistics reports

Statistic reports wizard will show the counts and sums on any specific modules. Statistical reports can be generated for all most all modules of Koha as shown in the home page of report in Koha staff client.

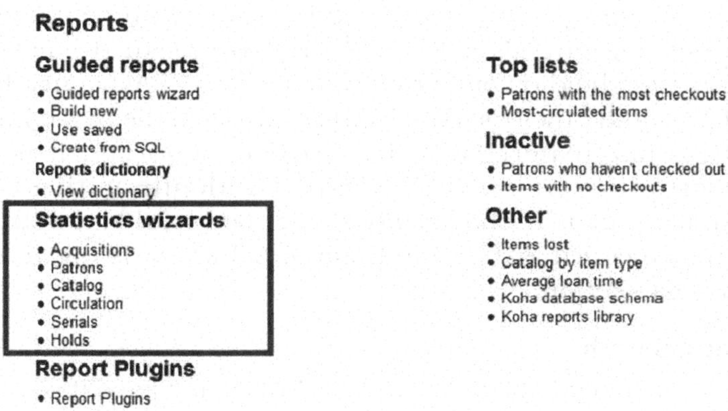

Fig. 5.51. Reports home page in staff client

For example if you wish to generate statistics on patrons then choose which value you would like to appear in the column and which will appear in a row as shown in the below form. There are several options like to download the statistics in csv file for further editing, can choose counting and summing as given in acquisition, etc. Similarly you can generate statistics for cataloguing, acquisition, circulation and serial.

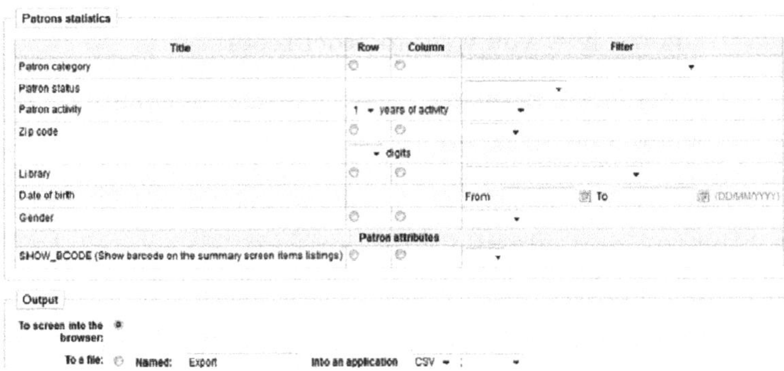

Fig. 5.52. Patron statistics screen

5.10. ONLINE PUBLIC ACCESS CATALOGUE

Online public access catalogue or library catalogue is nothing but it's a kind of database of all the library materials held by one or more libraries. OPAC is used by library and other users to locate and check the availability of reading materials in that particular library; it is an electronic version of the card catalogue with lot of improvements. Koha provides most powerful and web 2.0 based modern features in their OPAC which is discussed in next section.

Basic Search

When you open the Koha OPAC home page it provide the basic search interface with a search box on the top and you can limit your search with some basic fields like title, author etc. at the left side of search box and right side provide option to choose the library if it is multiple branch library as well as language select option. Koha provides option to search string as well as keyword so if user is not aware about full name of author he/she can use few initial character of the name and Koha will display the result with the same. On top of the search result it will display total number of results and the result will be sorted based on criteria you have selected in system preferences however you can modify the order alphabetically, accession date etc from the drop down options provided at the right of the search result.

The search result display title, type, availability of materials etc. in the basic search along with book jacket at right corner, to know the detail about the books like accession number, issue details etc. you have to click the title which will display the details as shown below.

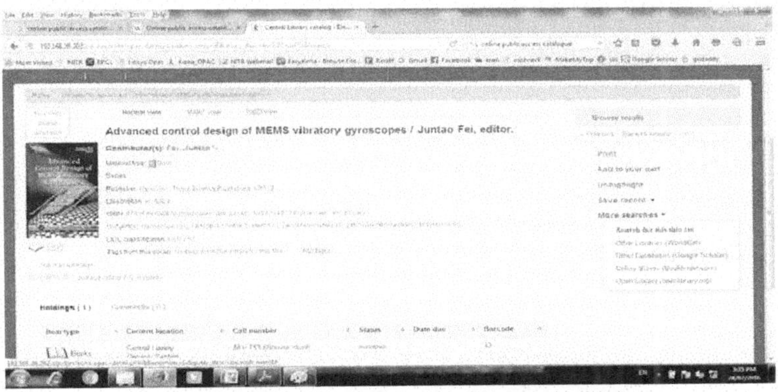

Fig. 5.53. Detail view of an item on OPAC

Detail view of a book provides lot of other values against the book entered by the library like page number, subject headings, notes, etc. You can see the MARC view as well as International standard book description (ISBD) view of the book. Browse shelf is an excellent feature through which user can see what is available/placed near this particular book on the library shelves which is nothing but a kind of virtual tour of a library. Patrons can comment and give star rating on the books as well as save the item in various formats like Bibtext, Dublin core, MARCXML, RIS etc. from the options provided at right side of the result. If social network has been allowed in system preferences then you can share the particular book directly from here to facebook, twitter etc.

Advance Search

Koha advance search is so powerful that it could bring particular results from millions of record available in the database. Search box provide lot of options for limiting the search like corporate author, title, barcode, added entry personal name etc. along with powerful Boolean operators.

User can limit the search by item types, language, and audience, group of library, format, content, date range and additional content.

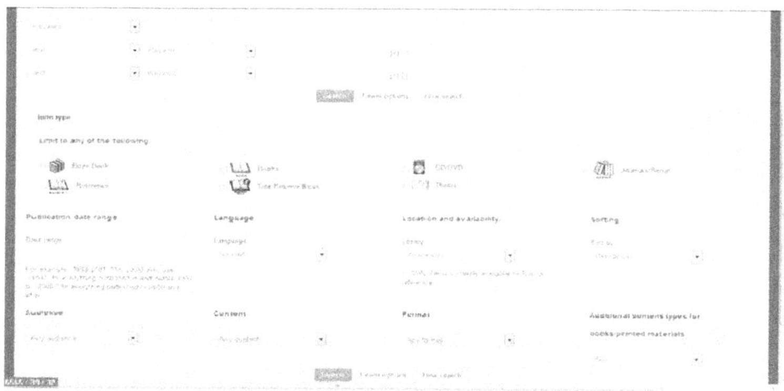

Fig. 5.54. Advance search option in Koha

Refine your search results at the left side provide the facet count from the search result as well as you can click any of the option to limit the result or get the filtered result from already searched results. Patrons can refine search with availability, item type, author, location, series and topics.

Customization of Koha Home page

Koha provide lot of flexibility to convert your library OPAC into a website for this the entire OPAC has been divided into six blocks which is named in system preferences as opaccredits, opacheader, opac main user block, opacnav, opacnavbottom and opacnavright. You may write the text or HTML and CSS codes to display various links and other texts in the various side of the OPAC. A typical example of Koha OPAC customization is displayed in the home page of NIT Rourkela Koha OPAC.

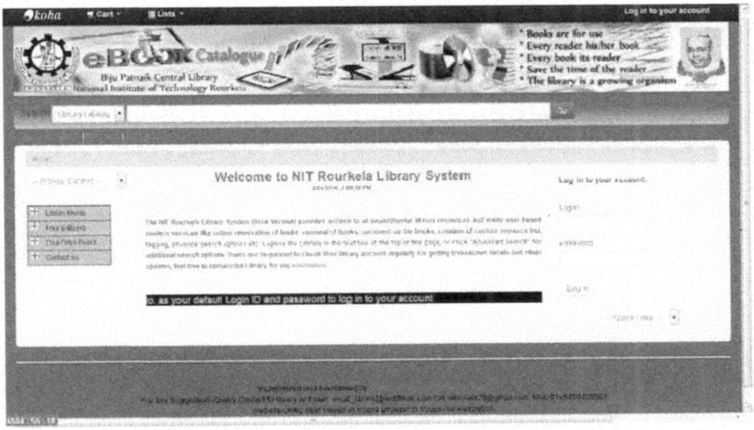

Fig. 5.55. Customized Koha OPAC home page

User services from OPAC

There are various login based features and services provided by Koha to the users which include the online web 2.0 based features as discussed above. User can login to his/her account with various methods of login like ID and password/Mozilla persona/Light directory access protocol (LDAP)/Central authentication system (CAS) which depends upon the Koha setup and facilities available at the concern institutes. On login user can see the accounts detail like total check-out books, renew the books, fine dues, make purchase suggestions, check search and reading history etc. They can create the public or private list and include the books in the list which can be accessible to the public to view the books included in that list for example a teacher can make the list of books recommended for particular semester and make it public to refer by his/her students.

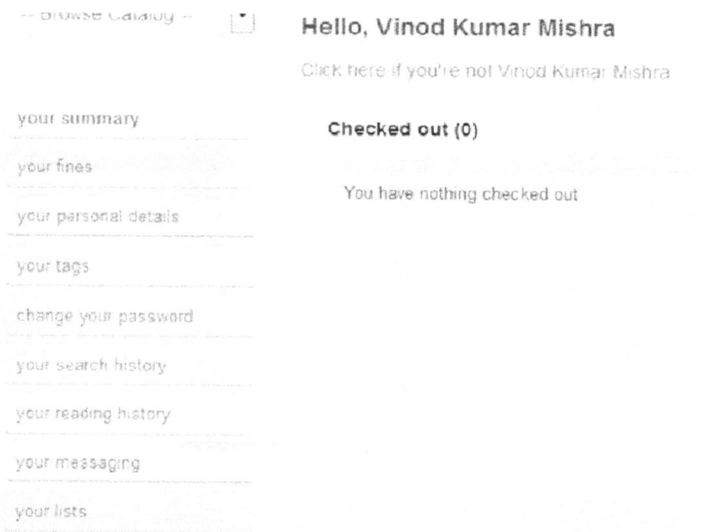

Fig. 5.56. User login based Koha services

5.11. TOOLS AND OTHER FEATURES OF KOHA

Tools module of Koha provide many useful additional features which is necessary for complete library automation system, the features included in this module are displayed below in the home page of tools module. Some most useful features are described below which is dived into three sections.

Patron and circulation

This section provides the options through which we can do bulk editing of information/data which is directly related to patron services of patrons like image upload, message settings etc.

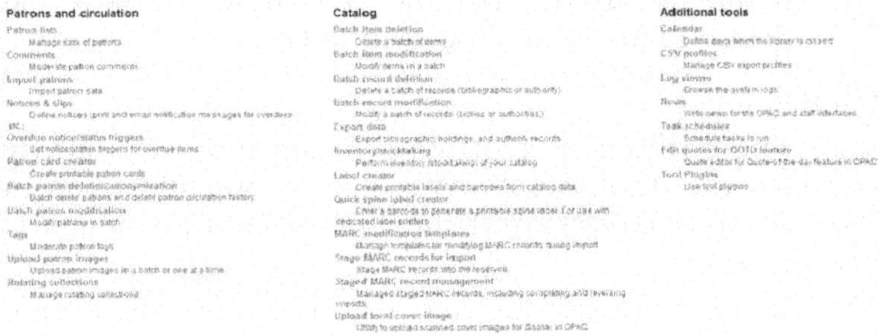

Fig. 5.57. Tools feature of Koha

- Patron list is a tool to manage list of specific group of patrons for easy modifications with batch patron modification option/report.
- Import patron is a ways through which you can import the patrons in the Koha in bulk to do this format is available in csv file and records needs to be filled accordingly.
- Notices and slips are the option through which you can customize the message contents like overdue / reminder /renewal etc. as well as activate or deactivate the same.
- Patron card creator provides facility to generate the library patrons customized ID card as per the requirements. You have options to display the image/logo/patron profile picture and the member bar-code on the Id card. To customize the ID card layout format and template settings needs to be defined properly usually this work takes lot of time to get the card in desired format but once the setting has been done it can be fixed permanently and shared among the Koha community so that others can use it.
- Batch patron modifications are a easy way to modify the members records in bulk in case of requirements. Similarly you can import the patron

image in bulk too provided the images must be in desired format like jpg, png, gif etc.

Catalogue

The catalogue section of tools module mainly provides the flexible options related to modifications in the catalogue records and some other features which is briefed below.

- Batch item deletion and modifications, some time library needs to delete/edit some items from the catalogue in bulk due to damage/write off etc hence this option provide provisions to do so.
- Batch record deletion and modification, similar to above if entire records need to be modified or deleted from the Koha this option is most suitable for bulk editing/deleting of records.
- Export data is the option through which users can export the Koha bibliographic and authority records along with items detail in MARC format. It also provides export of entire SQL backup also if configured in the Koha system files.
- Inventory/stocktaking is nothing but getting the report of stock verification in the library.
- Label creator, libraries needs barcode generation for pasting on the book for automatic circulations. This option configuration is almost similar to patron card creator hence library may create the barcode of varying size with desired data on it.
- Stage MARC record for import and Staged MARC record management provide the option to import the MARC record into the Koha from external sources. The conversion of MARC record which is compatible with Koha has been discussed in data migration chapter. Records once imported temporally exist in Koha but does not display in

OPAC unless it is not imported into the catalogue. Please note once the record is finally imported into the catalogue it can be reverted back.

Additional tools

There is many additional features and tools provided by Koha system like calendar, news, quote of the day, log viewer etc. which can be configured from here. Calendar has features to setup library holidays with great flexibility i.e. one can setup weekend holidays, holidays in same date each year etc. in one go as shown in the below screen.

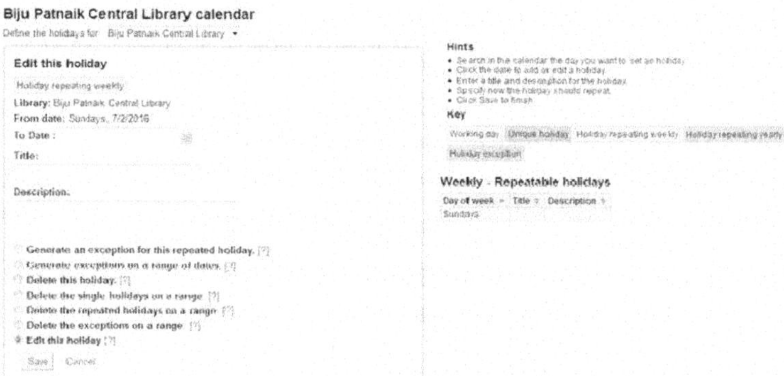

Fig. 5.58. Holidays setup screen in Koha

News and Quotes of the day have features to display any library related news on OPAC/Staff client as well as quotes from famous people. Log and task scheduler are the great way to track the changes made in the Koha system and setup of generating Koha reports on particular time/day respectively.

REFERENCES

1. Beginners/BashScripting. (n.d.). Retrieved February 22, 2016, from https://help.ubuntu.com/community/Beginners/BashScripting
2. Download Koha. (n.d.). Retrieved February 26, 2016, from 17. https://koha-community.org/download-koha/

3. Download Ubuntu Desktop. (n.d.). Retrieved February 21, 2016, from http://www.ubuntu.com/download/desktop

4. Free ISO burner. (n.d.). Retrieved February 24, 2016, from http://www.freeisoburner.com/

5. Holdings data fields (9xx). (n.d.). Retrieved February 09, 2016, from https://wiki.koha-community.org/wiki/Holdings_data_fields_(9xx)

6. How to Install Ubuntu Linux. (n.d.). Retrieved February 23, 2016, from http://www.wikihow.com/Install-Ubuntu-Linux

7. Install Koha on Ubuntu 14.04. (n.d.). Retrieved February 27, 2016, from http://kohageek.blogspot.in/2015/05/install-koha-on-ubuntu-1404.html

8. Install Ubuntu 14.04.4 LTS. (n.d.). Retrieved February 24, 2016, from http://www.ubuntu.com/download/desktop/install-ubuntu-desktop

9. Installation. (n.d.). Retrieved February 18, 2016, from https://help.ubuntu.com/community/Installation

10. Installation/SystemRequirements. (n.d.). Retrieved February 25, 2016, from https://help.ubuntu.com/community/Installation/SystemRequirements

11. Koha (software). (n.d.). Retrieved February 18, 2016, from https://en.wikipedia.org/wiki/Koha_(software)

12. Koha Library Software. (n.d.). Retrieved February 22, 2016, from https://koha-community.org/

13. Koha on ubuntu - packages. (n.d.). Retrieved February 24, 2016, from https://wiki.koha-community.org/wiki/Koha_on_ubuntu_-_packages#Install_Ubuntu

14. Koha. (n.d.). Retrieved February 21, 2016, from https://directory.fsf.org/wiki/Koha

15. MARC Standards. (n.d.). Retrieved February 06, 2016, from https://www.loc.gov/marc/

16. Official wiki of Koha. (n.d.). Retrieved February 19, 2016, from https://wiki.koha-community.org/wiki/Main_Page

17. Online public access catalog. (n.d.). Retrieved February 12, 2016, from https://en.wikipedia.org/wiki/Online_public_access_catalog

18. Ransom, J. (n.d.). The story of Koha, the first open source library management system. Retrieved February 22, 2016, from https://opensource.com/education/14/4/story-of-koha-lms

19. SQL Reports Library. (n.d.). Retrieved February 11, 2016, from https://wiki.koha-community.org/wiki/SQL_Reports_Library

20. Supported Architectures. (n.d.). Retrieved February 17, 2016, from https://help.ubuntu.com/community/SupportedArchitectures

21. Using The Terminal. (n.d.). Retrieved February 24, 2016, from https://help.ubuntu.com/community/UsingTheTerminal

22. Welcome to Bugzilla. (n.d.). Retrieved February 17, 2016, from https://bugs.koha-community.org/bugzilla3/

23. Zebra configuration for regional language searching. (n.d.). Retrieved February 18, 2016, from http://kohageek.blogspot.in/2013/10/zebra-configuration-for-regional_2.html.

6
Data Migration and Various Tools

The current section will describe the data migration tools and techniques with the help of MarcEdit and Microsoft Excel. Data migration is nothing but it is the process of shifting/transferring your existing data which may exist in any format/database like Excel, MySQL, Oracle, etc. Regarding library automation, we may describe data migration as importing/exporting process of existing bibliographic, member, etc. data from one ILMS system to another. There may be several reasons for migrating existing data from one system to another which is described in next subsections.

REASON FOR DATA MIGRATION

There are many reasons for migrating data from one system to another. Now a day's libraries are very dynamic and more concern towards providing a better state of the art services to their patrons with minimum efforts and cost. The huge increase in the cost of the licensed software solutions are growing year by year hence, many of the libraries in developing countries may not afford such costs, so they are looking for another cost effective solutions. There are several reasons for data migrations from one system to other which may be followed:

- High cost of the existing integrated library management system
- There are vendor locking/restrictions on data entry limits
- Lot of bug in the current system
- Poor vendor supports after sells
- Lack in ILMS features as per requirements
- Poor backend like RDMS, Web server, etc.
- Compatibility issues with other devices like RFID etc.

CHALLENGES IN DATA MIGRATION

Data migration is some time very risky and requires a lot of planning and tips and tricks rather than technical skills. The author of this book is having a lot of migration experiences and found that it require a lot of concentration and testing once the job is done. Data migration involves many repetitive works and verification of converted data in the desired format several times. The detail process and some complexities involve in migration have been discussed in detail in the case study of Indian Institute of Technology Roorkee. Before we go for data migration we need to plan and think on the following:

- Current ILMS and its features
- Existing data entry format like MARC21, CCF, Local etc.
- Total cost involve in data migration
- Existing in-house manpower to clean the data
- Skills in Microsoft excel or open office package or similar solution

- Possibility of exporting data in standard format to import in new system
- Depth knowledge of standard MARC21 format etc.

PROCESS OF DATA MIGRATION

Once the planning has been finalized to change the existing system and migration of data has been discussed then, we need to undergo several processes to ensure the successful data migration from one system to another. Data migration process does not involve only understanding the current system in which data lies, but it is also required to study the system which has been planned to adopt. In brief, the flow chart has been given below to understand the entire process of data migration to MARC21 standard format compatible ILMS.

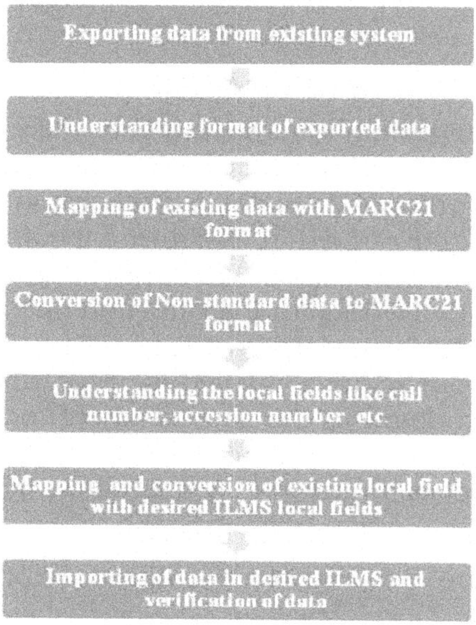

Fig. 6.1. Process of data migration

BENEFITS OF DATA MIGRATION

Author experienced that data migration is not only meant for changing the software to another, but it gives a lot of other opportunities to libraries for refinement/ purification of their data before migrating to a new system. It gives the very clear picture about the existing data and errors as well. Some of the advantages of data migration are as follows:

- Better ILMS solutions as per current market practices and compliance
- Total number of records with bibliographic detail and items available in the system
- Total number of blank records i.e. without item/ accession number
- Capitalization of words and sentences of available data
- Punctuation of existing data as per AACR 2
- Combining of same bibliographic records i.e. same titles scattered as many records
- Removal and addition of additional fields
- Subject heading assignments to records from Library of Congress
- Class number assignment to records in case of missing etc.

TOOLS OF DATA MIGRATION

There may be several tools and techniques available for data migrations, but we will describe in detail about the tools which are available for all and common worldwide. Microsoft Excel by Microsoft and MarcEdit developed by Terry Reese are two tools on which author has good expertise and mostly used for the data migration purposes among the library professionals and vendor who provides support for data migration to libraries. The sub-section of the current chapter describes in detail about data migrations using the above two tools.

6.1. APPLICATION OF MICROSOFT EXCEL IN DATA MIGRATION

Microsoft Excel is a spreadsheet developed by Microsoft for Windows, Mac OS X, and iOS. It provides features for calculation, graphing tools, pivot tables, and a macro programming language called Visual Basic for Applications. It has been a very widely applied spreadsheet for these platforms, especially since version 5 in 1993, and it has replaced Lotus 1-2-3 as the industry standard for spreadsheets. Excel forms part of Microsoft Office. Data files created with Excel is called workbook, when we open the Excel by default, it presents the three workbooks (sheet1, sheet2, and sheet3 and we can generate more) contradictory to Microsoft Word which opens only one blank page for editing. Excel files referred as spreadsheet and sometimes means workbook/ worksheet.

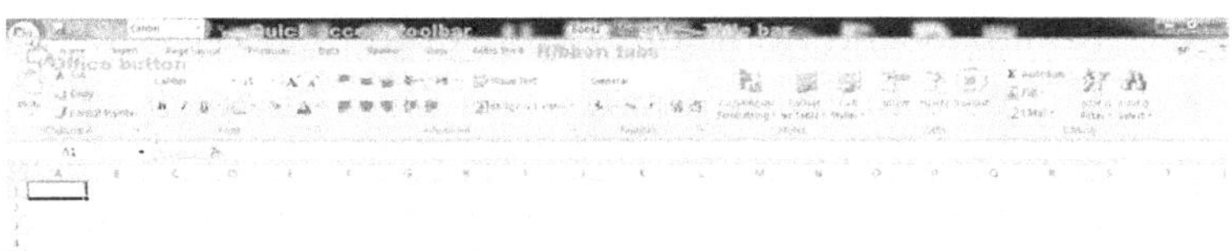

Fig. 6.2. Excel 2007 Home page

Why we need Microsoft Excel for data migration

Many libraries especially those who are not having ILMS are using the Microsoft Excel spreadsheet for data entry of Books and maintaining the accession register in Excel format. However, many libraries use the software which is having Ms-Access as the backend for data storage as well as some very old and popular propriety software like Libsys in India which uses the flat file system as the backend for data storage and provide the reports in the text file only. Many proprieties ILMS is either not having provision to export the data in MARC21 format, or sometimes they restrict the users to export the data in MARC21 format.

Keeping above limitations author has observed that once the data is available in Excel or have been converted in Excel than it would be much easier to convert the data in MARC21 format with the help of MarcEdit tool. Converting the data in Excel from Ms-Access is no issue, but another system may be difficult like software which provides reports in text file/PDF formats i.e. other than Excel format. In this section how text file from Libsys can be converted in Excel and prepared for conversion into MARC21 will be demonstrated.

Book data conversion from Libsys propriety ILMS to Excel

The following are the General steps to get your Libsys data in Excel format for final conversion into the MARC21 format. Please note that there are several other tips and tricks which you can use to convert your Libsys data in Excel so that you can migrate data in some other desired software like Koha, Newgenlib, and Evergreen, etc. The reports module given under Cataloguing, Circulation and Serial of Libsys software can be used to get the data in Excel format. In case you are not getting subject heading then it can be added at the time of Excel data conversion as well as you can also group together, all the same, titles, but you should have at least ISBN/ ISSN number for your records. MARC editor (http:// marcedit.reeset.net/downloads) is wonderful software which converts your data in MARC format as well as gives you the opportunity to make your data standard before importing in new ILMS. In the case of any help needed in this regard, please feel free to contact the author of this book. The steps are discussed below in detail:

a. Go to Acquisition module and click the accession register under the Reports option.

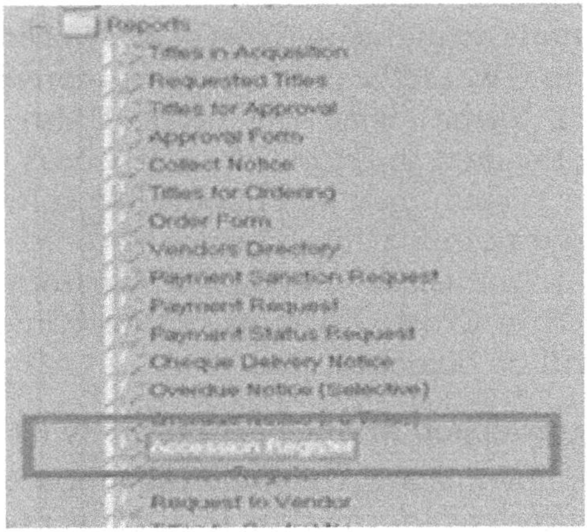

b. Click on the My Format option as shown in the below screen.

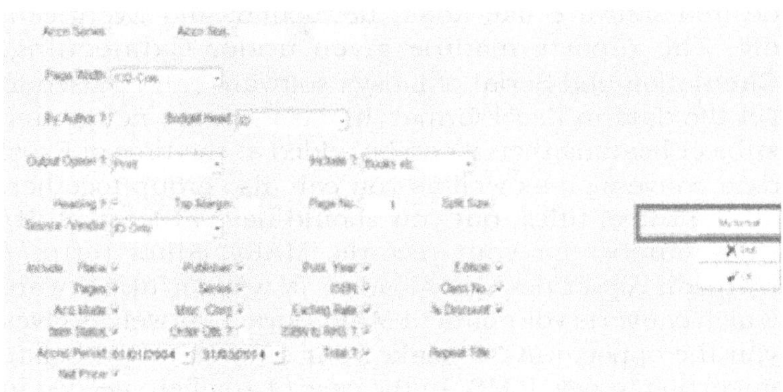

c. On display of the next screen click again the Format option as displayed in below screen and choose the range of accession number (you may leave this blank to get report of all records)

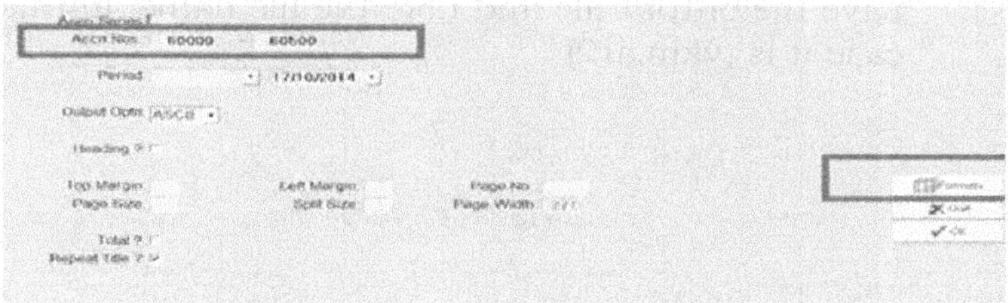

d. This is most important point, select the fields which you want to print and assign Seq (it is column number/sequence, refer the last screen shot to understand the concept) and Size (You may enter maximum size of the character length in the field like author, titles etc. however it will not accept more than 99 but it is sufficient). After careful selection of all the required fields click on OK to get the below screen.

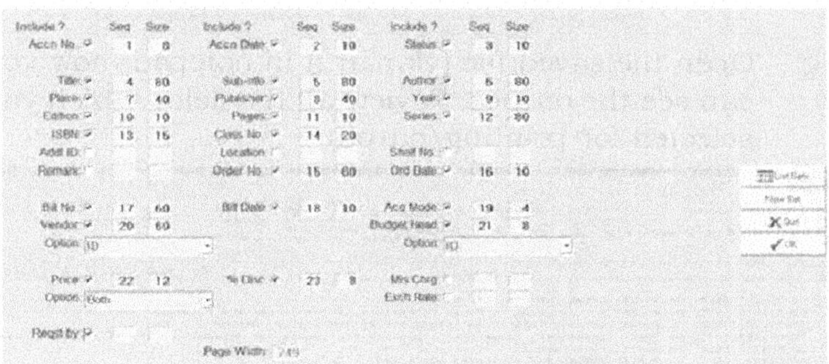

e. Again review the range of accession number and most important is select Output Option ASCII than click on ok

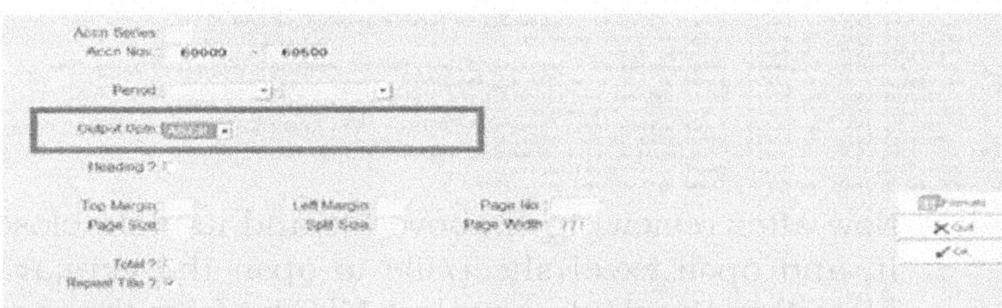

f. Save the output file and note the file name, in this case it is (vkm.ar2)

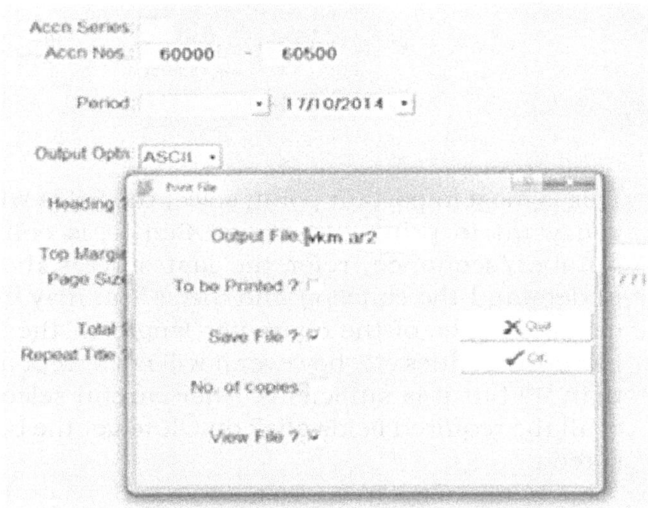

g. Open the saved file (vkm.ar2) in notepad, now you can see the output, Review all the fields which you selected for printing/output

h. Now after reviewing of above file and its data close it, and open excel sheet/file to open the vkm.ar2 file within Excel (please select All Files from the popup windows to view the vkm.ar2 file) as shown in the below screens and highlighted as well.

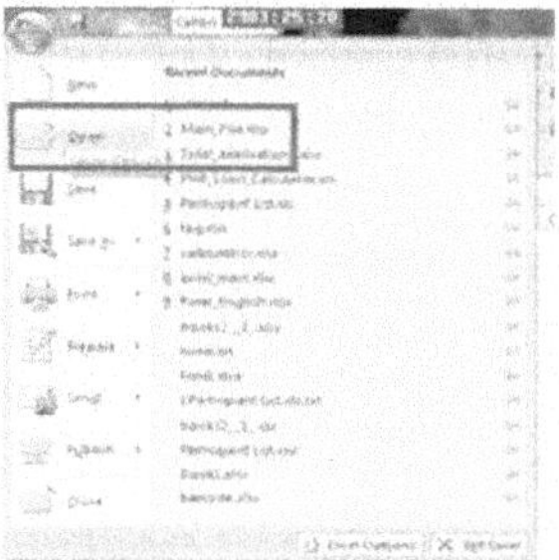

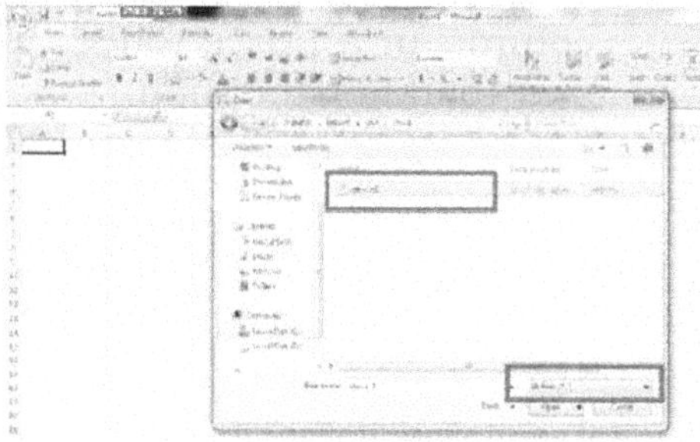

i. Once you click the open menu, system will presents the below screen with pop up window called Text import wizard, than you may select next as highlighted below.

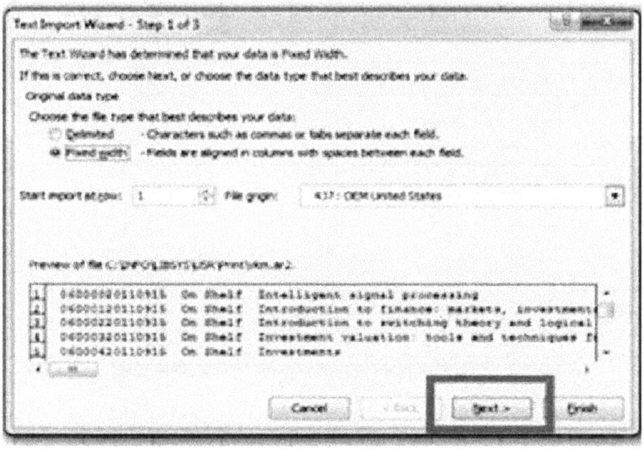

j. You can see a line with arrow dividing various fields/ data like author, accession number, title, etc but it is not properly separating, so you can just select irrelevant line arrow and drag upward to remove it similarly to divide/make new line in between different fields just click on the scale above to make a line with arrow as shown below. Please review this for all the data and see that all the fields are properly separated by the line because it is necessary to get all the fields under the different column in an excel sheet. Finally, click the next and then finish option.

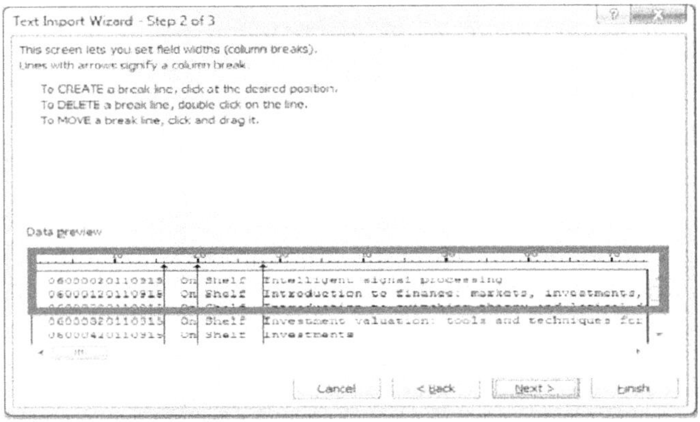

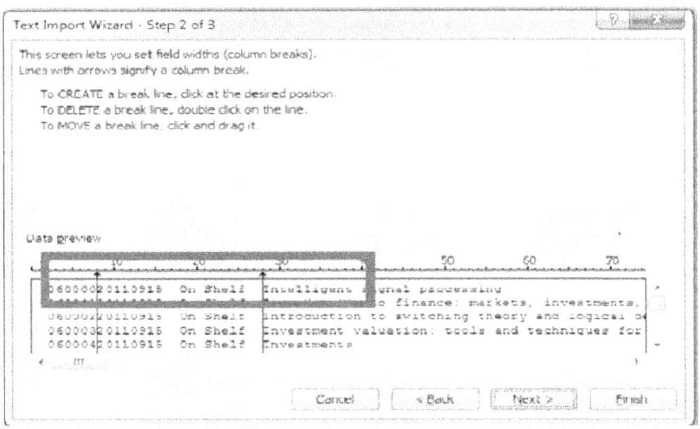

k. Now you can see your data in excel sheet. Make little changes if required with the help of options given under excel for more refinement of data.

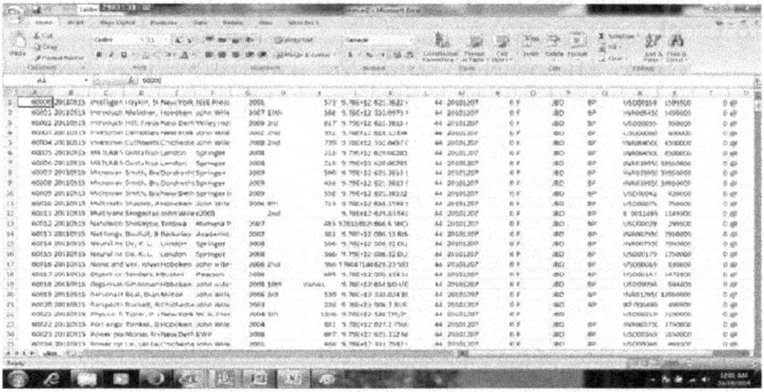

1. After necessary changes click save option and then select No, popup windows will ask to save the file in Excel format. Now your data is ready for converting from excel to MARC. Please note some refinement can be done in Marc editor software also for better output. For conversion from Excel to Marc refer next section of this book chapter or http://manual.koha-community.org/3.4/en/marceditexcel.html and many more sites which can be searched from Google website to give an idea of data conversion in Excel.

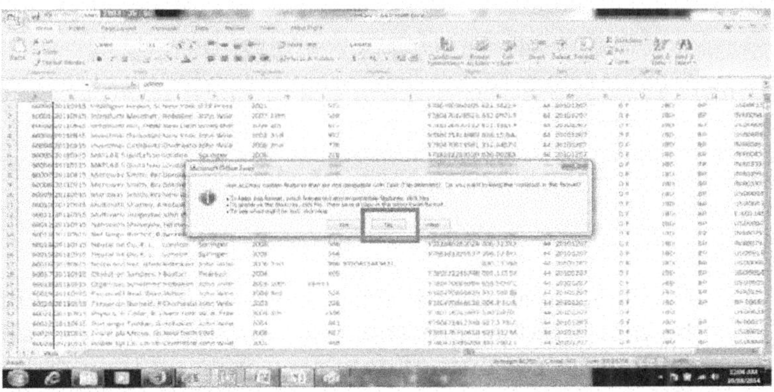

Periodicals bound volume data conversion from Libsys ILMS to Excel

a. Open the Serial modules and click the Bound Volumes / Issues option available under the: Serial > Reports > Miscellaneous >

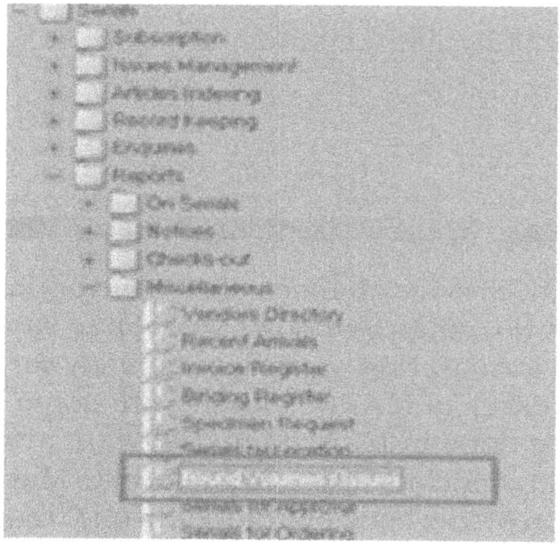

b. Select the options as shown in the below screenshot and specially (ASCII) and then click the record structure option:

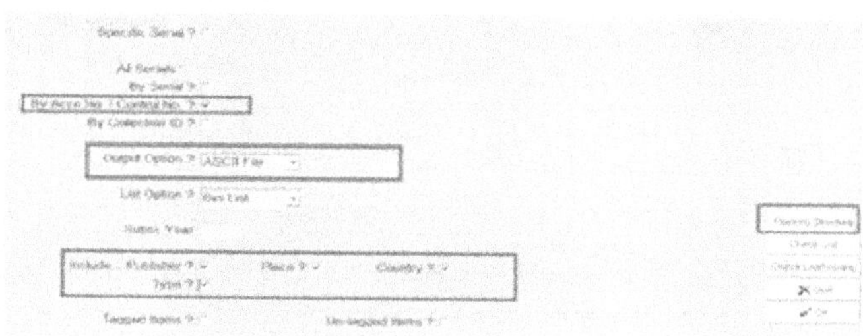

c. On clicking of record structure following screen will be displayed where you have to select almost all options as per output data required and then press OK:

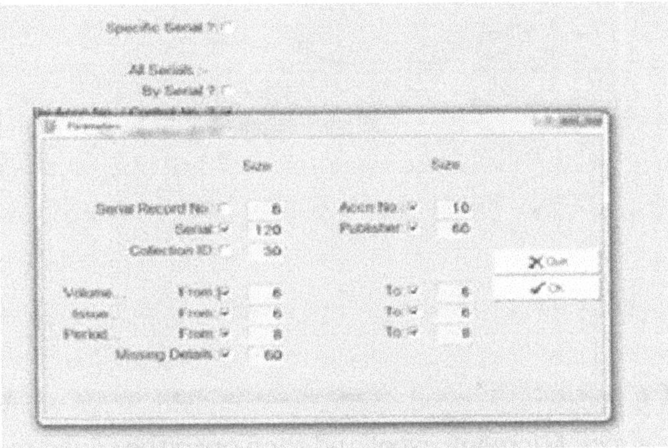

d. Then select the range of accession number which you want to take output for conversion into marc:

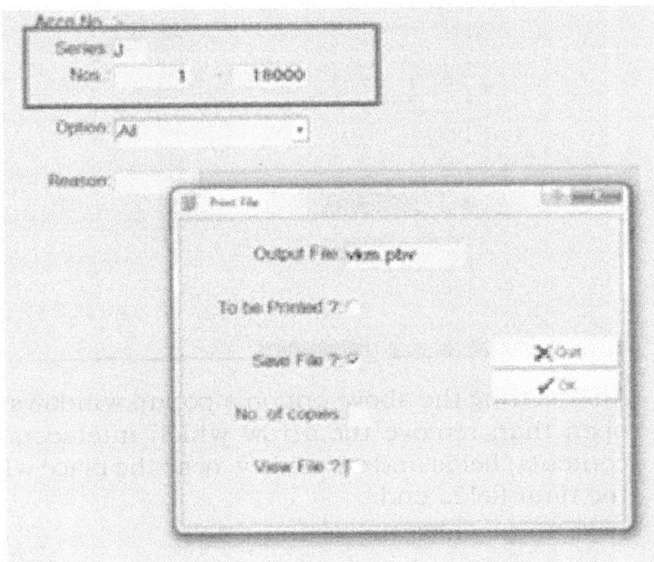

e. Now you can view your saved record in the following format in notepad.

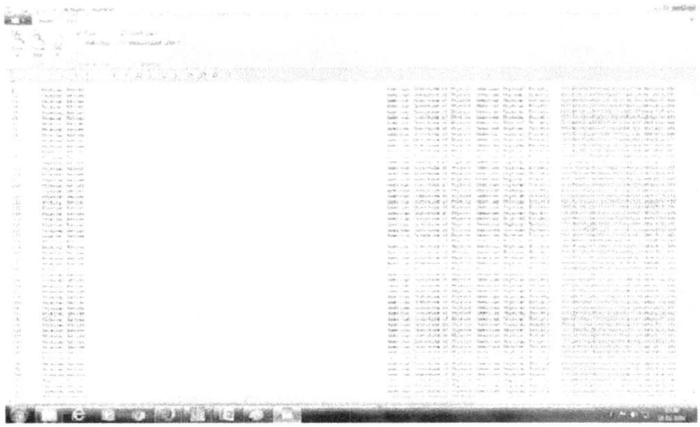

f. Open Microsoft excel and then open the saved record file of Bound Volumes as shown below:

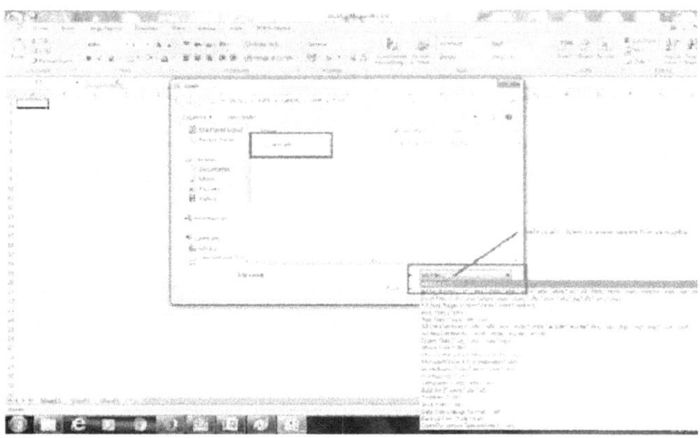

g. After setting the above option a popup windows will open than remove the arrow which intersects the contents/fields and create new near the place where the data fields end:

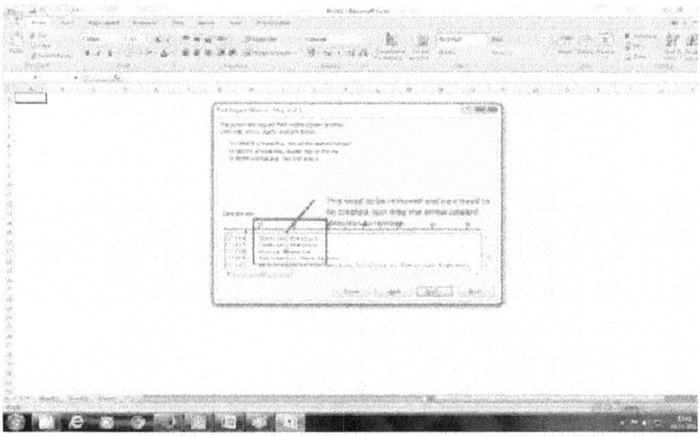

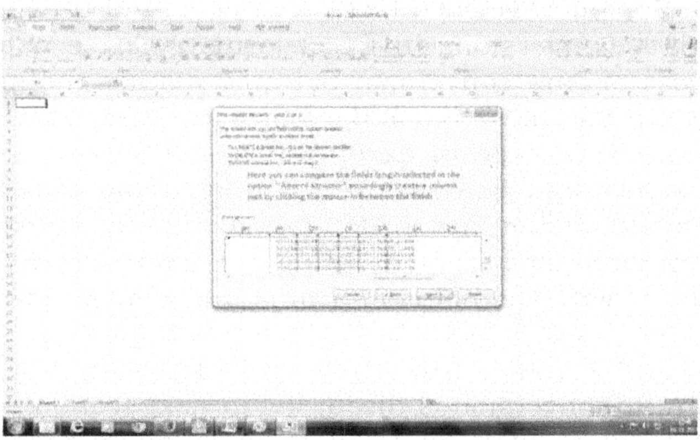

h. On clicking the finish button you can see and evaluate your excel converted data as follows than save the file in excel format as described in previous section.

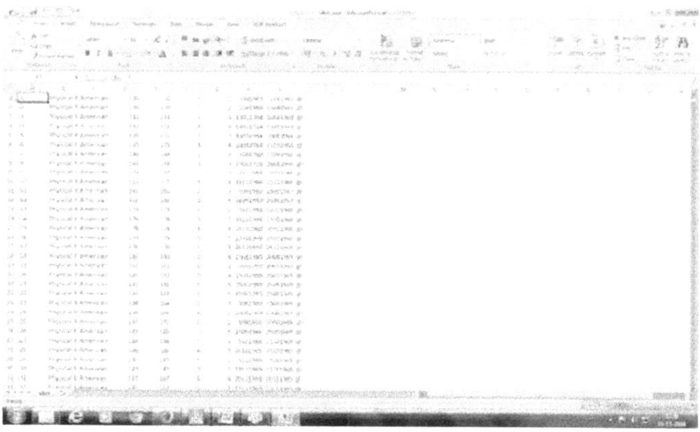

So you have seen how some tools and tricks work for data conversions in Excel format, please note the process of data conversion not only require the help of tools but you have to use the logics too. After converting few different type of excel sheets with data, a good experience can be developed for preparing data to be converted finally into MARC format. There are various techniques used for separating the data into different columns with the help of formula and options provided in Excel through its tools on the top header. Some of the tools and formulae which are useful for preparing Excel to MARC conversion is discussed in next section.

Useful Excel tools and formula

This section describes some of the tools/Formula which is frequently used during the preparation of Excel sheet before conversion into the MARC through MarcEdit software.

Table 6.1. Useful Excel formula for data refinement

Tool/Formula for	***Description***
Sort and Filter	It helps in sorting the selected columns data in ascending/descending order. The filter option provides flexibility in displaying only the selected field's data in entire worksheet.

Find and select	There are various options available under this icon, fine and replace provide option to search some specific set of character for editing as well as you can replace or remove the set of character with other character sets. "Go to special" option provide selection of blank rows and their deletions as well as many other advance options available under this menu.
Test to column	This is the more frequently used tool under the "data" menu of Excel. This tools help in separating various text into columns on the basis of some unique identifier inside the text for example if we want to separate Place and publisher available in same column "Delhi, Springer" than we can separate it with unique identifier ",". This type of separation will help in defining different data under the defined MARC tag field for it.
Copying same data in many cells	To copy the contents of one cell to a set of adjacent cells, select the initial cell and then move the cursor over the small square in the bottom right-hand corner (the fill handle). The cursor will change from a white cross to a black cross. Hold down the mouse button and drag to a range of adjacent cells. The initial cell contents will be copied to the other cells
Inserting or deleting columns	Select the column from top and right click the mouse than hit the insert option; it will insert one blank column to the left of selected column.
Formula to combine columns text	=CONCATENATE(A2," ",B2," ",C2) the said formula will combine the text of A2,B2 and C2 cell into the selected cell. Hence we can able to combine more than two texts in single cell that exist in different cells.
To add prefix in the text	= "Vol. "&D1 it helps in adding the prefix like "Vol." in text of a cell.
To combine the text of many columns	=E1&F1&H1 similar to =CONCATENATE(A2," ",B2," ",C2) this will also combine the texts of many cell into the one.
To add prefix and suffix in the text	="7"&A1&"8" This formula will add prefix 7 and suffix 8 in the text of cell A1
To compare similar data of two columns	=IF(ISERROR(MATCH(E1,$G$1:$G$20000,0)),"Unique","Duplicate")

Apart from above there are so many techniques and options available in Excel to prepare the standard data for final conversion into MARC21 format. In next section

I will demonstrate with example how Excel data and other MARC21 data can be made compatible for importing into the Koha system.

6.2. APPLICATION OF MARCEDIT WITH EXAMPLES

MarcEdit was initially conceived in the summer of 1999, and finished largely in response to a major database clean-up project that had been planned for the Oregon State University's electronic catalog. It is developed by Terry Reese. In 1999, MarcEdit started out as simple MARC=>plain text translation utility. Today, MarcEdit has become one of the more complete metadata edit suites available to librarians. MarcEdit presently includes a very rich feature set targeted at making metadata translation and editing easier for both the beginner and advanced users.

Features of MarcEdit

MARC Editing : MarcEdit includes a MARC Breaker and Maker to move MARC data into a friendlier mnemonic file format. It includes a dedicated MARC Editor, that provides a number of global editing functions, the ability to edit MODS and MARCXML data (in a mnemonic format) and integrate data from other data sources like OCLC, etc. into a batch set of MARC data.

MarcEditor : The MarcEditor is MarcEdit's built in metadata editor. It includes a number of global editing functions, full regular expression and UTF-8 support, as well as the ability to configure the editor to utilize any character set supported by the operating system. Included functions: Globally Add/Delete Fields, Edit Subfields, Swap Field Data, Copy Field Data, Edit Indicators, Generate Call Numbers, Validate Records, Generate Reports, Find/Replace, Direct Integration with Supported ILS systems, Macro support, Task Support, etc.

RDA Helper : The RDA Helper is both a standalone and integrated tool that allows users to take a set of MARC data and automatically generate RDA specific data. The RDA data is derived from the source record set using available control data, variable field data, and RDA specific assumptions.

Delimited Text Translator : The Delimited Text Translator is a tool that allows users to translate data in Excel, Access, or any delimited format into MARC.

Export as Tab Delimited : A tool that allows users to export their MARC data as delimited text.

Harvest OAI Data : MarcEdit has the ability to harvest metadata from an OAI data provider and convert the data directly to MARC. Supported formats are MARCXML, oaimarc, oai_dc, and MODS. However, the program allows the user to provide their own translation rules, so any format could be accommodated.

XML Translations : MarcEdit supports the facilitation of metadata from XML and non-XML formats into various forms, including MARC.

Characterset conversion : MarcEdit supports the ability to convert MARC records from one characterset to another. This includes the traditional charactersets like MARC-8 (ANSEL) and UTF-8. But it also includes support for any characterset currently supported by the operating system. So users with MARC data in Traditional Chinese can utilize MarcEdit to convert that data to UTF-8.

Z39.50/SRU Client : MarcEdit includes a built in Z39.50 and SRU client for interaction with other library systems.

MARC SQL Explorer : MarcEdit includes an SQL Explorer — a tool that allows users to export their data into either an SQLite or MySQL data and run SQL queries directly on the data to mine for information.

MARC Validator : MarcEdit includes a number of

tools to help users validate data and identify incorrectly structured MARC record data.

Many more features : Like the ability to split, join, sort, etc. data in various formats.

Technical requirements of MarcEdit

- Operating System: XP SP3 (32 & 64 bit) – present So long as Windows can support .NET 4.0+, MarcEdit will run on it.; Linux with Mono 4+; OSX 10.8+
- RAM: 8 MB (minimum); 32 MB+ (recommended)
- Disk space: 13 MB (setup); 5 MB (application)
- Windows Requirements: Primary Windows Requirement is the presence of .NET 4.0+.

Conversion of Excel data in MARC21 format

If Excel data is ready to be converted into the MARC then it is advisable to write exact MARC tag number along with sub-tag on header/Top of each column rather than writing its description like Title, Author, editor etc. This will help at the time of converting/assigning each column MARC tag number. For example one excel sheet is displayed here which will be converted into MARC format and detail step by step conversion of the same is given below.

	A	B	C	D	E	F	G	H	I	J	K	L	M	N	O
1	100a	245a	245b	250a	260a	260b	260c	300a	080a	080b	020a	650a	952c	952p	
2	Author Na	Title	SubTitle	Edition	Place of P	Name of I	Year of Pu	Pages/Vo	Classif. N	Book Num	ISBN	Subject	Type	Accession Number	
3	Hall, C Mi	The geogr	environ m	4th	United Kir	Routledge	2014	458p	338.4791	H14G	978041583	Tourism	General	09022	
4	Kotler, P	Marketing for hospit		6th	New Delh	Pearson E	2014	629p	647.9407	K79M	978933251	Hospitality Industry - N	General	09028	
5	Kotler, P	Marketing for hospit		6th	New Delh	Pearson E	2014	629p	647.9407	K79M	978933251	Hospitality Industry - N	General	09029	
6	Desai, V	Small-scla	in the twenty-first c		Mumbai	Himalaya	2014	570p	338.642	D451S	978935024	Small business	General	09030	
7	Sharma, A	Mon-Livre learn french in easy			Jammu	Saksham I	2011	84p	445.3421	S23M	SBIPB1001		General	09040	
8	Robinson,	Tourism			United Kir	CABI	2013	525p	338.4791	R565T	978184593	Tourism	General	09041	
9	Moutinho	Strategic manageme		2nd	United Kir	CABI	2011	313p	338.4791	M86S	978184593	Tourism-Management	General	09042	
10	Sirakaya-T	Research methods for leisure,			United Kir	CABI	2011	278p	790.07	S76R	978184593	Recreation-Research	General	09043	
11	Raj, Razaq	Cultural tourism			United Kir	CABI	2013	247p	910.68	R11C	978184593	Heritage Tourism-Man	General	09044	
12	Phillips, R	Tourism, planning and commu			Oxon	Routledge	2013	146p	338.4791	P546T	978041552	Tourism	Reference	09051	
13	Saarimen,	Tourism a	tourism, local comm		Oxon	Routledge	2013	241p	338.4791	S11T	978041552	Poverty--Government	General	09052	
14	Liburd, Ja	Understanding the sustainable			Oxford	Goodfello	2010	247p	338.4791	L1U	978190688	Sustainable developm	General	09053	

Fig. 6.3. Sample Excel data for Conversion in MARC format

a. First you have to open the installed MarcEditor for which you need to double-click the shortcut icon available on the desktop. The first screen will display various options on the screen along with icons like MARC tools, MarcEditor, etc. out of which we have to select first "Delimited Text Translator" as highlighted in the below screen.

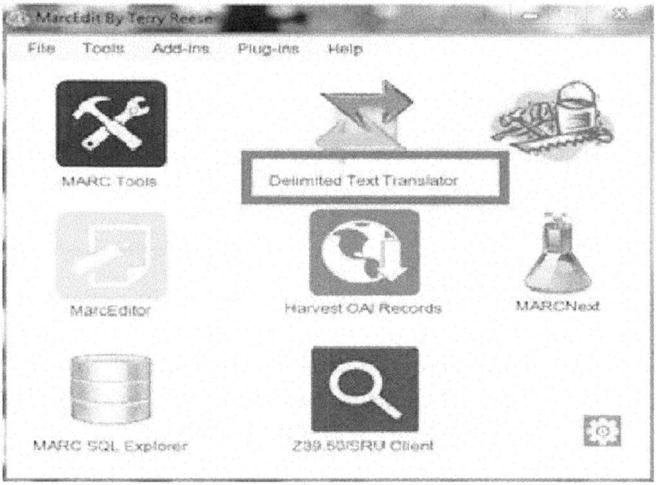

b. The delimited text translator screen will present many options out of which some are a very basic requirement for MARC data like Edit LDR/008. First we have to select the source file i.e. the Excel file which we have prepared for conversion into the MARC and the output file name than excel sheet name which may be sheet1. The delimiter value will remain only Tab although many options are given to the drop down list. The Edit LDR/008 option will present another small screen to choose the default type of material as per international standards, and you can modify the data of 008 fields but for beginners it is recommended to leave all the fields and data as it is just select the option Book and come back to the main screen now tick marc under UTF-8 Encoded option and select next.

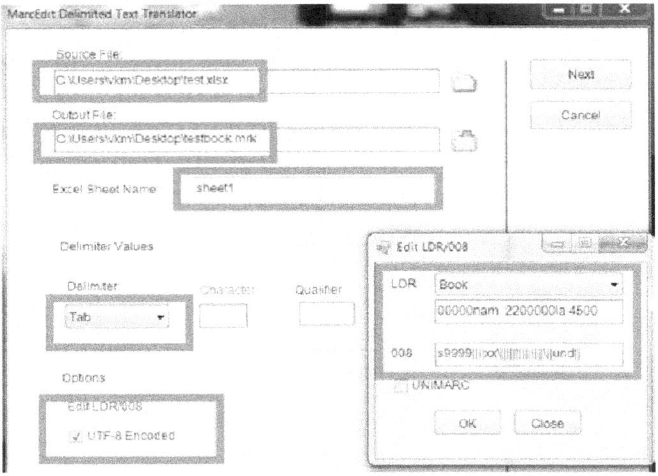

c. The next screen will display the main screen where you need to assign actual MARC tag to all the data which you have entered in the each column. The data snapshot display you each field and the MARC tag below it which you have assigned to the Excel original data sheet on top of each column. Please note that we have assigned a tag to each column as to just remember which tag number will be assigned to each field. Under setting we have to select the field number out of the drop down list one by one and assign the tag number as the display in the screen below, the indicator will remain \\ by default then finally click "Add Argument". Once you have assigned all the fields' marc tag number then next you need to join the same tag number which occurs more than once by selecting, the same tags join option appears after right click as shown in the below screen. At last, just click finish and it will confirm the generation of the .mrk file.

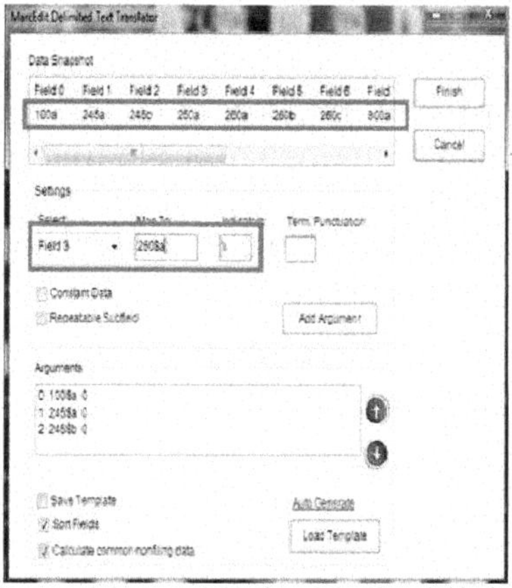

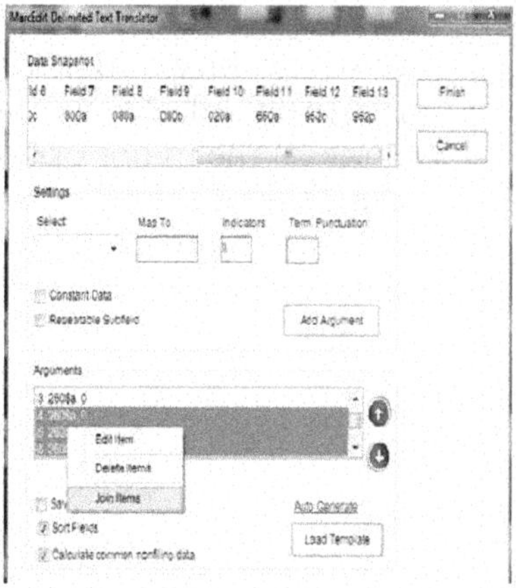

d. On double clicking the file which is finally saved in the above step the entire excel data will open in MarcEditor as shown in the below screen along with the MARC tag number assigned to us in the previous step. Each bibliographic data is separated by space and on top first data is nothing but tags only which we have assigned in Excel just for mnemonic purpose hence you can delete it.

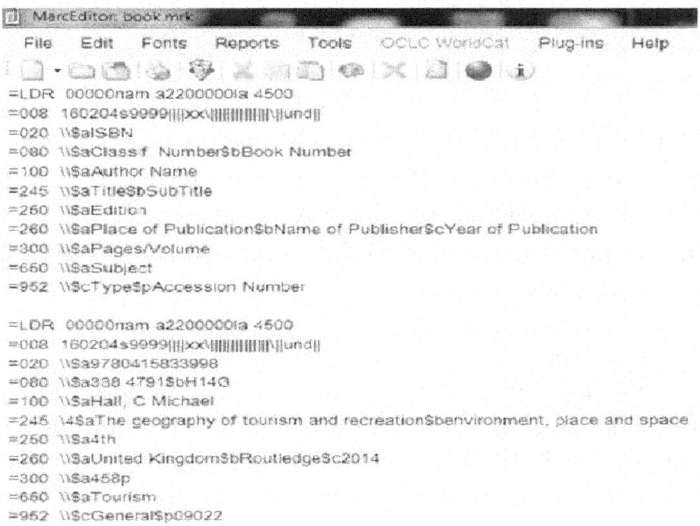

e. We have seen our data structure in above step, and now we have to refine it as per standard and requirement of Koha library management software. Some of the major options which are available under the MarcEditor are shown below, and important ones are highlighted which is frequently used during data refinements as per standards.

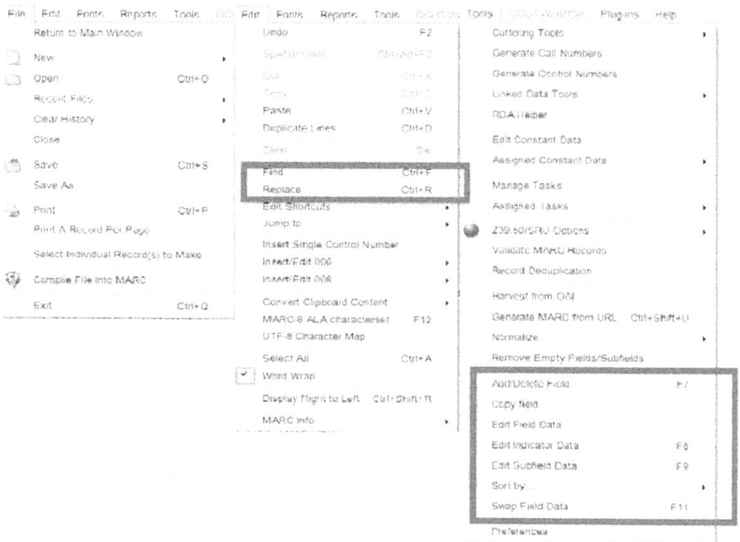

The major work in this data standardization which is left out as per Koha requirement is:

a. Assigning tag 952 to subfields for library codes, the location of the item, call number etc.

b. Replacing the year (9999) with an actual year from 008 tags.

c. Assigning new tag for Koha bibliographic record (942$c)

First of all we will assign 952 to subfields which is local field in Koha and mandatory to display item details, some of the subfields are $a (library code say if MAIN), $b (item current location code say if GEN/REF), $o (call number), etc. to assign these we will use the option edit subfield data option as shown below.

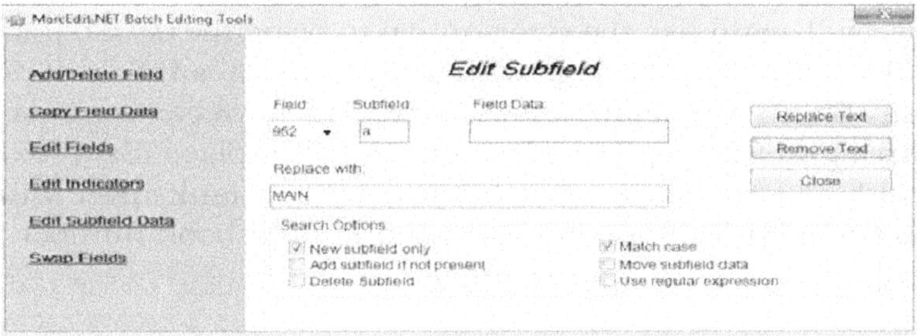

After addition of subfields code now we have to replace text data into the code from the subfield $c (General/Reference) to do this we will use find and replace option given under edit menu as the string $cGeneral/ $cReference) will be common everywhere in the file so we can do this job very easily. The call number is the combination of class number and book number hence we will use swap option along with some logic as we can only bring subfields separated by $ and field like ab but not the combination of two subfields like $ab. So first use the Swap field option to bring 080$a data in 952$o as shown in below screenshot.

Now we have to bring 080$b near the 952$o so that we will use some trick, first use the subfield edit option as shown below to place some dummy data near $o with a probable string of character which does not available in rest of the MARC record in existing file as displayed on next screen. So the final output will be now $o$zyyy. Now we will again use the swap option to bring the 080$b just like 080$a in 952 tags with some dummy subfield let's say $x, so now finally we will have $o$zyyy$x as common string in 952 tag out of which we will replace ($zyyy$x) with a blank space in such a way that a blank space will be created in between class number and book number.

Edit Subfield

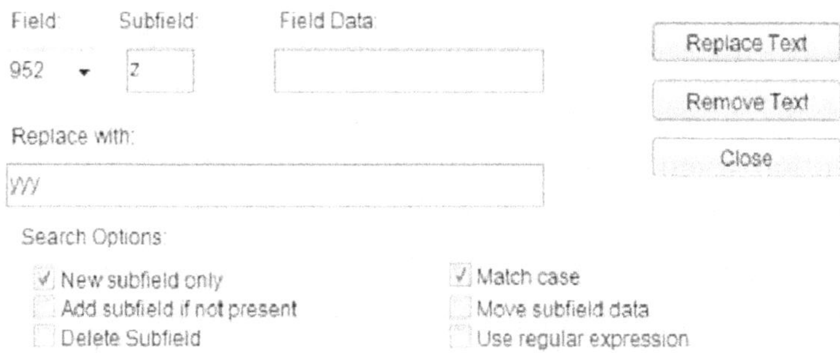

One of the major challenge I faced to bring all the year of publication data in 008 field, it mainly happen when we get the data from Excel sheet or from a non standard ILMS. During converting Excel file to MARC we have assigned 008 default field data where year was 9999. In Koha system there is a year wise searching option given which is indexed from 008 field, therefore we are bound to replace the data 008 data (9999) from year (260$c). Along with some MarcEditor tool we will use some logic like we created 952$o call number field.

First of all change 008 tags to any other non-mandatory tag like 801 with the help of find and replace and assign subfield $z so it should be now "*=801 \\$z160204s9999||||xx\||||||||||||||\||und||*. Now use the swap field option and bring 260$cYear to create 801$x field then create another subfield $y with edit subfield option and add data "160204s9999||||

xx\|||||||||||||||\||und||" so the entire field be =801 \\$z160204s9999||||xx\|||||||||||||||\|| und||$x2014$y160204s9999||||xx\|||||||||||||||\||und||. Next job is to remove the field $z from above with delete subfield option under edit subfield data hence it appears as =801 \\$x2014$y160204s9999|||| xx\|||||||||||||||\||und||. Now we will remove $y160204s9999 find and replace option then finally replace =801 \\$x with =008 160204s to get the final 008 field as desired (=008 160204s2014||||xx\|||||||||||||||\||und||). Therefore all the data refinement has been done so just add two more field with text (942$cGEN and 041$aeng)

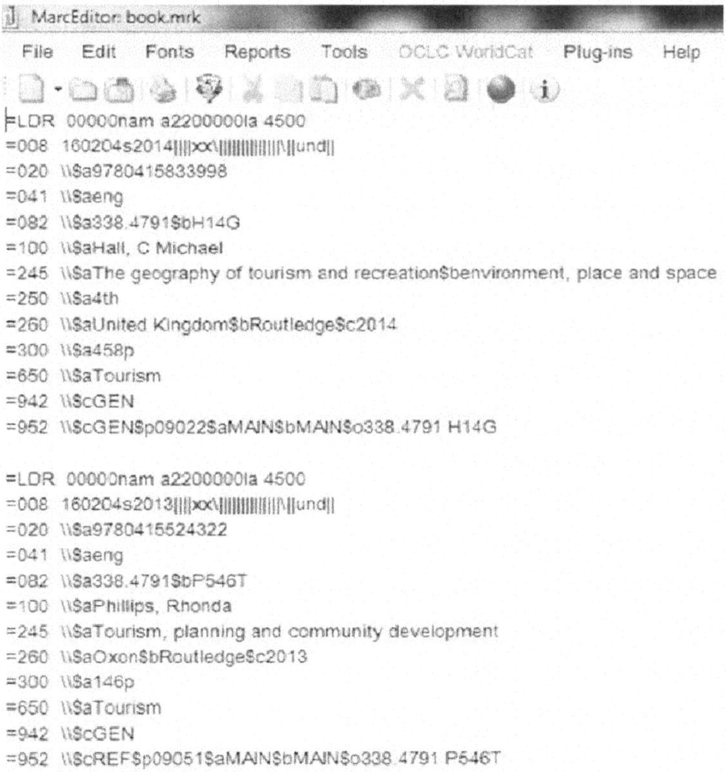

```
MarcEditor: book.mrk
File  Edit  Fonts  Reports  Tools  OCLC WorldCat  Plug-ins  Help

=LDR  00000nam a2200000Ia 4500
=008  160204s2014||||xx\|||||||||||||||\||und||
=020  \\$a9780415833998
=041  \\$aeng
=082  \\$a338.4791$bH14G
=100  \\$aHall, C Michael
=245  \\$aThe geography of tourism and recreation$benvironment, place and space
=250  \\$a4th
=260  \\$aUnited Kingdom$bRoutledge$c2014
=300  \\$a458p
=650  \\$aTourism
=942  \\$cGEN
=952  \\$cGEN$p09022$aMAIN$bMAIN$o338.4791 H14G

=LDR  00000nam a2200000Ia 4500
=008  160204s2013||||xx\|||||||||||||||\||und||
=020  \\$a9780415524322
=041  \\$aeng
=082  \\$a338.4791$bP546T
=100  \\$aPhillips, Rhonda
=245  \\$aTourism, planning and community development
=260  \\$aOxon$bRoutledge$c2013
=300  \\$a146p
=650  \\$aTourism
=942  \\$cGEN
=952  \\$cREF$p09051$aMAIN$bMAIN$o338.4791 P546T
```

Fig. 6.4. Refined converted data from Excel

then please review two/three times all the MARC tags for corrections and additions/missing etc. and finally arrange the bibliographic data tag number wise and compile file into MARC, the options are given under tools and file respectively. The final refined data appears as below and you can delete the first bibliographic record as it represents the excel headings only.

REFERENCES

1. MarcEdit Development. (n.d.). Retrieved January 02, 2016, from http://marcedit.reeset.net/
2. Microsoft Excel. (n.d.). Retrieved February 04, 2016, from https://en.wikipedia.org/wiki/Microsoft_Excel
3. Excel functions. (n.d.). Retrieved February 03, 2016, from http://www.techonthenet.com/excel/formulas/concat.php
4. About MarcEdit. (n.d.). Retrieved February 01, 2016, from http://marcedit.reeset.net/about-marcedit

7
Koha Implementations : Case Studies

The current chapter is the real implementation story of Koha at various educational institutes in India by the author Hence this chapter will describe the Koha implementation problems along with their solutions, data migrations and post implementation difficulties and their solutions. The book will cover the following case studies.

- Indian Institute of Technology Roorkee, Saharanpur Campus
- Assam University Silchar: a central university
- DAV Public School, CCL, NTS, Barkakana, Ramgarh, Jharkhand
- Central University of Jammu
- MGAHV, Wardha: a central university
- National Institute of Technology Rourkela
- Bhakti Vedanta Research Center, Kolkata

7.1. CASE STUDY OF INDIAN INSTITUTE OF TECHNOLOGY ROORKEE, SAHARANPUR CAMPUS

The Department of Paper Technology located at the Saharanpur Campus of IIT Roorkee offers academic programs at various levels in Pulp and Paper Technology, Polymer Science and Technology, Process Engineering and Management. The Department has well developed academic infrastructure. Its faculty is engaged in teaching, research and industrial consultancy. The Department is the predecessor of the School of Paper Technology established by the Government of India in 1964, with an aid from the Royal Swedish Government. This school was managed by a society created by the U.P. Government until its merger with the then University of Roorkee in 1978. The school was renamed as the Institute of Paper Technology in July 1968 and subsequently Department of Paper Technology in July 1992.The University of Roorkee converted into Indian Institute of Technology (IIT) and renamed as IIT Roorkee in 2001. Saharanpur Campus of IIT Roorkee has three departments which are recently trifurcated from Department of Paper Technology, so the campus library is basically having excellent collection of Paper Technology related resources in India, apart from this library is having good collections of books on engineering, management, humanities, science, Hindi and English literature etc. The library is having various types of collections like General books, reference books, Book bank, reserved collection, Theses, dissertations, B.Tech. Projects, CD/DVD's, journals, etc. The library serves more than 600 users who belong to various groups like Faculty, Under Graduate, Postgraduate, Research Scholar, nonteaching staff, etc. with various types of their circulation privileges. Library provides all the modern facility like internet access, Xeroxing, computing, etc. Library purchasing policy is centralized i.e. the reading material of library is being procured through Mahatma Gandhi Central Library (MGCL) located at IIT Roorkee main campus at Roorkee, but this library performs all the other housekeeping tasks like accessioning, cataloguing and other technical processing of books after receiving from the vendors/ MGCL.

Need for new ILMS

The library was semi-automated with commercial software Troodon3 which lacks many features, like setting up of circulation privileges for various type of documents, fine collection, web OPAC, compatibility for implementation of radio frequency identification (RFID), web-based user services, etc. because of which staff members and users were dissatisfied in modern context of library system and services. So library decided to go for the change of the ILMS, which has most modern features and could fulfill the user's and staff's requirements.

Selection of Koha

Mahatma Gandhi Central Library (MGCL) at IIT Roorkee main campus migrated from Troodon software to Libsys. It was decided that same system could be adopted for our library but due to a distance of several kilometers in between and some technical issues, the decision was dropped. This is how an idea for implementing Koha came into being. This software is quite popular and has immense commercial and open source support which could help in its implementation at our library.

Installation and testing of Koha

The major challenge was to gain reasonable knowledge of LAMP architecture and install Koha on LINUX. The Live CD/DVD on Ubuntu available on the internet made the task a lot easier. Live CD/DVD iso file was downloaded from the sourceforge website. With many interpersonal communications with the experts and discussions on the open forums Koha was installed on a 512 MB RAM PC for running a prototype and testing. Several issues were confronted in the configuration part but online community help resolved them too. Some minor corrections on live DVD were also informed to the concern person and discussed for other technical issues and their solutions. Sample data of all type of library materials and users category were created with different circulation privileges than thoroughly tested the software as per our requirements and discovered the solutions of the problem/requirements given beautifully in the Koha system.

Data migration

The trickiest part of the whole process was the migration of data from the existing system to the new one. The existing ILMS database was based on MS_Access, and there was no databasepassword to see the structure of data inside MS_Access, but luck favored those who worked hard so discovered one option in Troodon3 to export the whole data (Library materials except user data) in ISO 2709 format. But it was not sufficient because converting the ISO 2709 into MARC format was another challenge before the author hence again went to http://www.google.co.in/ and found MARC editor which can easily convert the CDS/ISIS iso format (Winisis) database to MARC format which is discussed in next section.

Application of Winisis (CDS/ISIS) in data migration

The author tried to convert the data which was got through Troodon import option in iso 2709 format through the option given in MARC editor and shown in Fig. 7.1

But unfortunately, fails to convert and got the blank .mrc file, realize the mistake that iso which is trying to convert belongs to Troodon iso 2709, but MARC editor needs iso from CDS-ISIS. So author imported Troodon iso to winisis (Windows version of CDS-ISIS) in existing default this.mst database as shown in fig.2, then first time saw iso data in winisis and found correct after checking in the original source (Troodon) as given in fig.3 than exported the whole data again in CDS-ISIS iso format as desired by MARC editor.

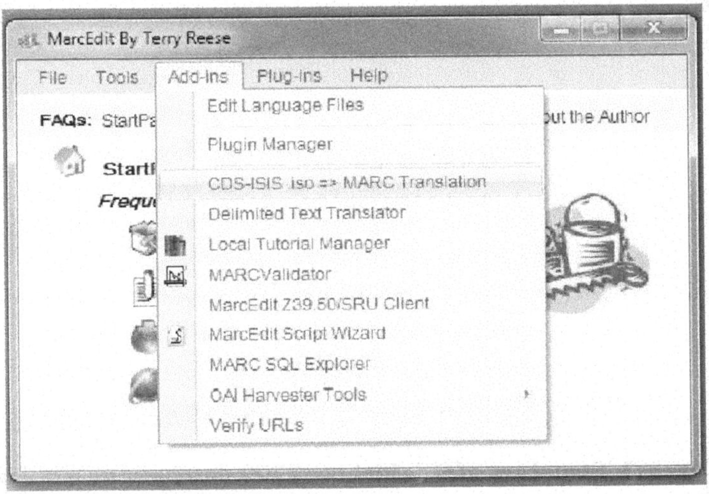

Fig. 7.1. The option available to convert CDS_ISIS.iso data in MarcEdit

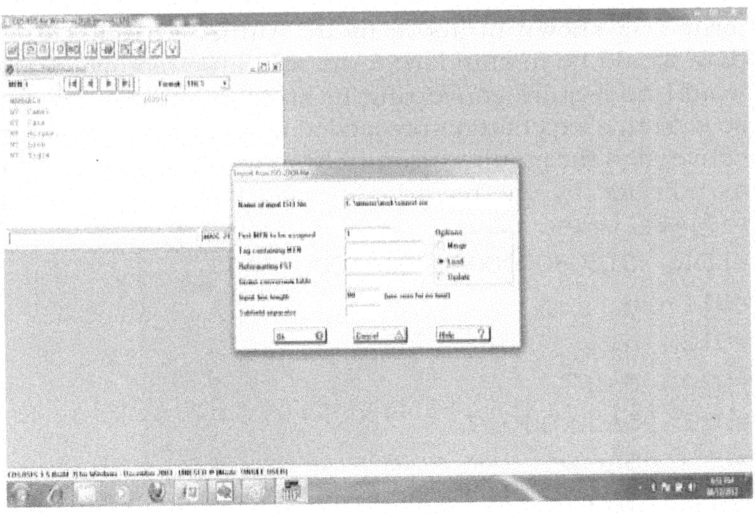

Fig. 7.2. Importing of Troodon iso 2709 to Winisis thes.mst database

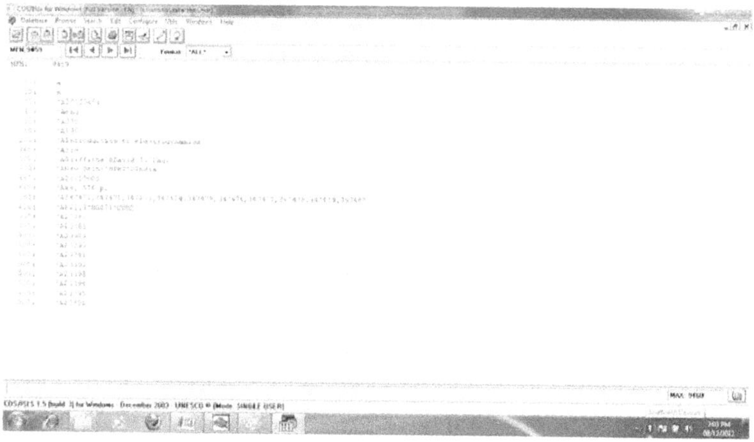

Fig. 7.3. Structure of Original iso-2709 database in Winisis

MarcEditor

MARC editor is a wonderful and user-friendly system to convert above CDS-ISIS iso data in MARC format as shown in above figure Author expected that data would be in standard form, and little modifications would be require converting in standard MARC format so with this expectation proceeded for next step, but after conversion the result was entirely against the expectation as reflected by one record converted from CDS-ISIS iso to MARC below:

=LDR 010080000000003610004500

=011 a

=012 m

=020 $AIPT

=022 $A20011019

=040 $Aeng

=050 $A010

=060 $A100

=200 $AEncyclopedia of chemical technology

=260 $A4th

=300 $AOthmer$BKirk

=400 $ANew York$BJohn Wiley

=440 $A19980000

=460 $AV 25- xxviii,912 V 8- xxviii,1093 V 23-xxviii,1118 V 14- xxviii,1115 V 18- xxviii,1073 V 21-24 148

=490 $AVol 25$CVitamins to zone refining

=490 $AVol 8$CDeuterium and tritium to elastomers, polyethers

=490 $AVol 23$CSugar to thin films

=490 $AVol 14$CImaging technology to lanthanides

=490 $AVol 18$CPaper to pigment dispersions

=490 $AVol 21-24$CIndex Recycling, oil to vinyl polymers

=500 $AIPT

=610 $A660.03$BK73$CDDC

=620 $AChemical technology- Encyclopedias

=900 $A17213$B25$CR

=900 $A17372$B8$CR

=900 $A17052$B23$CR

=900 $A17566$B14$CR

=900 $A16897$B18$CR

=900 $A17212$B21-24$CR

Therefore mental analysis and searching the process on how to make it standard helped in finding several useful files over the internet but all were just to convert good data into standard MARC not like ours. So the challenge was accepted and started systematic approach to achieving the standardization and most satisfaction which are described in next section.

Mapping and editing of bibliographic data in correct MARC format

It was the most challenging task due to less expertise/experience on MARC and other conversion tools and techniques but compared the different tags of Troodon and about the MARC tags of Koha from the details given on Library of Congress (LOC) website and made a description of Troodon tags and their equivalent in MARC/ Koha tags as given in below Table.

The various tags in Troodon and their equivalent in Koha/Marc

Description	***Troodon Tags***	***Marc/Koha Tags***
Leader	=LDR	LDR
	=011	
	=012	
Source of Record	=020	037 $b (May be in 952$e)
	=022	Need to remove
Language	=040	041 $a
Physical Medium	=050	
Type of material	=060	942 $a (Delete this number and insert fresh field)
ISBN	=100	020 $a
CODEN	=102	
Title	=200	245 $a
Journal Name	=201	
Edition	=260	250 $a
Name of persons	=300	100 $a ($F Au,comp. etc need to be removed)
Corporate body	=310	110 $a
Name of Meeting	=320	111 $a
Publisher	=400	260 $aPlace$bPublicher$cYear
Date of publication	=440	260 $c
Serial Number/Date	=450	
Physical Description	=460	300 $a
Price	=465	
Series statements	=480	490 $a
Part statement	=490	505 $a

Note	=500	500 $a
Bibliographical relation=510		
Frequency	=520	
Call Number	=610	082 $aClass$bBook No.
Descriptors/ Subject heading	=620	650 $a
Bill No./Date/ Vendor	=800	
Accession number	=900	952 $p

Wherever necessary made remarks in separate files for further job works, like what needs to be added, deleted and additional codes as per Koha requirements, so different type of codes for reading materials was added in MARC format which is given in below Table.

Item types and their codes used in Koha for data conversion

Item Type	***Code***
Books	BK
Reference Books	REF
Book Bank	BB
Reserve Books	RB
Location of Items	Code
General Section	GEN
Reference section	REF
TBLS/Books book section	TBLS
Reserve section	RS

The mapping was done only for the tags under which bibliographical data of library materials were present in the Troodon database as shown in below Table. After consultation on MARC website of LOC found that some mandatory fields were missing/wrong like 008 etc. Therefore fully exploited the options of MARC editor software and converted all basic Troodon tags one by one into standard MARC tags as shown in next figure.

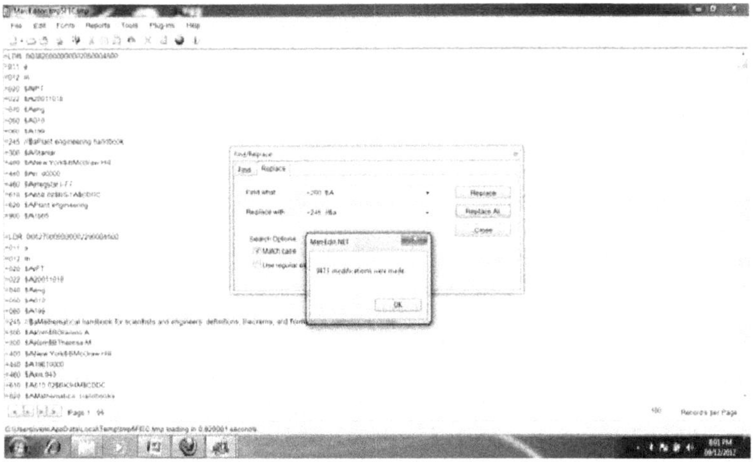

Fig.7.4. Find and replace option in MARC editor to convert tags in standard MARC tag

Inserting, editing, replacing, deleting etc. related work was more complex but some of the things has been done with the options available in MARC editor as shown in next screenshot (fig.7.5) but some works forced to solve the puzzles of converting rest of the data for which author

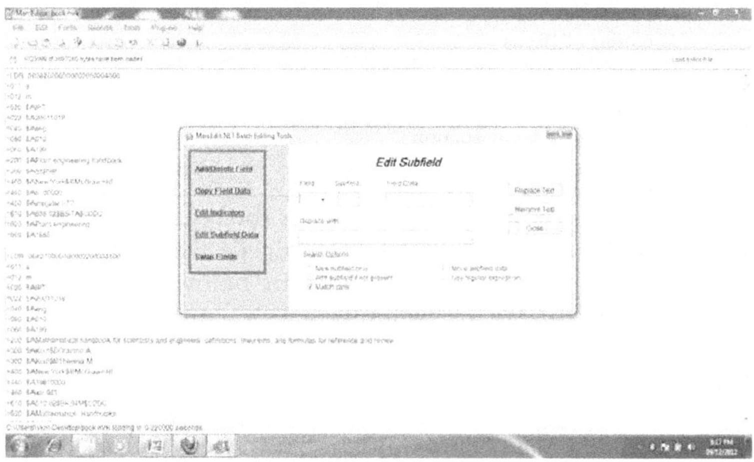

Fig. 7.5. Options under MarcEdit to add, remove, replace MARC tags and sub tags

started mental analysis and one by one all nonstandard data was successfully converted into standard MARC format which was just tricky rather than technical. It is difficult to mention all the process here but ensures the professionals that almost every solution is available through some mental analysis and MARC editor for converting data in standard MARC format which is compatible with Koha requirements.

The final converted data of Troodon as shown in above section now looks like below as per requirements of Koha software:

```
=LDR   01665nam a2200313Ia 4500
=008   101213s1998 utu o eng d
=037   \\$bIPT
=041   \\$aeng
=082   \\$a660.03$bK73
=100   \\$aOthmer, Kirk
=245   \\$aEncyclopedia of chemical technology
=250   \\$a4th
=260   \\$aNew York:$bJohn Wiley,$c1998
=300   \\$aV 25- xxviii,912 V 8- xxviii,1093 V 23-
       xxviii,1118 V 14- xxviii,1115 V 18- xxviii,1073 V
       21-24 148
=505   \\$aVol 14. - Imaging technology to lanthanides
=505   \\$aVol 18. - Paper to pigment dispersions
=505   \\$aVol 21-24. - Index Recycling, oil to vinyl
       polymers
=505   \\$aVol 23. - Sugar to thin films
=505   \\$aVol 25. - RBitamins to zone refining
=505   \\$aVol 8. - Deuterium and tritium to
       elastomers, polyethers
=590   \\$aIPT
=650   \\$aChemical technology- Encyclopedias
```

=942 \\$cREF

=999 \\$c3003$d3003

=952 \\$w2012-05-02$p16897$r2012-05-02$40$ 00$ 6660_ 030000000000000_K73$95167 $bMAIN$ 10$o660.03 K73$d2012-05-02$t18$ 70$cREF$yREF$aMAIN

=952 \\$w2012-05-02$p17052$r2012-05-02$40$00 $6660_ 030000000000000_K73$95168$ bMAIN 10o660.03K73$d2012-05-02$t23$70$ cREF$yREF$aMAIN

=952 \\$w2012-05-02$p17212$r2012-05-02$40$00 $6660_030000000000000_K73$95169$bMAIN$10$ o660.03K73$d2012-05-02$t21-24$70$cREF $yREF$aMAIN

=952 \\$w2012-05-02$p17213$r2012-05-02$40$00 $6660_030000000000000_K73$95170$bMAIN$10 $o660.03 K73$d2012-05-02$t25$70$cREF $yREF$aMAIN

=952 \\$w2012-05-02$p17372$r2012-05-02$40$ 00$ 6660_ 030000000000000_K73$95171$ bMAIN$ 10$o660.03 K73$d2012-05-02$t8$70$ cREF$yREF$aMAIN

=952 \\$w2012-05-02$p17566$r2012-05-02$40$ 00$6660_030000000000000_K73$95172$bMAIN$10$ o660.03 K73$d2012-05-02$t14$70$cREF$ yREF$aMAIN

Setup and configuration of Koha

The next process was to set up the Koha system as per MARC data which was needed to be imported, so set the system as per the instruction provided in Koha manual except user setup like circulation privileges, category etc. The various codes was configured like main library Code (MAIN), authorized value for location of different item type (Reserve section, Reference section etc,) and codes for Item types as given in below screenshot (Fig.7.6 and 7.7).

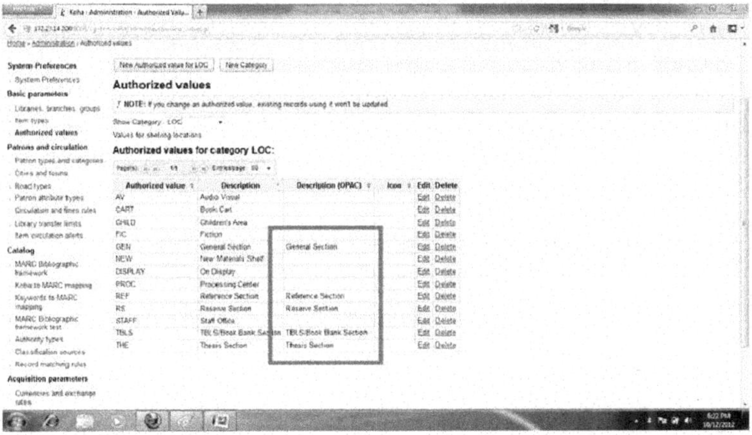

Fig. 7.6. Configuration of Item Locations in Library

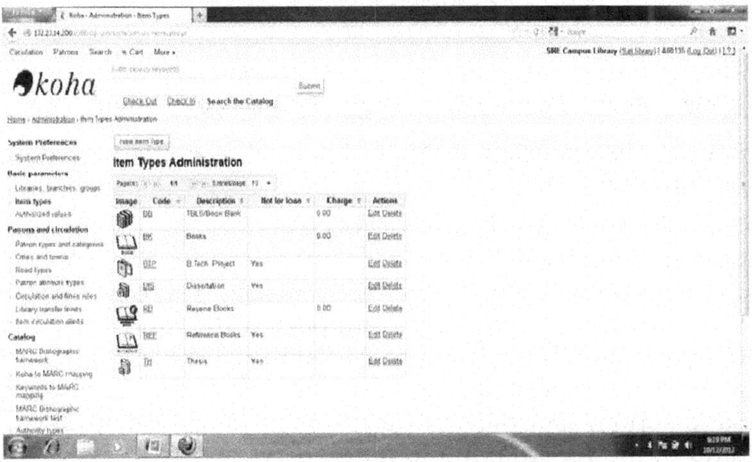

Fig. 7.7. Configuration of Various item types on the basis of circulation depends.

The MARC bibliographical framework for Book as shown in table 3 for different type of library books according to the converted MARC data was created to import all the converted MARC data in Koha.

Apart from above bibliographic framework some field for individual items (Tag 952 in MARC) as shown in screenshot (Fig. 8) was also selected which appears after feeding all the bibliographic details of the items in bibliographic framework for Books type of material.

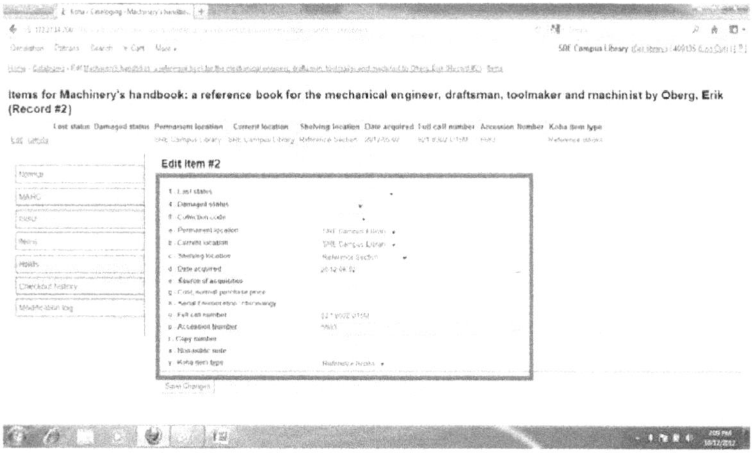

Fig. 7.8. MARC tag 952 selected for each individual item

Importing/exporting of MARC data and re-editing the data in Koha ILMS

After successful import of data in Koha through the option Stage MARC records for Import under Tools option we checked the data in real OPAC and found some errors, then again corrected and re-imported the data in Koha, the process of re-importing and editing of MARC record were done several times until achieved the maximum satisfaction/accuracy. The author found several duplicate data of the records due to data entry quality in previous software which was merged with the help of excellent merging option by bringing similar data at one place as shown in fig. 9 for reducing an unnecessary size of the database, circulation related issue and to avoid any reporting related problems.

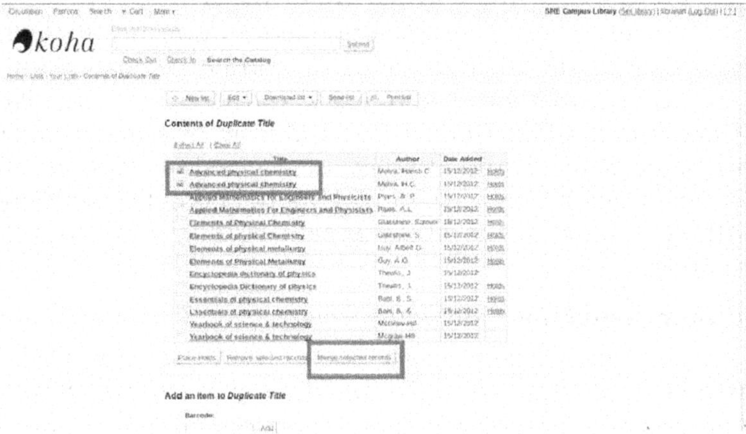

Fig. 7.9. Merging option under Koha

Importing of Users Data in Koha

Before discussing this issue author wish to share that user data was separately imported with no relationship with book issued to members this was done due to lot of corrections were needed to be done in Books database like changing of accession number which was non-uniformly entered in the Troodon database. It was suitable stage/step to perform this task at the time of MARC editing which made the job easy by tricks of MARC conversion, and there was no any circulation related issue because maximum books was already returned by users during vacations hence the circulation record was not imported in Koha. As there was no password for opening Ms_access record for user and book so planned to get all from academic section but luckily the password of Ms_access database was recalled by staff and then everything was visible in Troodon3 database. It was now simple to copy the needed records of users in new excel format and paste it in the .csv format as given in downloadable sample format in Koha staff client for patron import.

Customization of Koha Search and Display

After successful migration/correction of all Book and users data felt need of some additional search and display features for ease of work and user comfort, like browsing of whole item type, searching by acc. number in basic search and display of accession number in detailed display for ease of placing hold on specific item. All were done successfully which is discussed in sub section.

Customization for Catalogue browse

For browsing, discovered tip from the Koha OPAC available on various Koha websites and simply copied the code inside our Koha system preferences and changed the Items code which was assigned for our library item types. The detail code for browsing and our library item code is shown below in bold which were changed for execution of this excellent feature:

```
<!—Catalog search Begins—>
<p><form name="searchform" method="get" action="/cgi-bin/Koha/opac-search.pl">
<input type="hidden" name="idx" value="kw">
<input type="hidden" name="sort_by" value="acqdate_dsc">
<input type="hidden" name="do" value="OK">
<select name="limit" onChange="this.form.submit()"><option>— Browse Catalog —</option>
<option value="mc-itype:BK">General Books</option>
<option value="mc-itype:BB">TBLS Books</option>
<option value="mc-itype:REF">Reference Books</option>
<option value="mc-itype:RB">Reserve Books</option>
<option value="mc-itype:TH">Thesis</option>
<option value="mc-itype:DIS">Dissertation</option>
```

```
<option value="mc-itype:BTP">B.Tech. Project</option>
</select></form></p>
<!—Catalog search Ends—>
```

Customization for search by accession number

Searching by accession number is very frequently needed mainly by staffs for some technical reasons but lack of this feature on main Koha home page bound them to go for advance search and select the option search by barcode which takes much time to reach up to that option. Therefore found the code in file masthead.inc through which various search restriction options were given on Koha main home page. Carefully observed all the codes and successfully inserted the code which can facilitates searching by accession number on Koha main home page, the inserted code is highlighted below among all other existing code.

```
[% IF ( ms_callnum ) %]
<option selected="selected" value="callnum">Call Number</option>
[% ELSE %]
<option value="callnum">Call Number</option>
[% END %]
[% IF ( ms_bc ) %]
<option selected="selected" value="bc">Acc. Number</option>
[% ELSE %]
<option value="bc">Acc. Number</option>
[% END %]</select>
```

Customization for display of accession number

Other important feature related to display of accession number in detailed display was missing due to which patrons and staff had to click another option i.e. MARC view. Therefore it was necessary to add this feature which facilities ease in placing hold on specific item by patron and several data correction related work to library staffs. The code in opac-detail.tt file is responsible for display of some book related information like class number, location etc so to get the above effect new code was inserted which is highlighted below in between the already existing codes:

```
<th>Location</th>
[% IF ( itemdata_ccode ) %]<th>Collection</th>[% END %]
<th>Acc.Number</th>
<th>Call Number</th>
[% IF ( itemdata_enumchron ) %]<th>Vol/Pt Info</th>[% END %]
[% IF ( itemdata_ccode ) %]<td>[% ITEM_RESULT.ccode %]</td>[% END %]
<td>[% IF ( ITEM_RESULT.barcode ) %] [% ITEM_RESULT.barcode %]</td>[% END %]
<td>[% IF ( ITEM_RESULT.itemcallnumber ) %] [% ITEM_RESULT.itemcallnumber %][% IF ( OPACShelfBrowser ) %] (<a href="/cgi-bin/Koha/opac-detail.pl?biblionumber=[% ITEM_RESULT.biblionumber %]&amp;shelfbrowse_itemnumber=[% ITEM_ RESULT.itemnumber %]#shelfbrowser">Browse Shelf</a>)[% END %][% END %]</td>
```

Koha Home page customization

After concluding all the above works successfully author got idea to customize the Koha home page in such a way that Koha could also work like our library website and serves the users as Library website cum online public access catalogue. This idea was wonderful to have a website and OPAC on single server and on single web.2.0 based ILMS Koha, but it was more challenging due to lack of expertise in HTML, CSS etc. so it was more pain full to customize whole Koha home page. Keeping in view the importance of library website made list of links and contents which may be needed to display over the website and the possibility of putting that idea over the Koha OPAC home page. The whole things were discovered from various internet resources and some basic book on HTML and CSS which is described in sub-sections below.

Display of drop down menu

Creating drop down menu over the webpage is good to have more linking in minimum space of the page so author discovered the code which is available free of cost at http://www.spiderwebmastertools.com and modified as per library requirements after consulting some basic books on above requirements, the code which is used to display the drop down menu as shown in fig. 10 are as follows and pasted on Koha system preferences-OPAC-header option:

```
<!—-Drop Down Menu Begins—>
<style type="text/css">
#lib-logo{
background: #550000;
padding-left: 10px;
margin:-22px -10px 0 -10px;
font-weight:bold;
font-size: 16px;
color: #550000;
}
</style>
<div id="lib-logo"><center>.</center>
<style type="text/css">a.KohaMenu_csstopmenu{
color:black;
}
#KohaMenu_csstopmenu, #KohaMenu_csstopmenu ul{
padding:0;
```

```
margin:0;
list-style:none;
}
#KohaMenu_csstopmenu li{
float:left;
position:relative;
}
#KohaMenu_csstopmenu a{
text-decoration:none;
}
.KohaMenu_mainitems{
border:1px solid black;
border-left-width:0px;
background-color:yellow;
margin:-19px 0px 0 0;
font-size:0px
}
.KohaMenu_headerlinks a{
margin:auto 5px;
font-family:arial,verdana,sans-serif;
font-style:normal;font-weight:bold;
color:#000000;
font-size:14px
}
.KohaMenu_submenus{display:none;
width:150px;
position:absolute;
top:1.2em;
left:0;
background-color:pink;
border: 3px solid #000000;
```

```
}
.KohaMenu_submenus li{
width:100%;
}
.KohaMenu_submenus li a{
display:block;
width:100%;
text-indent:3px;font-size:14px;font-family:arialblack,
verdana,sans-serif;font-style:normal;font-weight:normal;
}
html>body .KohaMenu_submenus li a{
/* non IE browsers */
width: auto;
}
.KohaMenu_submenus li a:hover{
background-color:black;
color:white;
}
#KohaMenu_csstopmenu li>ul {
/* non IE browsers */
top:auto;
:auto;
}
#KohaMenu_csstopmenu li:hover ul, li.over ul {
display:block;
}
html>body #KohaMenu_clearmenu{
/* non IE browsers */
height: 3px;
}
</style>
```

```
<script type="text/javascript">
<!—
startMenu = function() {
if (document.all&&document.getElementById) {
KohaMenu_cssmenu =
document.getElementById("KohaMenu_csstopmenu");
for (i=0; i<KohaMenu_cssmenu.childNodes.length; i++) {
node = KohaMenu_cssmenu.childNodes[i];
if (node.nodeName=="LI") {
node.onmouseover=function() {
this.className+=" over";
}
node.onmouseout=function(){
this.className=this.className.replace(" over", "")
}
}
}
}
}
if (window.attachEvent)
window.attachEvent("onload", startMenu)
else
window.onload=startMenu;
//—>
</script>
<!— DHTML/CSS Drop Down Menu created with Spider
WebMaster Tools DDDMenu Wizard
http://www.spiderwebmastertools.com—>
<ul id="KohaMenu_csstopmenu">
<li class="KohaMenu_mainitems" style="border-left-
width:1px">
```

```
<div class="KohaMenu_headerlinks"><a href="http://172.23.14.200/" class="KohaMenu_csstopmenu">Home</a></div>
<ul class="KohaMenu_submenus">
<li><a href="http://www.iitr.ac.in" target="blank" class="KohaMenu_csstopmenu">IIT Roorkee</a></li>
<li><a href="http://mgcl.iitr.ac.in" target="blank" class="KohaMenu_csstopmenu">MGCL Home</a></li>
</ul>
</li>
<li class="KohaMenu_mainitems">
<div class="KohaMenu_headerlinks"><a href="" class="KohaMenu_csstopmenu">About Library</a></div>
<ul class="KohaMenu_submenus">
<li><a href="http://172.23.14.200/opac-tmpl/prog/www/01gen_rule.htm" target="blank" class="KohaMenu_csstopmenu">General Rules</a></li>
<li><a href="http://172.23.14.200/opac-tmpl/prog/www/03services.htm" target="blank" class="KohaMenu_csstopmenu">Services</a></li>
<li><a href="http://172.23.14.200/opac-tmpl/prog/www/02book_indent.doc" target="blank" class="KohaMenu_csstopmenu">Book Indent Form</a></li>
<li><a href="http://172.23.14.200/opac-tmpl/prog/www/04contacts.htm" target="blank" class="KohaMenu_csstopmenu">Contacts</a></li>
</ul>
</li>
<li class="KohaMenu_mainitems">
<div class="KohaMenu_headerlinks"><a href="" class="KohaMenu_csstopmenu">E-Standards</a></div>
<ul class="KohaMenu_submenus">
<li><a href="http://enterprise.astm.org/SUBSCRIPTION
```

```
/filtrexx40.cgi?-P+LANDING+true+complete_library.frm” target=”blank” class=”KohaMenu_csstopmenu”>ASTM Standards</a></li>
<li><a href=”http://192.168.125.8/iec/iec_cat.asp” target=”blank” class=”KohaMenu_csstopmenu”>IEC Standards</a></li>
<li><a href=”http://192.168.125.8/bis/start.shtml” target=”blank” class=”KohaMenu_csstopmenu”>Indian Standards</a></li>
<li><a href=”http://192.168.125.8/bs_eurocode/index.html” target=”blank” class=”KohaMenu_csstopmenu”>Eurocodes</a></li>
</ul>
</li>
<li class=”KohaMenu_mainitems”>
<div class=”KohaMenu_headerlinks”><a href=”http://mgcl.iitr.ac.in/e-books/e-books%20cliitr.htm” target=”blank” class=”KohaMenu_csstopmenu”>E-Books</a></div>
<ul class=”KohaMenu_submenus”>
<li><a href=”http://ebooks.cambridge.org/” target=”blank” class=”KohaMenu_csstopmenu”>Cambridge</a></li>
<li><a href=”http://www.crcnetbase.com/search/advanced_search.asp/” target=”blank” class=”KohaMenu_csstopmenu”>Taylor & Francis</a></li>
<li><a href=”http://www.sciencedirect.com/science/books” target=”blank” class=”KohaMenu_csstopmenu”>Elsevier Science</a></li>
<li><a href=”http://www3.interscience.wiley.com/browse/?type=BOOK/” target=”blank” class=”KohaMenu_csstopmenu”>John Wiley</a></li>
<li><a href=”http://www.oxfordscholarship.com/” target=”blank” class=”KohaMenu_csstopmenu”>Oxford</a></li>
```

```
<li><a href=”http://www.springerlink.com/home/
main.mpx/” target=”blank” class=”KohaMenu_
csstopmenu”>Springer Verlag</a></li>
<li><a href=”http://lib.myilibrary.com/home.aspx”
target=”blank” class=”KohaMenu_csstopmenu”>Tata
McGraw Hill</a></li>
</ul>
</li>
<li class=”KohaMenu_mainitems”>
<div class=”KohaMenu_headerlinks”><a href=”” class=”
KohaMenu_csstopmenu”>Databases</a></div>
<ul class=”KohaMenu_submenus”>
<li><a href=”http://search.proquest.com/index” target=”
blank” class=”KohaMenu_csstopmenu”>E-Dessert./
Thesis</a></li>
<li><a href=”http://www.engineeringvillage2.org/
controller/servlet/Controller?CID=quickSearch&
database=67/” target=”blank” class=”KohaMenu_
csstopmenu”>Engg.Village</a></li> <li><a href=”http:/
/www.ams.org/mathscinet/” target=”blank” class=”
KohaMenu_csstopmenu”>MathSciNet</a></li>
<li><a href=”http://mgcl.iitr.ac.in/e-databases/Scifinder.
htm” target=”blank” class=”KohaMenu_csstopmenu”>Sci
Finder Scholar</a></li>
<li><a href=”http://www.scopus.com/home.url”
target=”blank” class=”KohaMenu_csstopmenu”>
Scopus</a></li>
<li><a href=”http://apps.isiknowledge.com/WOS
_GeneralSearch_input.do?product=WOS&search_mode
=GeneralSearch &SID =Q2pnEGNkOMIGdj@ 7Kco&
preferencesSaved=&highlighted_tab=WOS” target=”
blank” class=”KohaMenu_csstopmenu”>Web of Science</
a></li>
<li><a href=”http://192.168.125.9/” target=”blank”
```

```
class="KohaMenu_csstopmenu">CD-ROM Databases</
a></li>
</ul>
</li>
<div id="KohaMenu_clearmenu" style="clear:left;"></div>
</div>
<!—-Drop Down Menu Ends—>
```

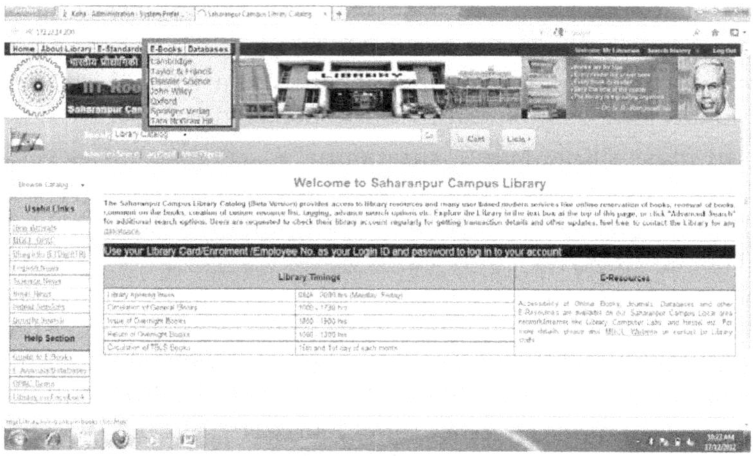

Fig. 7.10. Home page shows drop down menu in pink color

Display of Left navigation menu and Credits area

The left navigation of system preference used to provide most important frequently used informative links regarding help and updated information. Credit code used to display copyright and contact information is beautifully placed in the credits option of system preference. The left navigation and credit codes are shown in next sub sections.

Left navigation code

```
<!—Useful links Begins—>
<table border="1" style="border-color: #000000; border-
width: 1px; border-style: solid">
```

```
<tbody>
<tr>
<td align=”center” style=”border-color: #000000; border-style: solid; border-width: 1px; background-color: #6699ff”>
<h4>Useful Links</h4></td>
</tr>
<tr>
<td style=”border-color: #000000; border-style: solid; border-width: 1px”><a href=”http://172.23.14.200/cgi-bin/Koha/opac-shelves.pl?viewshelf=16&sortfield=title” target=”blank”>New Arrivals</a></td>
</tr>
<tr>
<td style=”border-color: #000000; border-style: solid; border-width: 1px”><a href=”http://192.168.125.7:8080/jopacv11/html/SearchForm” target=”blank”>MGCL OPAC</a></td>
</tr>
<tr>
<td style=”border-color: #000000; border-style: solid; border-width: 1px”><a href=”http://bhagirathi.iitr.ac.in/dspace/” target=”blank”>Bhagirthi (ETD@IITR)</a></td>
</tr>
<tr>
<td style=”border-color: #000000; border-style: solid; border-width: 1px”><a href=”http://news.google.co.in/nwshp?hl=en&tab=wn” target=”blank”>English News</a></td>
</tr>
<tr>
<td style=”border-color: #000000; border-style: solid; border-width: 1px”><a href=”http://news.google.co.in/
```

```
news/section?pz=1&cf=all&ned=in&topic=snc&ict=ln"
target="blank">Science News</a></td>
</tr>
<tr>
<td style="border-color: #000000; border-style: solid;
border-width: 1px"><a href="http://news.google.co.in/
nwshp?hl=en&tab=wn&edchanged=1&ned=hi_in&
authuser=0" target="blank">Hindi News</a></td>
</tr>
<tr>
<td style="border-color: #000000; border-style: solid;
border-width: 1px"><a href="http://paniit.iitd.ac.in/
indest/" target="blank">Indest Services</a></td>
</tr>
<tr>
<td style="border-color: #000000; border-style: solid;
border-width: 1px"><a href="http://google.co.in"
target="blank">Google Search</a></td>
</tr>
<!—Help section Begins—>
<tr>
<td align="center" style="border-color: #000000; border-
style: solid; border-width: 1px; background-color:
#6699ff">
<h4> Help Section</h4>
</td>
</tr>
<tr>
<td style="border-color: #000000; border-style: solid;
border-width: 1px"><a href="http://mgcl.iitr.ac.in/e-
books/e-books%20guidelines.pdf" target="_blank" title="
Click to get Guidelines on how to use e-books procured
by MGCL">Guide to E-Books</a><br />
```

```
</td>
</tr>
<tr>
<td style="border-color: #000000; border-style: solid; border-width: 1px"><a href="http://paniit.iitd.ac.in/indest/tutorial/index.html" target="_blank" title="Click to get information about how to use various e-resources">E-Journals/Databases</a><br />
</td>
</tr>
<tr>
<td style="border-color: #000000; border-style: solid; border-width: 1px"><a href="http://www.youtube.com/watch?v=ekjGvzeNu9Y&feature=related" target="_blank" title="Click to get help on how to search catalog and use its various features">OPAC Demo</a><br />
</td>
</tr>
<tr>
<td style="border-color: #000000; border-style: solid; border-width: 1px"><a href="https://www.facebook.com/iitrlibrary?sk=app_156218351098324" target="_blank" title="Click to access the library website/OPAC and updates via facebook">Library on Facebook</a><br />
</td>
</tr>
</tbody>
</table>
<!—Help section Ends—>
```

Credits code

```
<hr><br><center>Powered by <a href="http://Koha-community.org/" target=blank>Koha,</a> Implemented and Maintained by <a href="http://www.facebook.com/
```

```
mishravk79" target=blank>Mr. Vinod Kumar Mishra.</
a> <a href="http://172.23.14.200/opac-tmpl/prog/
www/04contacts.htm" target=blank>Our Team</a> <a
href="http://mgcl.iitr.ac.in/personnel/Personnel.htm"
target=blank>MGCL Team</a><br>For any Suggestions/
Query Contact to library or Email: ajaysfpt@iitr.ernet.in,
library.sre@iitr.ernet.in OR mishravk79@gmail.com.
<br>©Copyright 2012, IIT Roorkee, Saharanpur
Campus.<br>Website/OPAC best viewed in Mozilla
Browser in 1024X768 Resolution. </center>

<!—Facebook section Begins—>

<div class="fb-like" data-href="https://www.facebook.
com/iitrlibrary?sk=app_ 156218351098324" data-
send="true" data-layout=" button_count" data-
width="450" data-show-faces="true"> </div>

<!—Facebook section Ends—>

<!— Histats.com START (standard)—>

<div align="right"><script type="text/javascript">
document.write(unescape("%3Cscript src=%27http://
s10.histats.com/js15.js%27 type=%27text/javascript
%27%3E%3C/script%3E"));</script>

<a href="http://www.histats.com" target="_blank"
title="html hit counter" ><script type="text/javascript" >

try {Histats.start(1,1988226,4,5,172,25,"00010100");

Histats.track_hits();} catch(err){};

</script></a>

<noscript><a href="http://www.histats.com" target="
_blank"><img src="http://sstatic1.histats.com/0.gif?
1988226&101" alt="html hit counter" border="0"></a></
noscript></div>

<!— Histats.com END —>
```

Other customization

Apart from above customization, color of the home page changed by modification of color code in opac.css file, the logo of Koha is replaces by Indian national flag and the header image is beautifully constructed with the help of paint tool of windows. Several html and doc files related to information about library were placed in the newly created folder and linked through drop down menu which worked well. Facebook liking and send link code was also placed in credit area to popularize the library website cum OPAC. To check the popularity, traffic and other user access related behavior of Koha website cum webopac author also placed the free website counter/ monitor code.

Conclusion

The paper very well described the whole process of implementation of Koha at Saharanpur Campus Library of Indian Institute of Technology Roorkee, India. The paper also attempted to reveal step by step that, challenging work of data migration to final implementation can be successfully achieved by discovering the solutions available on web resources so it could be easily achieved by well team of library professionals. The Koha software facilitates many advance online features like renewal, reservation, comment on books etc. , it also fully automate the circulation work of the library in comparison to previous software Troodon3 and helped in reducing much time of the staff and students. The most important is all the process involved zero cost i.e. data migration, customization and final implementation of Koha successfully; hence it is most suitable software for libraries whose main concern is finance.

The paper reveals the problem associated with changing the ILMS and also discovered their solutions. The most modern zero cost solution has been successfully provided to the library by the library staff only i.e. without any commercial support hence paper motivates the professionals to discover zero cost solutions available in the market/web as per library automation needs. This paper also shares useful technical knowledge and resources for further development and implementation at needy libraries who seeks a cost effective solution for automation. Instead of technical knowledge tips and tricks worked more in the whole implementation process so professionals are encouraged to discover the solutions with little efforts and mental analysis works. The Final Koha website cum webopac home page screenshot is shown in fig.10 above which proves beautiful/eye catching customization of Koha at no cost.

7.2. ASSAM UNIVERSITY, SILCHAR : A CENTRAL UNIVERSITY

Assam University came into existence in 1994 through Assam (Central) University Act, 1989 (Established under an Act of Parliament), 1994, since then the University is steadily becoming an excellent centre of learning. The campus, situated in Dargakona, about 20 kilometers from Silchar, is set amid sprawling hillocks, a typical landscape in the North East. The campus in an area of 600 acres surrounded by lakes and mountains provides an ideal environment for academic pursuit. Drawing its 300 plus faculty from many disciplines, from all over the country, the university sustains a multidisciplinary approach to higher education. The University has Sixteen Schools on major disciplines. There are Thirty Five Departments under these Sixteen Schools.

About Assam University Library

Assam University Library was started with the establishment of the University in the year 1994 as a central facility for meeting the information requirements of the academic community of the University. The Central Library of Assam University was shifted to its new permanent Central Library-cum-Computer Centre building in January 2006 and renamed as RABINDRA LIBRARY. The new building has a total plinth area of 38,700 sq.ft. The main function of Library includes collection and development of knowledge resources, technical processing, organization, retrieval and dissemination of information to the end users including the academic community of Barak Valley in particular and the entire North Eastern Region in general.

Why Koha at Assam University Library

Assam University library was using software for university library (SOUL) which is propriety solution provided by Information and Library Network (INFLIBNET) Centre an Autonomous Inter-University Centre (IUC) of University Grants Commission (UGC), government of India. The librarian took the initiative to migrate the data of SOUL to Koha as SOUL were used for only data entry but circulation and other modules were not at all operational. Approximately 70 thousand records were available in the SOUL but books were placed on the shelves without the bar-coding, webopac was not customized as per requirements, records were not fully compatible with MARC and there were many other admin related issues. Hence keeping above in view library staffs and admin took the decision to implement the Koha, some of the reason for switching from SOUL to Koha are as follows:

- Lack of customised WebOPAC in SOUL
- Copy cataloguing through Z39.50
- Complex table structure in data entry
- Strong support from the Koha community
- User friendliness of Koha
- Low security due to Window platform
- The back end software (like MS/Windows & MS-SQL) are not free

- Need not to install the separate version on client machine
- Koha is browser based etc.

SOUL to Koha data migration

SOUL provides the option to export the record in MARC format under the cataloguing module hence all the records in MARC format was exported and send to the author. It was first experience of the author to prepare SOUL data to export in Koha but due to MARCEdit software and earlier works helped great and made the job easy. Since the provided data was in MARC format so almost all the data fields were same but some essential fields like 041$a (language) was missing which is necessary to search the document language wise on Koha, similarly all the local fields were different than SOUL in Koha like item type, accession number, location etc. so initially all the basic local fields were configured in the Koha system like library code, item type code, location code etc. and ultimately SOUL data was converted in Koha compatible MARC format. An example of original MARC data from SOUL which was converted for Koha is shown below.

Original SOUL MARC record Converted SOUL record for Koha

Table 7.1. Structure of SOUL data conversion for Koha

<table>
<tr><th>Original SOUL MARC record</th><th>Converted SOUL record for Koha</th></tr>
<tr><td>=LDR 00668cam a2200205ua 4500</td><td>=LDR 00674nam a22002171a 4500</td></tr>
<tr><td>=001 11764</td><td>=008 140405s2004||||xx\ ||||||||||||||||\||eng||</td></tr>
<tr><td>=008 130520n\\\\\\\\\ii\\ |||gr||||Z||||||eng</td><td>=020 \\$a8120320352</td></tr>
<tr><td>=020 \\$a8120320352</td><td>=041 \\$aeng</td></tr>
<tr><td>=082 \\$a005</td><td>=082 \\$a005.13$bPRA</td></tr>
<tr><td>=245 \\$aProgramming languages</td><td>=245 \\$aProgramming languages</td></tr>
</table>

design and implementation$h Textual Documents	design and implementation
=250 \\$a4th.	=250 \\$a4th.
=260 \\$aNew Delhi:$bPrentice Hall of India,$c2004.	=260 \\$aNew Delhi:$bPrentice Hall of India,$c2004.
=300 \\$axv, 649p.:$bill;$c24cm.	=300 \\$axv, 649p.:$bill;$c24cm.
=500 \\$aIncludes index	=500 \\$aIncludes index
=504 \\$aIncludes bibliographical references.	=504 \\$aIncludes bibliographical references.
=653 \\$aComputer programming, programs & data	=650 \\$aComputer programming languages
=653 \\$aComputer programming languages	=650 \\$aComputer programming, programs & data
=700 1$aPratt, Terrence W.	=700 \\1$aPratt, Terrence W.
=700 1$aZelkowitz, Marvin V.	=700 \\1$aZelkowitz, Marvin V.
=852 1$t1$p62278$aShelf$ bGeneral $k005.13$f00000 $cShelf$mPRA	=942 \\$cGEN
	=952 \\$aMAIN$bMAIN$p62278$ yGEN$cGENS$o005.13 PRA

The Koha was configured as discussed above which is very necessary before any data migration because it is one of the basic requirement, the various code needs to be defines in MARC tag 952 and 942 in order to push the record in proper library, item type, location etc. The various codes defined in Koha for the same is describing below.

Table 7.2. Item types and their codes used in Koha for data conversion

Item Type	***Code***
Books	BK
Reference Books	REF
Book Bank	BB
Reserve Books	RB
Location of Items	Code
General Section	GEN
Reference section	REF
TBLS/Books book section	TBLS
Reserve section	RS

Conclusion

All the record of SOUL was successfully imported in Koha with many standardization and correction of data like punctuations, capitalizations etc for which MarcEdit provide lot of options. Koha was installed on old server with package installation on Ubuntu 12.04 operating system. The librarian Dr. A.K. Sharma took lot of initiative after its implementations and regularly updating the Koha and fully exploiting its features for the benefit of library and its users. The screenshot of current home page of Koha of Assam University is shown below which is highly customized by library staffs.

7.3. DAV PUBLIC SCHOOL, CCL, NTS BARKAKANA, JHARKHAND

Dayanand Anglo-Vedic (DAV) Public School, NTS, Barkakana, a leading school in the coalfields belt of Jharkhand started functioning as a DAV institution from 1st November 1987 with an approximate strength of 250 students, 12 teachers and 5 other staff members. The school is jointly managed by the DAV College Managing Committee New Delhi and Central Coalfields Ltd, Ranchi. DAV is Senior Secondary School with two wings in the +2 level. With student strength of 1500 and classes from LKG-XII the school now boasts of catering two streams both Science & Commerce in the Senior Secondary level.

The campus spans in three buildings which houses all the sections the Principal's chamber, the office and the staff room. In addition school has four spacious and well equipped labs for demonstrations of Physics, Chemistry, Biology, Mathematics, and Audio Visual Lab. The library is having good collection of books, journals and reference materials it issues the books from class 8th to 12th students. The CCL authorities bestowed the school with ample number of buses of around 12 in number and one out of which is separately run for children coming from IAG & Ramgarh, the nearest district town.

Why Koha at DAV School, Barkakana

DAV school Barkakana has conducted workshop on Koha for all the DAV schools librarians which fall under the Zone of Hazaribagh district of Jharkhand during 20-22 February, 2016. During the workshop the school librarians and management felt very unhappy because of existing library software (Librarian) provided by CR2 an Indian company and its limited features. The software used at DAV school Barkakana has many limitations as discussed below:

- Stand alone for single personal computer only
- Provided with dongle to be used to access staff client
- MS-Access backend
- Web OPAC was missing
- Lack of support
- Lack of standard like MARC, Z39.50.
- Windows XP based installation etc.

Implementation steps of Koha at DAV School, Barkakana

Since the data was in MS-Access so it was not very difficult to get it in excel format to be converted into MARC. The data retrieved in excel was not appropriate for final conversion into MARC hence many data refinement has been done including addition and elimination of fields at excel level itself to make the job of excel data conversion easy and clear. The original data structure and refinement for MARC conversion is shown below in the table.

Table 7.3. Original Excel columns in CR2 and refined new columns in excel

Fields in CR2 (Librarian) excel data	***New Excel columns with MARC tag***
accession_no	952$p
class_no	082$a and 0952$o
Isbn	020$a
year1	008 and 260$c

author1	100$a, and 245$c
author2	245$c and 700$a
Remarks	505$a
ent_date	952$d
Vol	952$h
Editor	245$c and 700$a
Edition	250$a
Series	490$a
pub_place	260$a
Translator	245$c and 700$a
Compiler	245$c and 700$a
Illustrator	245$c and 700$a
Subtitle	245$b

Successful Conversion of Excel into MARC

The entire process of data conversion from excel has been already discussed in concern chapter and many places in this book hence I hope readers are very much aware about the steps and precautions taken before excel to MARC conversion. An example of data which was converted from excel to MARC for DAV school, Barkakana is shown below with proper codes of Koha configured for DAV School in MARC tag 952 and 942.

```
=LDR 00395nam a2200157Ia 4500
=008 160221s2002||||xx\||||||||||||||\||und||
=020 \\$a81-237-3985-0
=041 \\$ahin
=082 \\$aN
=100 \\$aManjari Joshi
=245 \\$aBhartiya sangeet ki parampara
=250 \\$a1 st
=260 \\$aNew delhi$bNational book trust$c2002
=300 \\$a83
=942 \\$cBK
```

=952 \\$p4151yBKq25$d2011-03-31$aMAIN$b MAIN$cBK$oN

The entire record of approximately four thousand books and reference book was successfully converted during the three days of workshop and WebOPAC was made accessible on entire intranet of the school campus. The personal computer with 2 GB of ram was chosen for the same and kept inside the computer lab for proper maintenance.

7.4. MGAHV CENTRAL UNIVERSITY, WARDHA

The Mahatma Gandhi Antarastriya Hindi Vishwavidyalaya (MHAHV) came into existence through an Act of Parliament which received the assent of the president on January 8, 1997. The purpose of the act was to establish and incorporate a teaching university for the promotion and development of Hindi language and literature, through teaching and research, with a view to enabling Hindi to achieve greater functional efficiency and recognition as a major international language. The establishment of the university was the long conclusion of a resolutions passed by the First World Hindi Conference organized in Nagpur in the year 1975 to establish an international Hindi university at Wardha, the land where Mahatma Gandhi experimented all programmes dear to his heart.

In the last decade of the twentieth century, the university started functioning. The university was established in the light of the philosopher Mahatma Gandhi Hindi language and literature as well as Gandhi's favorite themes based on the principles "of nonviolence and peace studies 'and' woman Adhyyn'- made the major part of their course. Hindi is the intent of the university through the various disciplines of knowledge and scope not only in India but in the world population and its deep penetration, create world-heart necklace made Hindi. Mahatma Gandhi International Hindi University is a unique university in nature. Hindi employed with the aim of promoting the world's only university where French, Chinese, Spanish and Japanese are taught as foreign languages in Hindi medium. There are eight different faculties at the University.

- Language School
- School of Literature
- Culture School
- School of Translation and Interpretation
- School of Humanities & Social Sciences
- School of Law
- Managing the School
- School of Education

Existing Koha at MGAHV, Wardha

MGAHV was already using the Koha with the help of commercial support provider vendor. The vendor has converted their data from previous local made software to Koha which was around 60/70 thousands including Hindi and English languages. Unfortunately Koha was not working properly and initial Koha system configurations was done very wrong as well as staffs were not properly trained in the handling of routine works through Koha. Some of the reasons why existing Koha were needed to revamped are as follows:

- Item categorization was done on language basis but transaction was different
- Multi-location library/departmental library was not configured properly
- Koha was installed on non-recommended operating system Centos
- Language wise searching was not proper
- It was difficult to auto-upgrade due to Centos
- Proper staff interface based backup was not configured

- OPAC was not configured properly to search the document in various libraries
- Member categorization and circulation rule was not properly defined
- Auto indexing was not working properly
- Data entry MARC bibliographic framework was not sufficient

Revamped Koha of MGAHV, Wardha

Keeping the non-satisfactory condition of Koha configurations and poor support of vendor as per their requirements and improper staff training, Librarian took the initiative to invite me and make the report for further improvements. Author visited the MGAHV and made the following recommendations:

- Category of books must be defined on the basis of circulation privileges i.e. Textbook, Reference book, thesis etc but it has been defined language wise like Hindi book; English book etc. which is wrong and it will create problem in circulation of books. For example reference books may be issued in extraordinary circumstances and it is necessary to correct it immediately which will also be applicable to departmental library.
- Sine Proper indexing is not properly configured the new entered books can't be searched same has been shown to staffs and resolved from Delhi by vender after complain which also reflect that vender is having server ID/Password.
- Concept of branch/departmental library is default feature of Koha hence no need of additional customizations, which is not properly configured at this moment.
- Web OPAC has been customized which is not basic requirement as compared to staff client features/ housekeeping operations although as per current

requirements no need of any customizations at housekeeping operations is required.

- Circulation privileges need to be defined properly i.e. category of book wise (textbook, general books, journals etc) but at present it is defined wrongly hence all books can be issue.
- Proper Onsite Training for 3/4 days needs to be provided to all the Staffs and system must be configured as per library current and future requirements.
- All the server and Administrative ID/Password must not be shared with the Vender.
- Short templates of limited fields for entering different type of books data like thesis, textbooks etc. need to be made separately for ease of data entry.
- Proper Staff client based mysql backup need to be configured so that a staff can also take backup as and when require, it's a default feature of Koha but not yet activated.

On the basis of above recommendations authority of MGAHV invited the author again and entire data was exported in MARC format, however the SQL backup taken for the restoration and changes but it was very difficult in editing the records from staff client Koha options as per requirements and making the changes in MySQL was too dangerous. Therefore the exported MARC record was the best option for editing since MARCEdit software provides great flexibility in editing/deleting/addition of records. It was very challenging task due to concept of multi branch library and multi languages hence lot of care and experiment was done before finalizing the data. Language like Sanskrit was not available in the Koha hence it was inserted in the MySQL database table at the appropriate place which helped in searching the document by Sanskrit language in WebOPAC. The major work done during revamping of existing Koha of MGAHV is described in the below table.

Table 7.4. Features of new Koha which has been achieved after revamping of Old Koha

Feature/Difference	*Old Koha*	*New Koha*
Version	Koha version 14	Koha version 20
Operating system	Centos	Ubuntu latest 14.04 which is recommended by developers of Koha
OPAC language searching	No such facility for Marathi and Sanskrit Language searching	Marathi and Sanskrit language searching feature has been added by hard coding
Search Departmental library collection in OPAC	No such feature was activated in Old version which was needed	Search by departmental library has been activated
OPAC look and Feel	—	More better look and feel of the OPAC with drop down navigation menu has been customized
Categorization of Library materials	Categorization was done very wrong (language wise)	Categorized as per library requirement and transaction policy (General book, Reference book etc.)
Location of Books	Proper Location (department) of Book was not entered	Incomplete Location of books has been corrected which is reflected in OPAC now
Proper Indexing	Indexing was very poor because of which newly entered books was not searchable	Much better and new books entered can be searched within one minute of its entry
Database Backup	It was not configured properly	Now any staff can take daily backup of Koha through Staff interface (Graphical User Interface)
Data entry format	Unnecessary/illogical fields were activated	Format designed as per requirements
Training	No proper training was given to staff	Brief but as per current requirement training has been provided

Support	—	Helping telephonic and online on voluntary basis
Koha Installation Live DVD	—	Koha installation Live DVD has been provided so in case of emergency they can install Koha and restore the backup in easy way.

7.5. CENTRAL UNIVERSITY OF JAMMU

The Central University of Jammu came into existence on August 08, 2011, with the appointment of the first Vice-Chancellor. It was established by the Central Universities Act, 2009 (Act No.25 of 2009 read with the Central Universities Act, 2009). The first academic session (2011-2012) commenced with three Post Graduate courses in English, Economics and Applied Mathematics at Temporary Academic Block-I (TAB-I) at Sidhra bypass road, Jammu. In the next academic session (2012-2013), five PG Courses were added: Computer Science, Educational Studies, Environmental Sciences, Human Resource Management and Travel & Tourism Management in Temporary Academic Block (TAB-II) at Sainik Colony Extension. Since the third session (2013-2014) all the departments are functioning from TAB at Sainik Colony. Four new post graduate courses were introduced in the academic session (2014-2015): National Security Studies; Public Policy & Public Administration; Social Work and Mass Communication & New Media. The University also offers Integrated M-Phil-Ph.D programme in eight subjects.

The University carries out its administrative functions from its head office at Bagla, Rahya-Suchani, Distt. Samba. The Central University of Jammu campus is under construction at Village Bagla, Raya Suchani in District Samba, which is at an approximate distance of 25 kms from Jammu.

KOHA AT CENTRAL UNIVERSITY OF JAMMU

Central University of Jammu (CUJ) is a new university hence initially there were no ILMS in the library but approximately 12 thousand data was available in the Microsoft excel. The university authority invited for the data migration and implementation of Koha from 06-09 June, 2015.

As usual the excel data was received and converted in MARC format similar to other cases mentioned above. Some of the difference with other case was arrangement of Books department wise in the central library and users/ staff used to locate the materials department wise. So to locate the book various authorized value for department was created in LOC (Authorized value) for this code of department is used to define code of authorized value for easy identification.

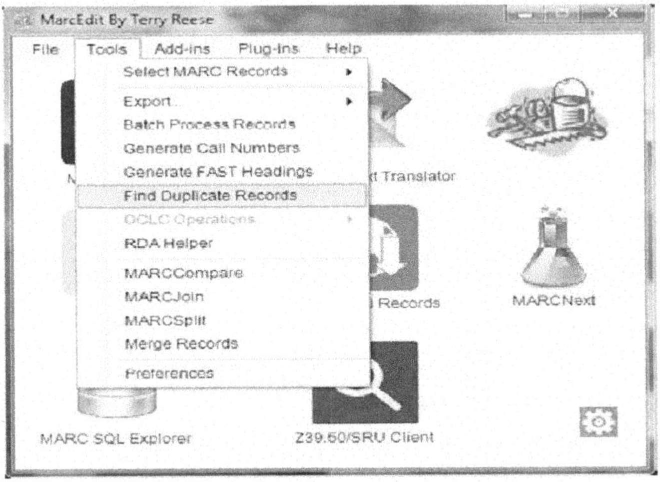

Fig. 7.11. Option to separate duplicate records with MarcEdit software

One of the major challenges was to bring together the same record with multiple items so after conversion of excel into MARC the mrc file was separated into two file (say A and B) i.e. one having the unique records indentified by ISBN number (file A) and another (file B) having duplicate records of previous file (file A) having same ISBN number, to do this MARCEdit option "Find duplicate records" were used as shown in the below screenshot.

Import of MARC records in Koha

To import the MARC records usual process was followed but in this case some filters were used to import the two different files (A and B) as discussed above. File A having all the unique records was imported in the Koha as usual but before final import of file B many filters were used in order to avoid import of same records which was already imported through file A as well as to merge the incoming items in already existing records, to do this the filters used are shown in below screenshot.

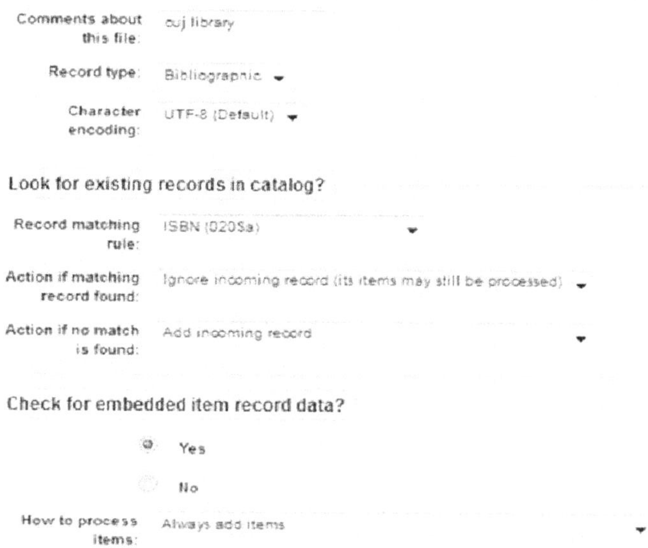

Fig. 7.12. Filters used to remove duplicate incoming records

So in screenshot above it is clearly shown that ISBN number (tag 020$a) is used to check for records matching rule and if matching records is found than it should be ignored however its item may still be processed so that it will be inserted in the already existing records. This is a very great option particularly when importing the records from Microsoft excels data and all the same titles/records are scattered.

Configuration of bar-code and patron cards

One of the major challenges which author faced during the implementation of Koha at central university of Jammu is generation of barcode for approximately 12 thousand books on 13X5 labels per sheet (A4) having 38.1X21.2 mm of each labels and generation of approximately three hundred members library ID card with printing on both the side. The target was perfectly achieved as desired by the university after configuration and testing on more than 30 label sheets. The configuration which was used for the above in Koha 3.18 is discussed below.

Table 7.5. Book barcode and Member Card settings

Field	***Configuration used***
Label layout setting for barcode	
Layout name	My barcode layout
Choose barcode type (encoding)	Code 39
Choose layout type	Biblio/Barcode
Choose order of fields to print	Only order 1 itemcallnumber was used
Split call number	Checked
Text justification	Center
Fonts	Times-Roman
Font size	11
Template layout setting for barcode	
Template code	My barcode Template
Units	US inches
Page height	11.69 inch
Page width	8.27 inch
Label width	1.5 inch
Label height	0.85 inch

Top page margin	0.1 inch
Left page margin	0.19 inch
Top text margin	0.236 inch
Left text margin	0 inch
Number of columns	5
Number of rows	13
Gap between columns	0.17 inch
Gap between rows	0.04 inch

Barcode printed on 13X5 A4 sheet

Patron card text layout

Layout name	Patron card layout
Units	PostScript points
Page side	Front
Guide box	On

Settings in text field 1

Text	Name: <firstname> <surname>
Font	Times-Roman
Font size	10 pt
Text alignment	Left
Lower left X coordinate	55 pt
Lower left Y coordinate	100 pt

Settings in text field 2

Text	Patron sign Librarian sign
Font	Times-Roman
Font size	6 pt
Text alignment	Left
Lower left X coordinate	8 pt
Lower left Y coordinate	5 pt

Settings in text field 3

Text	Dept: <address>
Font	Times-bold
Font size	10 pt
Text alignment	Left
Lower left X coordinate	60 pt

Lower left Y coordinate	80 pt

Patron card graphic layout

Barcode

Print card number as barcode	Checked
Lower left X coordinate	17
Lower left Y coordinate	18
Barcode type	Code 39
Print card number as text under barcode	Checked

Images 1

Image source	Patron image
Display height	45 pt
Lower left X coordinate	3 pt
Lower left Y coordinate	72 pt

Images 2

Image source	Other images
Image	Header1
Display height	31 pt
Lower left X coordinate	3 pt
Lower left Y coordinate	120 pt

Template settings

Template code	Patron Card Template
Units	US inches
Page height	11 inch
Page width	8.5 inch
Card width	3.37 inch
Card height	2.12 inch
Top page margin	0.6875 inch
Left page margin	0.5 inch
Number of columns	2
Number of rows	4
Gap between columns	0.4375 inch
Gap between rows	0.1875 inch

Member card generated after above settings

7.6. NATIONAL INSTITUTE OF TECHNOLOGY ROURKELA

President of India is the Visitor of NIT Rourkela and the Institute is managed by a Board of Governors (BoG) created as per NIT Act of 2007. Under the Act, the Director is the Principal Executive and Academic Officer. The Board of Governors is assisted by three other authorities, viz., The Senate, The Building and Works Committee and the Finance Committee. The Institute has different Departments, Centers and Technical Service Units (TSUs). Each Department or Centre is headed by a faculty member and each TSU is headed by a faculty member or an officer.

Biju Patnaik Central Library is the central library of the National Institute of Technology Rourkela. The Library caters to the educational and research needs of the academic community and its resources are consulted by scholars from all over the country. BPCL has started functioning since 1965. At present, the library holds about 74,000+ books and 18,000 back volumes of periodicals. Apart from the online journals and standards provided by INDEST-AICTE consortium, the library has purchased license to access more than 2000 online science and technology research journals to support local research activity. Prior to that, the BPCL has many ISI codes, educational video courses & cassettes and CD-ROMS etc. The BPCL is automated with integrated library software package called Libsys – LSmart and modernized with latest Radio Frequency Identification (RFID) based automation system that facilitates self check-in, self check-out and automatic security system. This technology offers fastest, easiest, most efficient way to track, locate and manage library materials.

Koha at NIT Rourkela

There is continues discussion ongoing at BPCL for fully implementation of Koha ILMS but it is not yet done till date mainly because of compatibility related issues with existing RFID devices and its high cost of integration with Koha. However Koha was already implemented at BPCL initially for e-book and other non catalogued materials like videocassette, CD/DVD etc. in the existing software Libsys. Till date following item types is available in the Koha at BPCL.

- Videocassette directly catalogued in the Koha
- Bound volume of periodicals migrated from Libsys
- Lecture noted in computer science through MARC provided by Springer
- E-book of Springer in engineering through MARC provided by Springer
- E-books by Elsevier through MARC provided by Elsevier

Bibliographic data conversions at BPCL for Koha

All the above data was refined and converted in MARC before importing into the Koha except videocassette. Bound volumes of journals were migrated from Libsys which has been already discussed in detail in data migrations chapter. The subscribed e-books available at Springer website in MARC format has been downloaded and little modifications were done as per requirement, some new MARC tag added in the downloaded record is 041$a and 942$c, the 041 is to ensure language wise searching of document from Koha web OPAC and 942 is to assign the records as item type (EB=e-book). Similarly some modifications were done for Elsevier e-books, the process of importing the e-book record is continues at some regular interval of time as BPCL is subscribing the resource continuously.

Member data conversions/migration at BPCL for Koha

Member data conversion/migration was another challenge from Libsys to Koha but it has been made possible with the help of Microsoft excel. Various categories of members created parallel to existing ILMS however the default password has been made much secure before importing with the help of various Microsoft excel formulae. In faculty and staff password employee number and date of joining has been combined with special character @ in between them (employeenumber@dateofjoining, 2131074@ddmmyear) similarly for students roll number and date of birth has been joined with @ in between them as discussed above. Further, it was also suggested to enable the member data editable through OPAC by users so that they can modify their contact number/email as and when require but with the restrictions to modify some of the fields like surname, first name, roll number, first email etc. So some codes have been inserted in Koha system preferences which will restrict the user to modify their details on OPAC like the example given below.

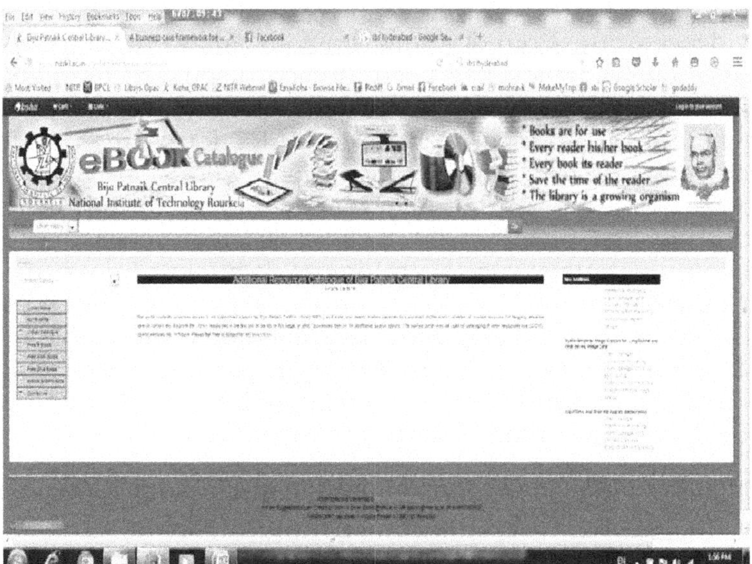

Fig. 7.13. Home page of Koha, ILMS at NIT Rourkela

$(document).ready(function(){

$("#borrower_surname").prop('disabled', true); = it will disable field surname to edit

$("#borrower_firstname").prop('disabled', true); = it will disable first name to edit

$("#borrower_city").prop('disabled', true); }); = it will disable city to edit

The book data migration of BPCL into the Koha system is under plan and it could be done once implementation of Koha will be finalized for the same.

7.7. BHAKTI VEDANTA RESEARCH CENTER, KOLKATA

The creation of BRC was the culmination of several ideas going back to His Divine Grace A.C. Bhaktivedanta Swami Srila Prabhupada, for whom the Centre is named. As early as 1972 Prabhupada instructed his followers to make film records of the original writings of the most prominent 19th century Gaudiya Vaisnava acarya Srila Bhaktivinoda Thakura which were found at his birthplace Ula Birnagar. He expressed a strong desire to preserve these ancient manuscripts and texts, describing it as a"treasure trove of Vaisnava lore"and stated his willingness to spend substantially to achieve this purpose.

In 1975 Prabhupada had discussed with one of his early folllowers, Dr. William Deadwyler, the possibility of opening a Vedic University in Sri Mayapur, WB. A preliminary requisite for that would be a firstclass library. In August 1976 Srila Prabhupada told his Bombay Juhu managers to create a Vedic library for the temple there. He said it should contain all his own books, those of all the acaryas, including other Vaishnava sampradayas, as well as the Upanisads, Puranas and other bona fide Vedic texts. Srila Prabhupada also discussed in detail about his biggest and boldest project, the Temple of the Vedic Planetarium (TOVP) in Sri Mayapur and again this would require an extensive cosmology library containing all available works on Puranic and Siddhantic cosmography and astronomy.

Bibliographic data conversions from excel

The bibliographic data conversion from excel to MARC was one of the biggest challenge during initial stage of learning the skills of data migrations. The excel data provided by the Librarian of BRC was one of the best and standard data maintained in excel sheets. The data was of almost very old and rare books with many responsibility/role against each bibliography like translator, editor etc. as shown in excel screenshot.

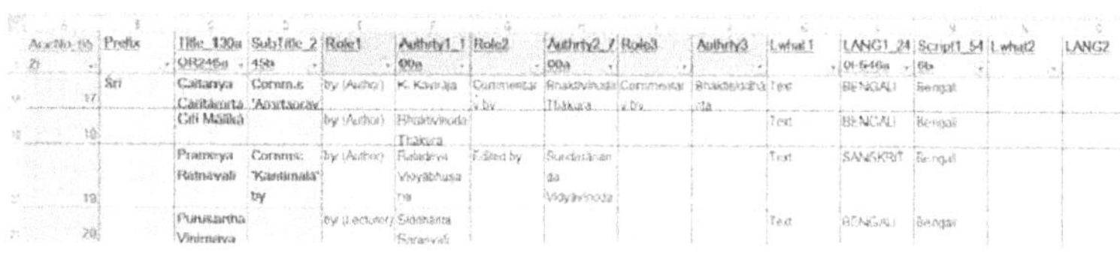

Fig. 7.14. Sample data screenshot of BRC

The data of rare books and manuscripts compel the author to do some exercise on MARC for such specialized conversion, hence all the excel fields were converted into the dummy MARC tags without combining the similar sub tags of same field because it gives more flexibility at the time of final data conversion. A sample data of original excel sheet and final conversion before importing into the catalogue is given below.

Table 7.6. Original data structure and converted data structure

Original excel data with dummy MARC tag	***Final converted data with MARC tags***
=LDR 00000nam a2200000Ia 4500	=LDR 00472nam a2200193Ia 4500
=008 140414s9999||||xx\\ |||||||||||||\\\||und||	=008 140414s2007||||xx\\\||||| |||||||||\\\||und||
=666 \\\\$a3404	=041 \\\\$aeng
=666 \\\\$bThe	=100 \\\\$aSasmal, R.P$eEditor

=666 \\$eEdited by
=666 \\$fSasmal, R.P
=666 \\$gTranslated by
=666 \\$hSasmal, R.P
=666 \\$kText
=666 \\$lENGLISH
=666 \\$mLatin-Roman
=666 \\$t1st ed.
=666 \\$vBKAS Sevasrama
=666 \\$wNadia
=666 \\$y2007
=666 \\$z108 p.
=777 \\$dHardbound
=777 \\$mMaiNCollectn
=777 \\$n4B2L
=777 \\$pExcellent

=666 \\$cCall of the flute
=245 \\$aThe Call of the flute$cEdited by Sasmal, R.P ; Translated by Sasmal, R.P
=250 \\$a1st ed.
=260 \\$aNadia$bBKAS Sevasrama$c2007
=300 \\$a108 p.
=546 \\$bLatin-Roman
=563 \\$aHardbound
=700 \\$aSasmal, R.P$e Translator
=942 \\$cBK
=952 \\$p3404$3Hardbound$8MAIN$o4B2L$aMAIN$bMAIN$yBK

REFERENCES

1. About the Bhaktivedanta Research Centre. (n.d.). Retrieved MARCh 01, 2016, from http://brcindia.com/about-us/
2. Assam University. (n.d.). Retrieved February 28, 2016, from http://www.aus.ac.in/
3. Basic Ubuntu commands. (n.d.). Retrieved May 05, 2012, from http://freshtutorial.com/basic-ubuntu-command-tutorial-for-beginners/
4. Bhaktivedanta Research Centre Library. (n.d.). Retrieved MARCh 04, 2016, from http://library.brcindia.com/
5. CR2. (n.d.). Retrieved MARCh, 01, 2016, from http://www.cr2.in/products/products-library.html
6. DAV, Public School, CCL, NTS, Barkakana. (n.d.). Retrieved February 29, 2016, from http://davbarkakana.in/5D3C8B0A-85B4-4C44-9BAA-8FF90B3C9351/CMS/Page/About-School

7. IIT Roorkee. (n.d.). Department of paper technology, IIT Roorkee. Retrieved November 11, 2012, from http://www.iitr.ac.in/departments/DPT/pages/About_Us History.html
8. Koha Live DVD. (n.d.). Retrieved November 11, 2012, from http://sourceforge.net/
9. Koha wiki. (n.d.). Retrieved April-June, 2012, from http://wiki.Koha-community.org/wiki/Main_Page
10. Koha. (n.d.). Retrieved April 02, 2012, from http://Koha-community.org
11. Koha: Customized live DVD. (n.d.). Retrieved January 18-31, 2013, from http://sourceforge.net/project/vkmKoha/files/
12. Kohageek. (n.d.). Retrieved April-June, 2012, from http://Kohageek.pbworks.com/w/page/28248118/FrontPage
13. Mahatma Gandhi Antarrashtriya Hindi Vishwavidyalaya. (n.d.). Retrieved MARCh 02, 2016, from https://en.wikipedia.org/wiki/Mahatma_Gandhi_Antarrashtriya_Hindi_Vishwavidyalaya
14. Mahatma Gandhi Antarrashtriya Hindi Vishwavidyalaya. (n.d.). Retrieved MARCh 03, 2016, from http://www.hindivishwa.org/contentdtl.aspx?category= 1&cgid=1 &csgid=29
15. MARC standards. (n.d.). Retrieved May 01-30, 2012, from http://www.loc.gov/MARC/
16. MARCEdit. (n.d.). Retrieved May 01-30, 2012, from http://people.oregonstate.edu/~reeset/MARCedit/html/index.php
17. Mysore University library OPAC. (n.d.). Retrieved June 06, 2012, from http://libcat.mysore-univ.org/
18. Rabindra Library, Assam University. (n.d.). Retrieved February 28, 2016, from http://www.aus.ac.in/library.html
19. Sharma, A.K., Mishra, V.K. and Tripathi, D.P. Koha in action: a case study of implementing Koha in Assam University, Silchar. IASLIC bulletin. 60(03), September, 2015. P.143-152
20. w3schools.com:the world largest web development site. (n.d.). Retrieved June 02-30, 2012, from http://www.w3schools.com/

8

Koha Live DVD

A live CD, live DVD, or live disc is a complete bootable computer installation including operating system and may be some applications which runs in a computer's memory, rather than loading from a hard disk drive; the CD/DVD itself is read-only. It allows users to run an operating system for any purpose without installing it or making any changes to the computer's configuration. Live CD/DVDs can run on a computer without secondary storage, such as a hard disk drive, or with a corrupted hard disk drive or file system, allowing data recovery. A live ISO is an ISO image of a Live CD/DVD which needs to be burn on the blank CD/DVD to make it bootable. Live CDs, ISOs, and images usually include an operating system available without charge or restrictive license such as Linux. Live DVD does not alter any files of a computer machine and once we remove the live DVD it leaves the system as it is. Further we can permanently install the programs/operating system of a live DVD on computers hard disk so that next time same can be used.

Live DVD may be some time refer as good entire system backup/image which can be restored in case anything serious happens with the working operating system/files and folders i.e. data loss or system crash.

Live DVD is some time designed and packed with much application software along with operating system like Koha, DSpace, Joomla etc. So it basically helps the beginners to test and work on application software without worrying of complicated Linux command based installations of each application software. The term "live CD" was coined because, after typical PC RAM was large enough and 52x speed CD drives and CD burners were widespread among PC owners, it finally became convenient and practical to boot the kernel and run X11, a window manager and GUI applications directly from a CD without disturbing the OS on the hard disk. The first Linux-based 'Live CD' was Yggdrasil Linux first released in beta form 1992~1993 (ceased production in 1995); though in practice its functionality was hampered due to the low throughput of contemporary CD-ROM drives. DemoLinux, released in 1998, was the first Linux distribution specially designed as a live CD.

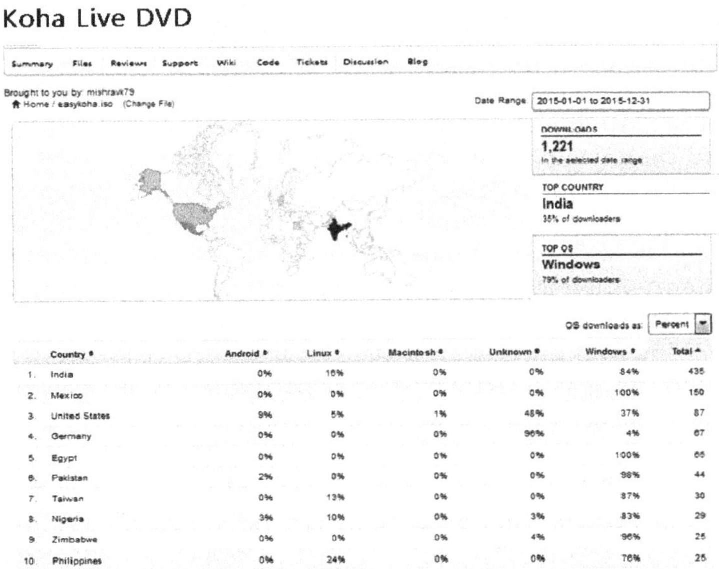

	Country	Android	Linux	Macintosh	Unknown	Windows	Total
1.	India	0%	16%	0%	0%	84%	435
2.	Mexico	0%	0%	0%	0%	100%	150
3.	United States	9%	5%	1%	48%	37%	87
4.	Germany	0%	0%	0%	96%	4%	67
5.	Egypt	0%	0%	0%	0%	100%	66
6.	Pakistan	2%	0%	0%	0%	98%	44
7.	Taiwan	0%	13%	0%	0%	87%	30
8.	Nigeria	3%	10%	0%	3%	83%	29
9.	Zimbabwe	0%	0%	0%	4%	96%	25
10.	Philippines	0%	24%	0%	0%	76%	25

Fig. 8.1. Download statistics of Koha live DVD

Author is producing the Live DVD of Koha since three years of his experience which is available at *http://sourceforge.net/projects/vkmkoha/files/* (easykoha.iso) and its video on how to install live DVD on dual booting mode (along side windows operating system) is also available in YouTube at *https://www.youtube.com/watch?v=2mg8h394E28*. The download statistics (top ten country) of the live DVD (easykoha.iso) can be seen in the below screen from 01/01/2015 to 31/12/2015. It reflects the popularity of the live DVD among the people from all corners of the globe and popularity of Koha too among the professionals.

Detail of Koha Live DVD

At the time of writing this book author has uploaded the Koha live DVD of version 3.22.01 at *http://sourceforge.net/projects/vkmkoha/* on Ubuntu latest long term support operating system version 14.04 LTS. The detail of the live DVD is as follows which is also available along with this book as accompanying material.

Koha Version- 3.22.1 on Ubuntu 14.04 LTS

OPAC - http://127.0.0.1

Staff Client - http://127.0.0.1:8000

System/Ubuntu Login Information

Username: koha

Password: koha123

Koha Staff Client Login

Username: koha

Password: india

MySQL

Root Password: mysqlkoha

Database Name: koha_library

Username: koha_library

Password: vkmkoha

Database Backup

- Each day backup will be deposited in /var/spool/koha/library folder and it stores two days backup by eliminating older ones automatically.
- Alternatively you can download backup from Koha staff interface through Tools modules under the export option

Database Restoration

Copy koha_library.sql.gz database backup to /home/koha folder and extract the file in the same folder (file name would be koha_library.sql)

Open Terminal and apply the following commands:

sudo su

Enter Koha login Password: koha123

mysql -uroot -p koha_library < koha_library.sql

Enter the MySQL root password "mysqlkoha"

Rebuild Zebra

Run following command in a terminal:

sudo koha-rebuild-zebra -v -f library

Upgrade Koha (You may use the command to upgrade old Koha LiveDVD)

Execute following commands in a terminal:

sudo apt-get update

sudo apt-get upgrade

sudo apt-get install koha-common

Customization of Koha Home page

The home page of Koha has been highly customized in such a way that one can use Koha as their library OPAC cum Website with little efforts.The code of all koha home page effects given in koha-administration-Global system preference under the options: Opaccredits, opacheader, OpacMainUserBlock, OpacNav, opacusercssr and OpacNavBottom.Therefore if you need to display contents and links as per your requirement than you have to modify just the links and contents of the code or Completely remove all the codes to get the koha default home page view.

Steps of Koha Live DVD installation on dual mode (Windows and Linux)

Steps/procedure of installing the Koha live DVD is similar to installation of Ubuntu operating system as described in previous chapter. However the below procedure is for installing the Ubuntu based Koha live DVD on machine which is already having Windows operating system installed. So for installing the Live DVD on windows first you can delete your one drive from windows machine like D/E/F then same free space can be utilized for the installation of live DVD as described in below steps.

Steps with description

Table 8.1. Koha Live DVD installation steps

Insert the live DVD in CD/DVD driver and restart the computer, than select the computer to boot from CD/DVD driver. You will get the following screen. Please select the third option if you want to install it on computer OR first option if you want to test koha without installation on computer than press Enter.

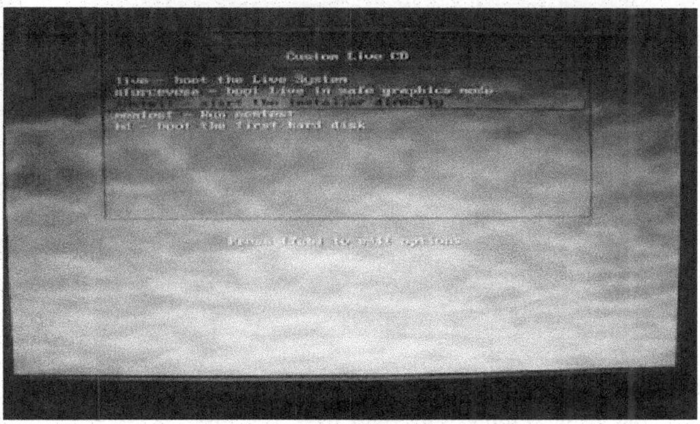

Screenshot

You will get the following option to choose the Language so just click the Continue option.

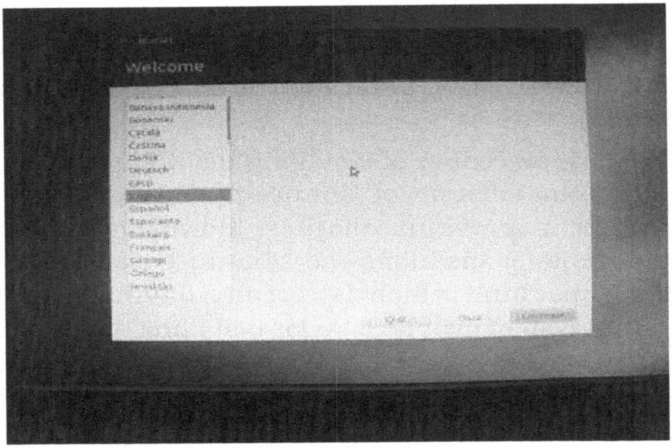

Screenshot

It will analyse Disk space, power source and internet connectivity and you need choose, whether to install updates and other third-party software's while installing OS (it may slow down the installation). Do not select anything just Continue.

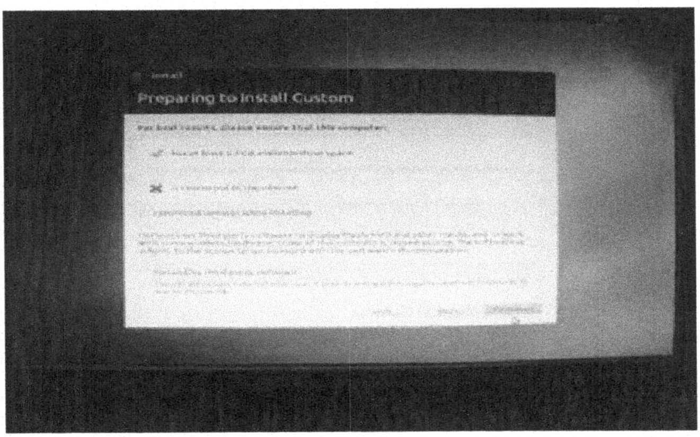

Screenshot

This is most important step, here you have to choose one option out of three, if you want to use computer only for koha installation (Single boot) than select option Second (erase everything and reinstall) or select option third (something else) as shown in the below screen if you want dual boot i.e. windows and Koha and continue. PLEASE NOTE IF YOU CHOOSE SECOND OPTION THAN YOU NEED NOT TO FOLLOW PARTITION STEPS.

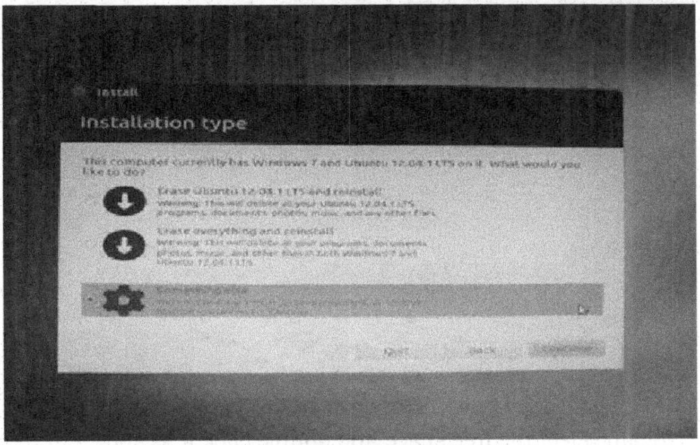

Screenshot

You can see free space in the next screen which is due to deletion of any windows driver (D/E/F etc.) for the installation of koha/ubuntu through windows os. Select the free space and double click over it/New partition table.

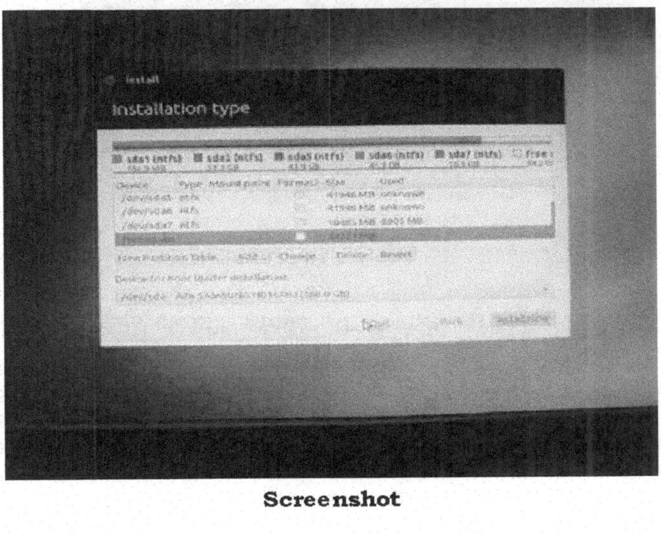

Screenshot

Enter 500 and select "/boot" as shown in the next screen and press OK

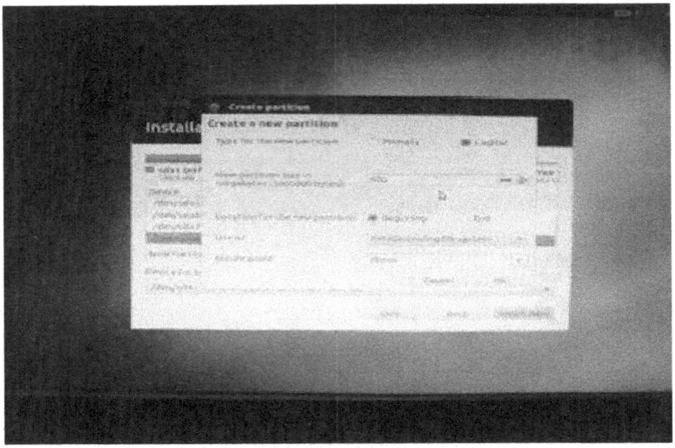

Screenshot

Again select the free space and double click it as shown in the next screen.

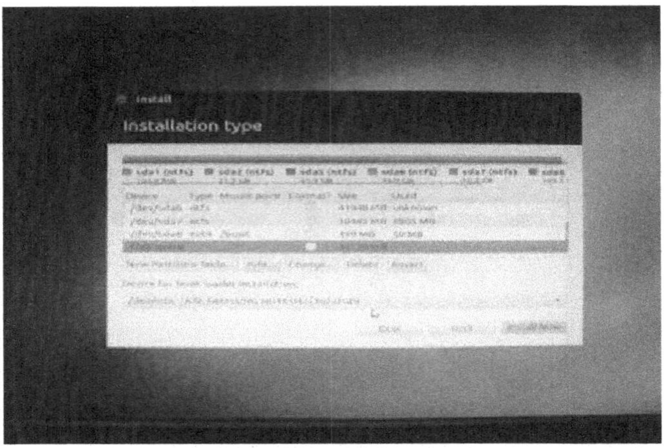

Screenshot

In this step enter all the figures by subtracting double of your RAM, for example if your computer RAM is 1 GB than subtract approx. 2000 from the rest space as shown in the below screen and select '/' (root) from the drop down menu than press OK.

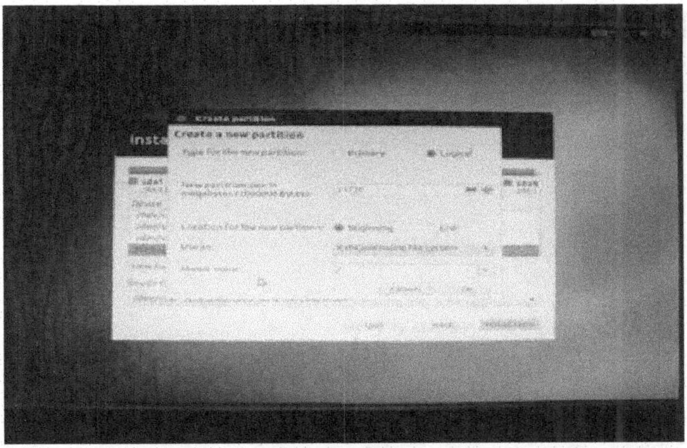

Screenshot

Select the free space and repeat the above step.

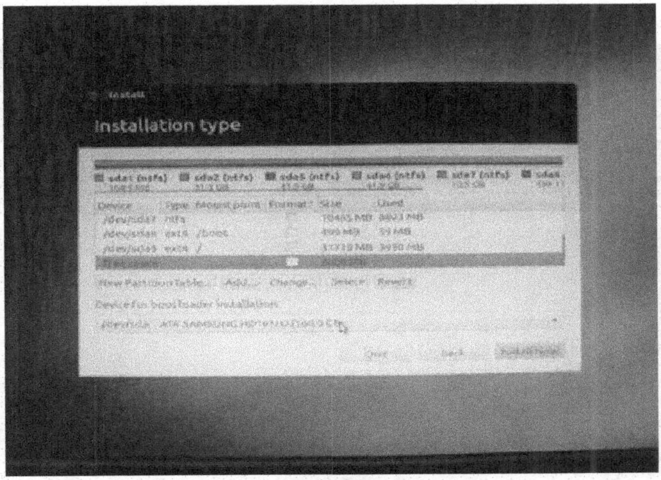

Screenshot

Just you have to select swap from drop down list than press OK

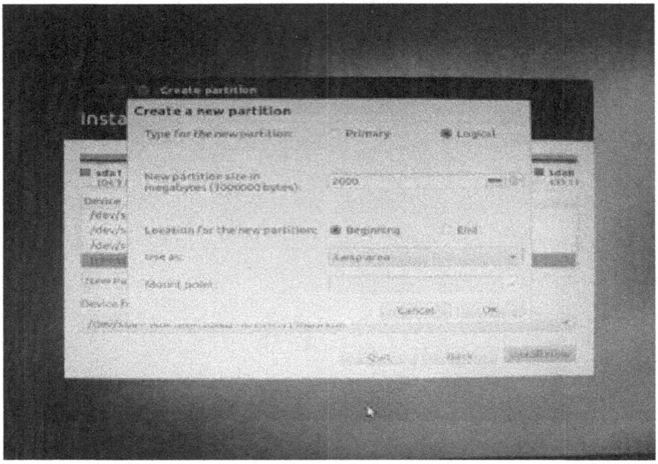

Screenshot

Now just hit install now as shown in next screen.

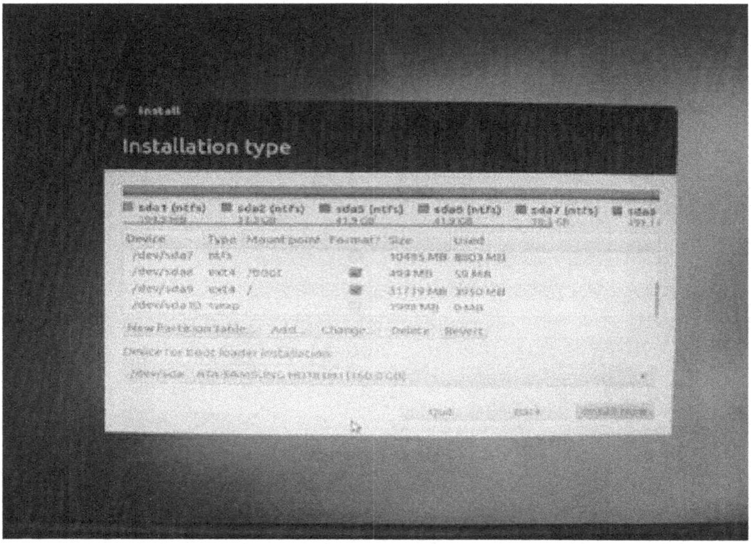

Screenshot

Click over your country to set the timings zone as shown in below screen and continue.

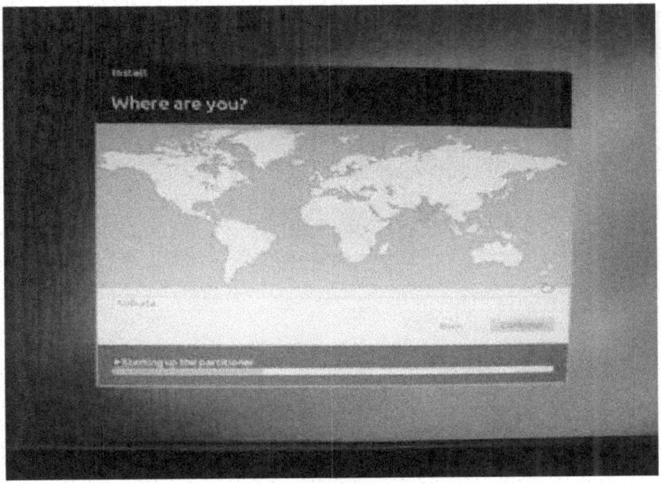

Screenshot

Press continue if asks for Kew board layout or select as per your layout

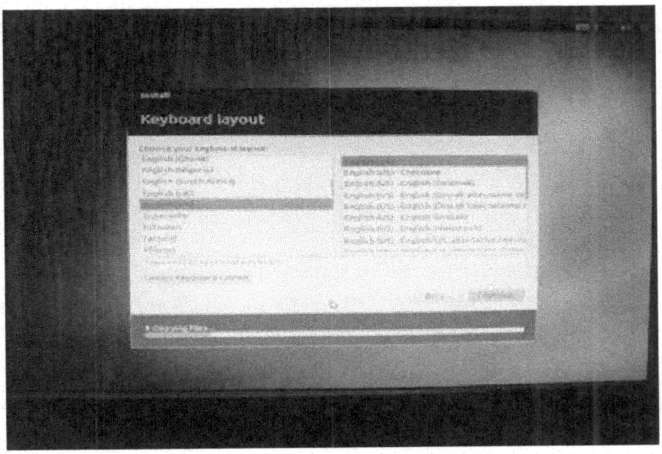

Screenshot

The below screen will take some time depending upon the speed of computer so please wait until you are not getting massage of installation complete and restart your computer. If computer asks to fill some fields please enter user name "koha" and password "koha123"

Screenshot

REFERENCES

1. Live CD. (n.d.). Retrieved March 06, 2016 from https://en.wikipedia.org/wiki/Live_CD

2. LiveCD. (n.d.). Retrieved March 05, 2016, from *https://help.ubuntu.com/community/LiveCD*

Bibliography

Abdelrahman, O. H. (2009). The State of ICT Implementation and Training at the University of Khartoum Library System. khartoumspace.uofk.edu. Retrieved from http://khartoumspace.uofk.edu/handle/123456789/16611

Abdussalam, A. T. B., & Saliu, U. A. (2014). Using Koha for cataloging and classification: A case study. Library Hi Tech News, 31(2), 15–21. http://doi.org/10.1108/LHTN-11-2013-0070

Adhikari, I. P. (2013). Factors impeding information processing works in TU college libraries in Kathmandu. 182.93.84.134. Retrieved from http://182.93.84.134:9991/lisd/handle/123456789/82

Adigun, A., Ojo, G., Salvador-Olayokun, S., & ... (2011). An Assessment of Online Public Access Catalogue (OPAC) Utilization in Two Selected University Libraries in Lagos State, Nigeria. Information Manager (.... Retrieved from http://www.ajol.info/index.php/tim/article/view/83645

Adoma, P., & Ponelis, S. (2015). Open source integrated library systems in academic libraries in Uganda: initial results. conferences.sun.ac.za.

AGRAWAL, P. (2014). Open source software and open access resources for enhancing library services: an exploratory study. 14.139.121.106.

Ahammad, N. (2014). Implementing the Koha integrated library system at the Independent University, Bangladesh: A practical experience. Electronic Library, 32(5), 642–658. http://doi.org/10.1108/EL-04-2012-0036

Ahmed, S. Z. (2014). The use of IT-based information services: An investigation into the current status of public university libraries in Bangladesh. Program. Retrieved from http://www.emeraldinsight.com/doi/abs/10.1108/PROG-08-2012-0048

Akpokodje, V. N., & Akpokodje, T. E. (2015). Assessment and Evaluation of KOHA ILS for Online Library Registration at University of Jos, Nigeria. irepos.unijos.edu.ng. Retrieved from http://irepos.unijos.edu.ng/jspui/handle/123456789/648

Alemayehu, F. (2010). The Practice of Opting for Open Source Solutions in Higher Education Institutions of Ethiopia. etd.aau.edu.et. Retrieved from http://etd.aau.edu.et/handle/123456789/8625

Ali, S. (2014). Difficulties in Use & Implication of Open Source Software in Academic Libraries of Gulbarga: A Study. Indian Journal of Library and Information Science. Retrieved from http://search.proquest.com/openview/96b2ebe281e097c6996e5ce7036dd69d/1?pq-origsite=gscholar

Amekuedee, J. O. (2005). An evaluation of library automation in some Ghanaian university libraries. The Electronic Library. Retrieved from http://www.emeraldinsight.com/doi/abs/10.1108/02640470510611508

Amin, S., & Prasad, A. R. D. (2003). Open Source Software for Libraries. Citeseer.

Amollo, B. A. (2013). Feasibility of adaptation of open source ILS for libraries in Kenya: A practical evaluation. Electronic Library, 31(5), 608–634. http://doi.org/10.1108/EL-12-2011-0171

Ansari, I. A. (n.d.). Open Source Software is A Boon for Library and Information Management Centers. Innovative Library Services for Dynamic Knowledge ... .

Anuradha, K. T., Sivakaminathan, R., & Kumar, P. A. (2011). Open-source tools for enhancing full-text searching of OPACs: Use of Koha, Greenstone and Fedora. Program, 45(2), 231–239. http://doi.org/10.1108/00330331111129750

Archana, S. N., Padmakumar, P. K., & Beena, C. (2014).

Catalogue interfaces of integrated library management systems (ILMS): Experiences in a proprietary and open source software. DESIDOC Journal of Library and Information Technology, 34(1), 16–22.

Arriola Navarrete, O., Tecuatl Quechol, G., & Gonzalez Herrera, G. (2011). Free software vs proprietary software: an assessment of integrated systems for library automation. Investigacion Bibliotecologica, 25(54), 37–70.

Arriola Navarrete, O., Tecuatl Quechol, G., & González Herrera, G. (2011). Software propietario vs software libre: una evaluación de sistemas integrales para la automatización de bibliotecas. Investigación Bibliotecológica, 25(54), 37–70.

Aryal, J. C. (2010). Open source softwares for libraries. INFOLIB JOURNAL.

Asemi, A., & Hosseini, Z. S. (2010). A survey on the library open source software in the University of Isfahan, Iran: Viewpoint of librarians. Information Sciences and Interaction .... Retrieved from http://ieeexplore.ieee.org/xpls/abs_all.jsp?arnumber=5534809

Atri, Y. K. (2012). Free/open versus commercial software: a study of some selected library management software. shodhgangotri.inflibnet.ac.in.

Aute, G., & Ghumare, S. (2014). Library Management Softwares: LIBSYS 7 & KOHA. ir.inflibnet.ac.in. Retrieved from http://ir.inflibnet.ac.in/handle/1944/1808

Awoyemi, A. R., & Olaniyi, S. T. (2012). A survey of the availability and use of koha open source software by academic libraries in Nigeria. COCLIN Journal of Library and Information Science.

Babu, P. B., & Krishnamurthy, M. (2013). Library automation to resource discovery: A review of emerging challenges. The Electronic Library. Retrieved from http://www.emeraldinsight.com/doi/pdf/10.1108/EL-11-2011-0159

Bailey, A., Lener, E., O'Brien, L., & Stovall, C. (2013). Automation and Collection Management: A Short History and Recent Trends. Retrieved from http://www.scopus.com/inward/

record.url?eid=2-s2.0-84944208358&partnerID=40&md5=6b206b50430bb3ef31bec41cb9701a79

Bakar, A. A., Rahmad, F., & Amin, Z. M. (2015). KOHA ILS: The Next Level. eprints.usm.my. Retrieved from http://eprints.usm.my/29517/

Bakar, A. A., & Yusoff, T. M. (2010). Open source in libraries: Implementation of an open source ILMS at Asia e-University library. repo.uum.edu.my. Retrieved from http://repo.uum.edu.my/538/

Balasooriya, A. H. K. (2012). A Sustainable Free and Open Source Software Solution for Library Automation in Sri Lankan Library Environment. NILIS Symposium 2012.

Bal, B. K., Shrestha, A., Hyoju, D., Adhikari, R. C., & Shrestha, V. (2008). Review Report on Cataloguing Module of Library Management System (LMS). Citeseer.

Balnaves, E. (2008). Open source library management systems: a multidimensional evaluation. Australian Academic & Research Libraries. Retrieved from http://www.tandfonline.com/doi/abs/10.1080/00048623.2008.10721320

Bapte, V. D. (2015). Copy Cataloguing through SOUL 2.0. DESIDOC Journal of Library & Information .... Retrieved from http://desidoc.drdo.gov.in/ojs/index.php/djlit/article/view/8578

Baruah, B. G. (2007). Role of Open Access, Open Standards and Open Sources in Libraries: A Study. researchgate.net.

Barve, S., & Dahibhate, N. B. (2012). Open source software for library services. DESIDOC Journal of Library and Information Technology, 32(5), 401–408.

Bavousett, D. R., & Iglesias, E. (2013). Who Ever Said that ILS Migrations Had to be Stressful? ... / : Advancements in Library Automation. Retrieved from http://books.google.com/books?hl=en&lr=&id=c9CeBQAAQBAJ&oi=fnd&pg= PA90&dq=koha+library +automation+open+source+software&ots=WcnZoxypp5&sig=4q5t_mTQR1Fg3GGFmKkAxqld6i8

Bennett, M. (2009). Koha with LibLime. Instructor.

Bidwell, P. S. (2011). E-learning and breaking barriers: teaching online cataloguing by distance. repository.usp.ac.fj. Retrieved from http://repository.usp.ac.fj/4647/

Biju, V. V., Jasimudeen, S., & Kumar, V. V. (2012). A study on managing Koha Open Source library management system using Live CD. eprints.rclis.org. Retrieved from http://eprints.rclis.org/handle/10760/17513

Bilal, D. (2014). Library Automation: Core Concepts and Practical Systems Analysis: Core Concepts and Practical Systems Analysis. books.google.com.

Birchall, A. J., & Hopkinson, A. (2007). Open source software in higher education. eprints.mdx.ac.uk. Retrieved from http://eprints.mdx.ac.uk/6305/

Bissels, G. (2008). Implementation of an open source library management system: Experiences with Koha 3.0 at the Royal London Homoeopathic Hospital. Program, 42(3), 303–314. http://doi.org/10.1108/00330330810892703

Bissels, G., & Chandler, A. (2010). Two years on: Koha 3.0 in use at the CAMLIS library, Royal London Homoeopathic Hospital. Program. Retrieved from http://www.emeraldinsight.com/doi/abs/10.1108/00330331011064276

Biswas, G., & Paul, D. (2008). NewGenLib, The First Indian Open Source Software: a Study of Its Features And Comparison With Other Software. ... at Bose Institute on Library ... .

Biswas, G., & Paul, D. (n.d.). A Study on the Open source Integrated Library Management Software: special reference to NewGenLib. Goutambiswasresearch.yolasite.com.

Borgman, C. L. (1997). From acting locally to thinking globally: A brief history of library automation. Library Quarterly, 67(3), 215–249.

Breeding, M. (2002). The open source ILS: still only a distant possibility. Information Technology and Libraries. Retrieved from http://go.galegroup.com/ps/i.do?id=GALE% 7CA84594450&sid=googleScholar&v=2.1&it=r&linkaccess=fulltext&issn=07309295&p=AONE&sw=w

Breeding, M. (2004). Integrated library software: a guide to multiuser, multifunction systems. Library Technology

Reports. Retrieved from http://go.galegroup.com/ps/i.do?id=GALE%7CA113563970&sid=googleScholar&v=2.1&it=r&linkaccess=fulltext&issn=00242586&p=AONE&sw=w

Breeding, M. (2009a). Major open source ILS products. Library Technology Reports.

Breeding, M. (2009b). Next-generation flavor in integrated online catalogs. Library Technology Reports.

Breeding, M. (2009c). Next generation library automation: Its impact on the serials community. Serials Librarian, 56(1-4), 55–64. http://doi.org/10.1080/03615260802679028

Breeding, M. (2009d). Open Source and the ILS. Library Technology Reports. Retrieved from http://scholar.google.comhttps://www.journals.ala.org/ltr/article/download/4707/5601

Breeding, M. (2012). Cloud computing for libraries. books.google.com.

Breeding, M. (2014). Smarter Libraries Through Technology: Community Source at the Crossroads. journals.ala.org.

Breeding, M., & Yelton, A. (2011). Librarians' Assessments of Automation Systems Survey Results, 2007-2010. books.google.com.

Brink-Drescher, J. (2014). VuFind: A NextGen Overlay. The Charleston Advisor. Retrieved from http://www.ingentaconnect.com/content/charleston/chadv/2014/00000016/00000002/art00016

Britton, C. J., Level, A. V., & Gardner, M. A. (2013). Crowdsourcing: divide the work and share the success. Library Hi Tech News. Retrieved from http://www.emeraldinsight.com/doi/abs/10.1108/LHTN-03-2013-0017

Brooke, T. (2013). Open source integrated library systems in public libraries. iSchool Student Research Journal. Retrieved from http://scholarworks.sjsu.edu/slissrj/vol3/iss2/3/

Brown-Syed, C. (2011). Parents of Invention: The Development of Library Automation Systems in the Late 20th Century: The Development of Library Automation Systems in the Late .... books.google.com.

Carassiti, A., & Tajoli, Z. (2009). Koha: un software gestionale open source per le biblioteche. Bollettino Del CILEA. Retrieved from http://bollettino.cilea.it/article/view/7018

Chandra, D. G., Kathing, M., & ... (2013). Library Automation in Cloud. ... Networks (CICN), 2013 5th .... Retrieved from http://ieeexplore.ieee.org/xpls/abs_all.jsp?arnumber=6658039

Chang, N., & Tsai, Y. (2009). An evaluation of multi-language/multi-script functions in Koha. World Library and Information Congress: 75th ....

Chang, N., Tsai, Y., Dunsire, G., & Hopkinson, A. (2013). Experimenting with implementing FRBR in a Chinese Koha system. Library Hi Tech News, 30(10), 10–20. http://doi.org/10.1108/LHTN-09-2013-0054

Chang, N., Tsai, Y., & Hopkinson, A. (2010). An evaluation of implementing Koha in a Chinese language environment. Program, 44(4), 342–356. http://doi.org/10.1108/00330331011083239

Chaudhari, B. (2012). Open Source Software and Librarianship. spmlib.pdpu.ac.in. Retrieved from http://spmlib.pdpu.ac.in:8080/jspui/handle/123456789/392

Chawner, B. (2004). Free/open source software: new opportunities, new challenges. 12th VALA Biennial Conference E Breaking ....

Chawner, B. (2005). F/OSS in the library world: an exploration. ACM SIGSOFT Software Engineering Notes. Retrieved from http://dl.acm.org/citation.cfm?id=1083262

Chawner, B. (2011). Factors influencing participant satisfaction with free/libre and open source software projects. researcharchive.vuw.ac.nz. Retrieved from http://researcharchive.vuw.ac.nz/handle/10063/1710

Chawner, B. L. (2005). Participant satisfaction with open source software. Victoria University, Wellington.

Chelatayakkot, V. (2013). Koha 3 Administration: Some Easy Tools Using PHP. dspace.cusat.ac.in. Retrieved from http://dspace.cusat.ac.in/xmlui/handle/123456789/6539

Chen, H., & Albee, B. (2012). An open source library system

and public library users: Finding and using library collections. Library & Information Science Research. Retrieved from http://www.sciencedirect.com/science/article/pii/S0740818812000321

Chisenga, J. (2006). Information and communication technologies: opportunities and challenges for national and university libraries in Eastern, Central and Southern Africa. eprints.rclis.org. Retrieved from http://eprints.rclis.org/handle/10760/9579

Choi, N., & Pruett, J. A. (2015). The characteristics and motivations of library open source software developers: An empirical study. Library & Information Science Research. Retrieved from http://www.sciencedirect.com/science/article/pii/S0740818815000341

Chouhan, L. B. (2010). Open Source Software (OSS) for Library Management-A Study. eprints.rclis.org. Retrieved from http://eprints.rclis.org/22633/

Chowdhury, M. H. H., Shoeb, M. Z. H., Rahman, M. M., & ... (2015). Information communication technology use in the library of Independent University, Bangladesh: Past, present and future plan. dir.iub.edu.bd. Retrieved from http://dir.iub.edu.bd:8180/handle/123456789/204

Chudasma, P., & Shastri, D. (2013). Reengineering Library Services with Emerging Technologies. ir.inflibnet.ac.in. Retrieved from http://ir.inflibnet.ac.in/handle/1944/1732

Clark, J. R. (2008). The Internet Connection: Open Source Library Software—Ready for Prime Time? Behavioral & Social Sciences Librarian. Retrieved from http://www.tandfonline.com/doi/full/10.1080/01639260802365905

Cleoda, L. M., Jeyapragash, B., & Ragavan, D. S. (n.d.). Automation of Physical Education Department Library at Bharathidasan University. 14.139.186.108.

Conc, T. (2013). Choosing free library software: Experiences of the Faculty of Humanities and Social Studies in Zagreb. In 2013 36th International Convention on Information and Communication Technology, Electronics and Microelectronics, MIPRO 2013 - Proceedings (pp. 647–653). Retrieved from http://www.scopus.com/inward/

record.url?eid=2-s2.0-84886872518&partnerID=40&md5= 33e8484d05a629e248303a64e88e7666

Corbly, J. E. (2014). The free software alternative: freeware, open-source software, and libraries. Information Technology and Libraries (Online). Retrieved from http://search.proquest.com/openview/c4c7dea71b30e02d67b304083feeef30/1?pq-origsite=gscholar

Corrado, E. M. (2004a). Open Source Library Automation: An Introduction.

Corrado, E. M. (2004b). Open Source Library Management Systems.

Corrado, E. M. (2007). An open source, open access journal database appliance: a proposal.

Corrado, E. M. (2008). Evaluating Open Source Software.

Crotty, A. (2006). Would you like a LOMS with your ILMS? Converging the library and learning management systems. ... Exhibition. Victorian Association for Library Automation ....

Dalling, J., & Rafferty, P. (2013). Open source, open minds? An investigation into attitudes towards open source library management systems in UK higher education libraries. Program. Retrieved from http://www.emeraldinsight.com/doi/abs/10.1108/PROG-06-2012-0034

Das, A. K., & Mandal, S. (2013). Standards Requirement for Integrated Library System. Asian Journal of Multidisciplinary Studies. Retrieved from http://www.ajms.co.in/sites/ajms2015/index.php/ajms/article/view/105

Das, S. C. (2014). Interoperability among university libraries in Bangladesh: Data exchange feasibility. repository.library.du.ac.bd.

Dehinbo, K., Pretorius, P., & ... (2012). Strategic Analysis Towards Deriving Competitive Advantage with the Use of FOSS: The Case of a South African University. .../ : New Generations (ITNG), ... Retrieved from http://ieeexplore.ieee.org/xpls/abs_all.jsp?arnumber=6209175

de Smet, E. (2009). ABCD: A new FOSS library automation solution based on ISIS. Information Development, 25(1),

61–67. http://doi.org/10.1177/0266666908101265

de Smet, E. (2011). Special features of the advanced loans module of the ABCD integrated library system. Program, 45(3), 323–332. http://doi.org/10.1108/00330331111151629

Devi, G. R., & Raghuveer, K. (n.d.). Hardware and Software Selection for Library Automation. Ijsr.net.

DeVoe, K. (2013). Innovations Affecting Us–Open Source in the Library: An Alternative to the Commercial ILS? Against the Grain.

Dhamdhere, S. N. (2011). ABCD, an open source software for modern libraries. Chinese Librarianship: An International ... .

Dimant, N. (2010). Breaking the barriers: The role of support companies in making open source a reality. Library Review, 59(9), 662–666. http://doi.org/10.1108/00242531011086980

Dione, B., & Savard, R. (2008). Managing Technologies and Automated Library Systems in Developing Countries: Open Source vs Commercial Options/Le Management des technologies et .... books.google.com.

Dora, M., Maharana, B., & Jena, S. (2008). Open Source movement in Indian libraries: an analytical study. eprints.rclis.org. Retrieved from http://eprints.rclis.org/handle/10760/16845

Dora, M., Maharana, B., & Jena, S. (n.d.). Open Source Movement in Indian Libraries: An Analytical. Core.ac.uk.

Dougherty, W. C. (2009). Integrated library systems: Where are they going? Where are we going? The Journal of Academic Librarianship.

Ebenezer, C. (2002). Trends in integrated library systems. Vine. Retrieved from http://www.emeraldinsight.com/doi/abs/10.1108/03055720210471139

Eckert, K., Hänger, C., & Niemann, C. (2009). Tagging and automation: Challenges and opportunities for academic libraries. Library Hi Tech, 27(4), 557–569. http://doi.org/10.1108/07378830911007664

Egunjobi, R. A., & Awoyemi, R. A. (2012). Library automation with Koha. Library Hi Tech News, 29(3), 12–15. http://doi.org/10.1108/07419051211241868

Eneya, D. D. (2008). A long walk to automation: experiences and challenges of the university of Malawi libraries. IFLA Publications. Retrieved from http://www.degruyter.com/dg/viewbooktoc.chapterlist.resultlinks.fullcontentlink:pdfeventlink/$002fbooks$002f9783598440953$002f9783598440953.2.74$002f9783598440953. 2.74.pdf?t:ac=product/38506

Engard, N. (2010). Practical open source software for libraries. books.google.com.

Erb, R. A. (2008). The Evolution of a Technical College Regional Library Network. Community & Junior College Libraries. Retrieved from http://www.tandfonline.com/doi/abs/10.1080/02763910802336480

Erturk, E., & Iles, H. R. E. (2015). Case Study on Cloud Based Library Software as a Service: Evaluating EZproxy. arXiv Preprint arXiv:1511.07578. Retrieved from http://arxiv.org/abs/1511.07578

Espiau-Bechetoille, C., Bernon, J., Bruley, C., & Mousin, S. (2011). An example of inter-university cooperation for implementing Koha in libraries: Collective approach and institutional needs. OCLC Systems and Services, 27(1), 40–44. http://doi.org/10.1108/10650751111106546

Eyler, P. (2003). Koha: A gift to libraries from New Zealand. Linux Journal.

Farahi, M. T., & Gandhi, R. T. (2011). Adoption of information technologies in medical libraries in Karnataka, India and Iran: A comparative study. International Journal of Library and .... .

Foote, A. (2010). The Myth of Free: The Hidden Costs of Open Source Software. dalspace.library.dal.ca.

Frigimelica, G., & Marchitelli, A. (2010). Library automation and Open source software in Italy: an overview. ... Role of the Systems Librarian, ... Retrieved from http://books.google.com/books?hl=en&lr=&id=y0lWAgAAQBAJ&oi=fnd&pg= PA29&dq=koha+library +automation+open+source+s oftware&ots=bInjnDPBmX&sig=ei5CCsjYnv43TSFZNTFHCmyEKAI

Genoese, L., & Keith, L. (2011). Jumping ship: One health science library's voyage from a proprietary ILS to open source. Journal of Electronic Resources in Medical Libraries, 8(2), 126–133. http://doi.org/10.1080/15424065.2011.576605

Giri, R. (2012). NewGenLib 3: an integrated open source library management system that makes your library visible in web. Library Hi Tech News. Retrieved from http://www.emeraldinsight.com/doi/abs/10.1108/07419051211294464

Giri, R., & Sengar, D. S. (2011). Use of open source software in the learning resource centre of Indira Gandhi Institute of Technology: a case study. Annals of Library and Information Studies. Retrieved from http://eprints.rclis.org/handle/10760/18058

Goddard, L. (2008). The Future of the OPAC. core.ac.uk.

Gong, R. H., & Gong, D. R. (2013). Lending and Borrowing Library Materials: Automation in the Changing. ... / : Advancements in Library Automation: .... Retrieved from http://books.google.com/books?hl=en&lr=&id=c9CeBQAAQBAJ&oi=fnd&pg=PA207&dq =koha+library+automation+open+source+software &ots=WcnZoxzgn7&sig=VXhz4zK9SZ6Agtel36Qt0U1ZNJc

Goodman, A., & Bucknall, T. (2010). ILS Selection for an Academic Library. godaisies.com.

Goyal, L. C., & Jatav, P. K. (n.d.). Open Source Software-Library with Special Reference to NewGenLib 3.0 Its Features and Functional Modules. Innovative Library Services for Dynamic Knowledge ... .

Grothkopf, U., & Erdmann, C. (2010). Lessons Learned: Implementing an Open-Source Library System. Library and Information Services in ... .

Gwynn, D. (2009). Open Source Web Content Management Systems in a Library Environment. David Gwynn.

Hall, K., Ames, C. M., & Brice, J. (2013). Open Source Library Software Development in a Small Rural Library System. Code4Lib Journal.

Haneefa, M. K., & Shukkoor, C. K. A. (2010). Information and communication technology literacy among library professionals in Calicut University, Kerala. DESIDOC Journal of Library & .... Retrieved from http://search.proquest.com/openview/3a0efce80106c8d7d7de157d073fff8d/1?pq-origsite=gscholar

Hanumappa, A., Dora, M., & Navik, V. (2014). Open Source Software solutions in Indian libraries. Library Hi Tech, 32(3), 409–422. http://doi.org/10.1108/LHT-12-2013-0157

Haravu, L. J. (2009). Comparison of two open source integrated Library Systems (ILS): Koha (version. 3.0) and NewGenLib (version. 2.2 beta). Retrieved June.

Hasan, N. (2011). Issues and challenges in open source software environment with special reference to India. ... of International Conference on Academic Libraries (....

Hastings, R., Braum, H., Willems, H., Hutchinson, C., & ... (2016). The Kansas Story: A Sea of Koha Green on the Plains. eprints.rclis.org. Retrieved from http://eprints.rclis.org/28918/

Hazel, W., & Rowland, F. (2011). The history of library automation in the United Kingdom. Retrieved from http://www.scopus.com/inward/record.url?eid=2-s2.0-84881783676 &partnerID=40&md5=e8df019e4d0662ae16bc6b5e94e4b87a

Helling, J. (2010). Cutting the proprietary cord: A case study of one library's decision to migrate to an open source ILS. Library Review, 59(9), 702–707. http://doi.org/10.1108/00242531011087024

Herrera, G. G. (2010). Software libre vs. propietario: una evaluación de sistemas Janium vs. Koha. eprints.rclis.org. Retrieved from http://eprints.rclis.org/id/eprint/14590

Hettiarachchi, N., & Fernando, K. I. (2011). Assuring the security and accuracy of data using a MySQL driven database in an automated library environment: case study for the Library of University of .... University Library Association.

Hoebeke, C. H. (2012). The Economics of Open Source. works.bepress.com. Retrieved from http://works.bepress.com/cgi/viewcontent.cgi?article= 1063&context= christopher_hoebeke

Horne, A. S., Ragon, B., & Wilson, D. T. (2012). An Innovative Use of Instant Messaging Technology to Support a Library's Single-Service Point. Medical Reference Services Quarterly, 31(2), 127–139. http://doi.org/10.1080/02763869.2012.670557

Horton, V., & Pronevitz, G. (2014). Library consortia: Models for collaboration and sustainability. books.google.com.

Huang, H. C., & Chen, Y. N. (2010). Evolutionary Development of Library Information Systems. ... of Educational Media & Library .... Retrieved from http://search.ebscohost.com/login.aspx?direct=true&profile=ehost&scope= site &authtype= crawler&jrnl= 1013090X&AN= 56565954& h=gITOMp3oYwcIN1FAslmNPz0kBP41T8vOErlxbHsUFrj8IX2Om TJOh2kXlVI% 2BrHXWjEtiVhsAPLV2bUKB1HMWuA% 3D%3D&crl=c

Hunter, P., & Guy, M. (2004). Metadata for Harvesting: The Open Archives Initiative, and how to find things on the Web. The Electronic Library. Retrieved from http://www.emeraldinsight.com/doi/abs/10.1108/02640470410533434

Hvass, A. (2008). Cataloguing with LibraryThing: as easy as 1, 2, 3! Library Hi Tech News. Retrieved from http://www.emeraldinsight.com/doi/full/10.1108/07419050810949995

Iglesias, E. (2013). The inevitability of library automation (Vol. 1). Retrieved from http://www.scopus.com/inward/record.url?eid=2-s2.0-84944895707&partnerID= 40& md5=d43e6cefe34ec5a3a9d7e8bf663be103

Igun, S. E. (2005). Implications for electronic publishing in libraries and information centres in Africa. The Electronic Library. Retrieved from http://www.emeraldinsight.com/doi/full/10.1108/02640470510582763

Igwe, K. N. (2013). Academic Libraries in Nigeria and the Challenges of Application of Information and Communication Technologies. Challenges of Academic Library Management in .... Retrieved from http://books.google.com/books?hl=en&lr=&id= 8dWe BQAAQBAJ&oi=fnd&pg=PA152&dq=koha+library +automation+open+source+software&ots=fzK-e373o6 &sig=i7aB39VhNLmcYeJJxWd7ptSn3bY

Illangarathne, S. K. (2012). Managing Automation in a Multi-Library Environment. repository.rjt.ac.lk.

Iqbal, M. (2008). A zero-budget strategy for innovation and ICTs' promotion in Pakistani libraries: The case of Pakistan Library Automation Group (PakLAG). International Conference for Information and ... .

Iroaganachi, M., James, J. I., & ... (2015). Software Selection and Deployment for Library Cooperation and Resource Sharing Among Academic Libraries in South-West Nigeria. ... Journal of Library & ... . Retrieved from http://search.proquest.com/openview/6b67476eb43e593c6f45bf83ab300d19/1?pq-origsite=gscholar

Islam, M. (2015). Assessing information needs and user satisfaction of private university libraries in Dhaka city. repository.library.du.ac.bd.

Ismail, N. R., & Mansor, Y. (2014). Building school library networks using open source technology: Teacher-librarians' awareness and perception. Information and Communication ... . Retrieved from http://ieeexplore.ieee.org/xpls/abs_all.jsp?arnumber=7020613

Jamaludin, A., Yusop, Z. M., & Bakar, A. A. (2012). Open source software as an integrated library management system: a study on the suitability and applicability of KOHA open source (KOHA OSS) for academic library ... . ir.uitm.edu.my. Retrieved from http://ir.uitm.edu.my/8229/

Jayakanth, F., Sharada, B., & Minj, F. (2007). An OAI-based approach to build and maintain union catalogue of OPACs. eprints.iisc.ernet.in. Retrieved from http://eprints.iisc.ernet.in/10263/

Jayakrishnan, J. S. (2013). Kerala Public Library Network: A Project Report. eprints.rclis.org. Retrieved from http://eprints.rclis.org/20451/

Jharotia, A. K. (2014). The Open Source Software for Library Management: An Overview. Tecnia Institute of Advanced Studies ... .

Jharotia, A. K., Behera, P. C., & Sharma, O. P. (n.d.). Usage of Open Source Software in Libraries: An Overview. Innovative Library Services for Dynamic ... .

Ji, Z. G. (2011). A Automation Library Management Method Based on Knowledge Management Tools. Advanced Materials Research. Retrieved from http://www.scientific.net/AMR.143-144.23

Joshi, S. K., & Baikady, M. R. (2014). Library Automation: Why and How? ... on Management of Modern Libraries (.... Retrieved from http://books.google.com/books?hl=en&lr=&id=42a8CQAAQBAJ&oi=fnd&pg=PA33&dq=koha+library+automation+open+source+software&ots=5WMModRXMp&sig= s6XFsQuGVVVvddgCBzZd2XpWRY4

Joy, B. (n.d.). KOHA and LIBSYS: A Comparative Study. Jalis.in.

Kaloyanova, S., Betti, G. L., Castellani, F., & ... (2008). Achieving OAI PMH compliancy for CDS/ISIS databases. ... Electronic Library. Retrieved from http://www.emeraldinsight.com/doi/abs/10.1108/02640470810879545

Kanagarasu, R., Lavanya, R., Umamaheswari, D., & Pandi, S. (2011). Need of the IT skills for Library and Information Science professionals. 14.139.186.108. Retrieved from http://14.139.186.108/jspui/handle/123456789/3549

Kari, K. H., & Baro, E. E. (2014). The use of library software in Nigerian University Libraries and challenges. Library Hi Tech News, 31(3), 15–20. http://doi.org/10.1108/LHTN-09-2013-0053

Keast, D. (2011). A survey of Koha in Australian special libraries: Open source brings new opportunities to the outback. OCLC Systems and Services, 27(1), 23–39. http://doi.org/10.1108/10650751111106537

Keats, D. (2008). Free and Open Source Software for librarians and libraries. Innovation.

Kemdarne, S. (2014). Library automation and networking of dental college libraries in Karnataka: A study. International Journal of Information .... Retrieved from http://search.proquest.com/openview/1ede2ff9a590a7f8187d2a11649f92f4/1?pq-origsite=gscholar

Kemdarne, S. B. (2014). A Survey of Library Automation and Networking of Dental College Libraries in Karnataka. International Journal of Information .... Retrieved from http://search.proquest.com/openview/1ede2ff9a590a

7f8187d2a11649f92f4/1.pdf?pq-origsite=gscholar&cbl=1036413

Kemp, R. (2008). MARC record services: A comparative study of library practices and perceptions. The Serials Librarian. Retrieved from http://www.tandfonline.com/doi/abs/10.1080/03615260802056367

Kennedy, P. (2004). Dynamic web pages and the library catalogue. The Electronic Library. Retrieved from http://www.emeraldinsight.com/doi/pdf/10.1108/02640470410570776

Khan, A., Idrees, H., & Mudassir, K. (2015). Library Web sites for people with disability: accessibility evaluation of library websites in Pakistan. Library Hi Tech News. Retrieved from http://www.emeraldinsight.com/doi/abs/10.1108/LHTN-01-2015-0010

Khan, M. A., & Mahmood, K. (2010). A study of the usefulness of Pakistan Library Automation Group's (PakLAG) services. Library Philosophy and Practice (e ....

Khatun, A. (2015). Open source integrated library system and usability issues: A study of Koha interfaces. repository.library.du.ac.bd. Retrieved from http://repository.library.du.ac.bd/xmlui/handle/123456789/734

Khode, S., & Chandel, S. S. (2015). Adoption of open source software in India. DESIDOC Journal of Library and Information Technology, 35(1), 30–40.

Khor, J. H., Widad, I. R., Md Rashid, M. N., Wan Ismail, A. A., Omar, M. Q., & Mohd Zanal, F. H. (2015). UHF RFID proof of concept (POC) with open-source ILS at Universiti Sains Malaysia (USM) libraries. Program, 49(2), 135–150. http://doi.org/10.1108/PROG-11-2012-0060

Khurshid, Z. (1996). Managing a library automation project. Aslib Proceedings, 48(1), 23–28.

Khurshid, Z., & Al-Baridi, S. A. (2010). System migration from horizon to symphony at king fahd university of petroleum and minerals. IFLA Journal, 36(3), 251–258. http://doi.org/10.1177/0340035210378712

Kiriyanant, P. (2012). Survey of Open Source Integrated Library System in Thai University Libraries in Bangkok and

Pathumthani. cseas.kyoto-u.ac.jp.

Kohli, R. (2014). Automation of Academic Libraries in ICT Environment: Issues and Challenges. Asian Journal of Multidisciplinary Studies. Retrieved from http://ajms.co.in/sites/ajms2015/index.php/ajms/article/view/778

Kohn, K., & McCloy, E. (2010). Phased migration to Koha: Our library's experience. Journal of Web Librarianship, 4(4), 427–434. http://doi.org/10.1080/19322909.2010.485944

KOLLE, S. (2015). Application of NewGenLib (OSS) for Automation of Librar y of College of Horticulture, Kolar, India. ... LIBRARIES ISSUES AND CHALLENGES.

Konnur, P. V., & Abidi, H. J. (2009). Transforming Libraries into Learning Centres using Open Source Technologies. inflibnet.ac.in.

Kumara, B., & Ravivenkat, B. (2015). Use of ICT and best practices for Tumkur university library: a study. Indian Journal of Science.

Kumar, A., & Rani, R. (n.d.). Automation of Library System. Erpublications.com.

Kumar, B. (2015). Academic Library in Transition from Library as a Place to Library as a Learning Centre: A Case Study of Indian Institutes of Management. DESIDOC Journal of Library & Information .... Retrieved from http://search.proquest.com/openview/a58cddb779d58848e81052b61c017572/1?pq-origsite=gscholar

Kumar, D. (n.d.). Overview of Open Source Virtual Learning Environment for Scientific Research. Researchgate.net.

Kumar, D. A., & Mandal, S. (2013). Development of cloud computing in integrated library management and retrieval system. International Journal of Library and ....

Kumar, K., & Atchamamba, L. (2013). Comparative Study of Opensource Software in Library Automation Network in Academic Institutions of Andhra Pradesh: A Survey. Pearl: A Journal of Library and .... Retrieved from http://www.indianjournals.com/ijor.aspx?target= ijor:pjolis&volume=7&issue=4&article=003

Kumar, K., & Raghunadha, R. T. (2013). Analytical study on knowledge about open source software in technological institutional LIS professionals. International Journal of Library ... .

Kumarsan, P. (2010). Automation of M. Phil Dissertations in Computer Science in Bharathidasan University Library. 14.139.186.108. Retrieved from http://14.139.186.108/jspui/handle/123456789/352

Kumar, T. G. (2015). Viability of Adopting Open Source Integrated Library Systems in Indian Libraries: Perspectives of Commercial ILS Users. ... Journal of Information Sources and Services. Retrieved from http://eprints.rclis.org/28781/

Kumar, T. K. G., & Jayapradeep, M. (2015). Perceptions of LIS Professionals on open source integrated library system and adoptability of Koha over LibSys in India. International Journal of ... . Retrieved from http://search.proquest.com/openview/d6d55f2afd6a05544f13f1613144f1f2/1?pq-origsite=gscholar

Kumar, V. (2008). Next generation catalogue: A user's expectation. International CALIBER. Retrieved from Http://www. ... .

Kumar, V. (n.d.). Open source Integrated Library Management Systems.

Kumar, V. V. (2005). Free/Open source integrated library management systems: comparative analysis of Koha, PHPMyLibrary and OpenBiblio. eprints.rclis.org. Retrieved from http://eprints.rclis.org/handle/10760/8578

Kumar, V. V. (2007). Selection and Management of Open Source Software in Libraries. eprints.rclis.org. Retrieved from http://eprints.rclis.org/handle/10760/8967

Kumar, V. V., & Abraham, T. (2009). Eight Things you should Know about Open Source Integrated Library Systems. eprints.rclis.org. Retrieved from http://eprints.rclis.org/handle/10760/13858

Kushwah, S. S., Gautam, J. N., & Singh, R. (2008). Library Automation and Open Source Solutions Major Shifts & Practices: A Comparative Case Study of Library Automation Systems in India. INFLIBNET Centre.

Lee, Y., & Yang, S. Q. (2012). Folksonomies as Subject Access- A Survey of Tagging in Library Online Catalogs and Discovery Layers. IFLA Publication Series. Accepted for ... .

Li, A. (2008). Investigation of ILS in Chinese main academic libraries. Library Collections, Acquisitions, and Technical ... . Retrieved from http://www.tandfonline.com/doi/abs/10.1080/14649055.2008.10766209

Little, M. (2009). Open source conversion: From preaching to practice. eprints.rclis.org. Retrieved from http://eprints.rclis.org/handle/10760/13737

Liu, G., & Zheng, H. (2011). Access to serials: Integrating SFX with Evergreen open source ILS. Library Hi Tech, 29(1), 137–148. http://doi.org/10.1108/07378831111116967

LIU, L., JIA, G., & SUN, Y. (2007). The Library's Management Software Based on Open-source [J]. Sci-Tech Information Development & ... .

Li, X. C. (2014). What would be the future of the Integrated Library Systems? docs.lib.purdue.edu. Retrieved from http://docs.lib.purdue.edu/iatul/2014/libservsys/3/

Macan, B., & Fernández, G. V. (2010). ABCD vs. KOHA: open source library options. fulir.irb.hr. Retrieved from http://fulir.irb.hr/326/

Macan, B., Fernández, G. V., & Stojanovski, J. (2013). Open source solutions for libraries: ABCD vs Koha. Program, 47(2), 136–154. http://doi.org/10.1108/00330331311313726

Mahajan, P., & Singh, N. K. (2014). RFID and It's Use in Libraries: A Literature Review. International Journal of Information Dissemination ... . Retrieved from http://www.ijidt.com/index.php/ijidt/article/view/4.2.4

Makori, E. O. (2013). Adoption of radio frequency identification technology in university libraries: A Kenyan perspective. The Electronic Library. Retrieved from http://www.emeraldinsight.com/doi/pdf/10.1108/02640471311312384

Mandal, S. (2015). Barcode Generation Tools in Integrated Library Management and Retrieval System. Asian Journal of Multidisciplinary Studies. Retrieved from http://ajms.co.in/sites/ajms2015/index.php/ajms/article/view/1379

Marijan, R., & Leskovar, R. (2015). A library's information retrieval system (In) effectiveness: case study. Library Hi Tech. Retrieved from http://www.emeraldinsight.com/doi/abs/10.1108/LHT-07-2015-0071

Maua, M., & Mwiti, T. (2013). Motivation for the adoption of open source software in Kenya academic libraries. IST-Africa Conference and Exhibition (IST- .... Retrieved from http://ieeexplore.ieee.org/xpls/abs_all.jsp? arnumber=6701712

McMahon, M. D. (2009). History of Koha and LibLime. Instructor.

Mêgnigbêto, E. (2012). A UNIMARC bibliographic format database for ABCD. Program. Retrieved from http://www.emeraldinsight.com/doi/pdf/10.1108/00330331211276503

Mêgnigbêto, E. (2013). The MARC tags and ISBD display formats for the ABCD UNIMARC bibliographic database. Information Development. Retrieved from http://idv.sagepub.com/content/29/3/265.short

Mehta, D., & Bhat, M. I. (2014). Use of Open Source Softwares in Indian Libraries. ir.inflibnet.ac.in. Retrieved from http://ir.inflibnet.ac.in/handle/1944/1806

Michaud, C. (2011). Cloud Computing and Software-as-a-Service in the Library Automation Marketplace. michaudcapstoneportfolio.yolasite. ....

Michaud, C., & Liu, J. (2011). Evergreen Integrated Library System (ILS). michaudcapstoneportfolio.yolasite. ....

Migliaccio, F., Carrion, D., & Zambrano, C. (2012). Tools based on proprietary and free/open source geospatial software for CO emission maps analysis and comparison. Applied Geomatics, 4(2), 105–112. http://doi.org/10.1007/s12518-011-0075-8

Mirza, M. S. (2014). Library Services at International Islamic University Islamabad: Academic Excellence in 21 Century. Pakistan Library & Information Science Journal. Retrieved from http://search.ebscohost.com/login.aspx?direct=true&profile=ehost&scope=site&authtype=crawler&jrnl=

00309956&AN= 101143317&h= st417ZH4Ag4j9len6I s5VhP66% 2B7ZvfQpm9MA0EHfROkhtD6TEhdcx K5L7b2Ydki56f2jFj9HI2sHIes7Z3 s4Sg%3D%3D&crl=c

Mishra, P. (2015). Successful Implimentation of Open Source Software in Libraries. dspace.nitrkl.ac.in. Retrieved from http://dspace.nitrkl.ac.in:8080/dspace/handle/2080/2299

Mishra, V. K. (2015). Systematic Approach of Data Migration, Customization and Implementation of Koha: A Case Study of Saharanpur Campus Library, IIT Roorkee. dspace.nitrkl.ac.in. Retrieved from http://dspace.nitrkl.ac.in/dspace/handle/2080/2261

Mitchell, E. T. (2013). Cloud-Based Services for Your Library. books.google.com.

Mnjama, N., & Wamukoya, J. (2007). E-government and records management: an assessment tool for e-records readiness in government. The Electronic Library. Retrieved from http://www.emeraldinsight.com/doi/pdf/10.1108/02640470710754797

Mondal, A. K., & Bandyopadhyay, A. K. (2010). Application of ICT and related manpower problems in the college libraries of Burdwan. DESIDOC Journal of Library .... Retrieved from http://search.proquest.com/openview/d71c734049e6cc8b09a95172fc207305/1?pq-origsite=gscholar

Morshed, M. (2008). Open source library management system. 123.49.46.157. Retrieved from http://123.49.46.157/handle/10361/176

Morton-Owens, E. G., Hanson, K. L., & Walls, I. (2011). Implementing open-source software for three core library functions: A stage-by-stage comparison. Journal of Electronic Resources in Medical Libraries, 8(1), 1–14. http://doi.org/10.1080/15424065.2011.551486

Mukhopadhyay, P. (2006). Five laws and ten commandments: the open road of library automation in India. ... of the National Seminar on Open Source ....

Mulla, K. R., Chandrashekara, M., & ... (2010). Usage and performance of various library software modules in engineering colleges of Karnataka. ... Journal of Library & .... Retrieved from http://search.proquest.com/

openview/33c7b15f6ba2d3fe18baeef3c50f2291/1?pq-origsite=gscholar

Müller, T. (2011). How to choose a free and open source integrated library system. OCLC Systems and Services, 27(1), 57–78. http://doi.org/10.1108/10650751111106573

Muruganandham, G., Pandian, N. M., & Selvaraju, R. (2015). Perception and Application of Open Source Software among LIS Professionals of Engineering Colleges in Tamil Nadu: A Study. ... of Advances in Library and ... .

Mutula, S. M. (2012). Library automation in sub Saharan Africa: case study of the University of Botswana. Program. Retrieved from http://www.emeraldinsight.com/doi/abs/10.1108/00330331211244832

Nassali State, E., & Åsmul, A. B. (2013). Building cataloging capacity for Libraries in South Sudan: A North-South-South collaboration. Cataloging and Classification Quarterly, 51(1-3), 194–201. http://doi.org/10.1080/01639374.2012.736123

Nazmul, I., & Islam, S. (2007). Use of ICT in libraries: An empirical study of selected libraries in Bangladesh. Library Philosophy and Practice. Retrieved from http://dialnet.unirioja.es/servlet/articulo?codigo=2472862

Neupane, C. (2014). Current Status of Library Networking and Resource Sharing Within TU Library Systems of Kathmandu Valley. 107.170.122.150. Retrieved from http://107.170.122.150:8080/xmlui/handle/123456789/50

Nghiêm, H. (n.d.). Implementing a new library management system.

Niu, X. (2012). Beyond text queries and ranked lists: Faceted search in library catalogs. gradworks.umi.com.

Niu, X. (2014). Faceted Search in Library Catalogs. New Directions in Information Organization (Library ... . Retrieved from http://www.emeraldinsight.com/doi/abs/10.1108/S1876-0562(2013)0000007013

Niu, X., & Hemminger, B. (2015). Analyzing the interaction patterns in a faceted search interface. Journal of the Association for Information ... . Retrieved from http://

onlinelibrary.wiley.com/doi/10.1002/asi.23227/full

Noonan, H. (2015). FLOSS in New Zealand Public Libraries. researcharchive.vuw.ac.nz. Retrieved from http://researcharchive.vuw.ac.nz/handle/10063/4638

Obajemu, A. S., Osagie, J. N., & ... (2013). Library software products in Nigeria: A survey of uses and assessment. ... Journal of Library ... .

Oberg, S. (2003). Open source software: An introduction from a serialist's perspective. Serials Review, 29(1), 36–39. http://doi.org/10.1016/S0098-7913(03)00002-9

ODONGO, M. (2012). Adoption of Open Source and Open Standards in Academic Libraries in Kenya. SCECSAL XXth Conference Hosted by KLA.

Ogbenege, J., & Adetimirin, A. (2013). Selection and use of KOHA software in two private Nigerian universities. Library Hi Tech News, 30(6), 12–16. http://doi.org/10.1108/LHTN-04-2013-0020

Omeluzor, S. U., Adara, O., Ezinwayi, M., & ... (2012). Implementation of Koha Integrated Library Management Software (ILMS): The Babcock University Experience. Canadian Social ... . Retrieved from http://www.cscanada.net/index.php/css/article/view/2750

Omeluzor, S. U., Bamidele, I. A., & ... (2013). The relevance of a library in the 21 st century: Students' perception. ... Journal of Library ... .

Ondoro, C. B. (2015). Adoption of integrated information management systems in Kenya: A case study at the Kenya Bureau of Standards Library. erepository.uonbi.ac.ke. Retrieved from http://erepository.uonbi.ac.ke/handle/11295/93153

Otunla, A. O., & Akanmu-Adeyemo, E. A. (2010). Library automation in Nigeria: The Bowen university experience. African Journal of Library Archives and Information Science, 20(2), 93–102.

Palmer, A., & Choi, N. (2014). The current state of library open source software research: a descriptive literature review and classification. Library Hi Tech. Retrieved from http://www.emeraldinsight.com/doi/abs/10.1108/LHT-05-2013-0056

Parab, N. (2004). A Strategic Analysis of Eloquent Systems. summit.sfu.ca. Retrieved from http://summit.sfu.ca/item/7863

Patel, P. I., & Patel, B. A. (2012). Library Automation and Planning. gnu.inflibnet.ac.in.

Poulter, A., Molyneux, R. E., & Rylander, M. (2010). The state of Evergreen: Evergreen at three. Library Review. Retrieved from http://www.emeraldinsight.com/doi/abs/10.1108/00242531011086999

Poulter, A., Payne, A., & Singh, V. (2010). Open source software use in libraries. Library Review. Retrieved from http://www.emeraldinsight.com/doi/pdf/10.1108/00242531011087033

Poulter, A., & Poulter, A. (2010). Open source in libraries: an introduction and overview. Library Review. Retrieved from http://www.emeraldinsight.com/doi/pdf/10.1108/00242531011086971

Pradhan, D., & Raj, M. (2011). Data Migration from CDS/ISIS to Koha (Integrated Library System). INFOLIB JOURNAL.

Pratheepan, T. (2011). Integrated Library Management Systems (ILMS)-Open Source and Commercial Software: An assessment of the merits and demerits. ... of the University Librarians Association of Sri .... Retrieved from http://papers.ssrn.com/sol3/papers.cfm?abstract_id=2215414

Pruett, J., & Choi, N. (2013). A comparison between select open source and proprietary integrated library systems. Library Hi Tech. Retrieved from http://www.emeraldinsight.com/doi/pdf/10.1108/LHT-01-2013-0003

Rafiq, M. (2009). LIS community's perceptions towards open source software adoption in libraries. The International Information & Library Review. Retrieved from http://www.tandfonline.com/doi/abs/10.1080/10572317.2009.10762808

Rafiq, M. (2011). Book Review: Practical Open Source Software for Libraries. Ariadne.

Rafiq, M., & Ameen, K. (2014). Issues and lessons learned in open source software adoption in Pakistani libraries. Electronic Library, 27(4), 601–610. http://doi.org/10.1108/02640470910979561

Rahman, M. (2014). Use and applications of library software in university libraries of Bangladesh. repository.library. du.ac.bd.

Rajani, N., Rekola, J., & Mielonen, T. (2003). Free as in education: significance of the free/libre and open source software for developing countries. Citeseer.

Rajan, V. R., Sekar, K., & ... (2015). Emerging Technological Innovations in Library Management and Services. Indian Journal of Library & .... Retrieved from http://search. ebscohost.com/login.aspx?direct=true&profile=ehost& scope= site&authtype= crawler&jrnl= 09739548 &AN= 111229967&h=MsiwqXcViN%2Bc7GDhxghbf8y% 2FCkaT2iyZyFYYeaT7H%2FX2JLt7igSo4at18 joylYiaLkwa3 exVX1kmKyCTwz4GCw%3D%3D&crl=c

Raju, R., Moodley, S. R., Jagarnath, O., & ... (2007). The migration of integrated library systems with special reference to the rollout of Unicorn in the province of KZN. ... Journal of Libraries .... Retrieved from http:// search.ebscohost.com/login.aspx ?direct= true& profile= ehost&scope=site&authtype=crawler&jrnl=02568861&AN= 28746544&h= EOM7wUYiZDvRi%2B %2F8PhUYn TplR1u4 MHtW1DV jputayaet6urBvpiFukWMOxexe KhVsKJGPHjtfS% 2BZ6EYx%2F6PXOw%3D%3D&crl=c

Ramzan, M., & Singh, D. (2009). Status of information technology applications in Pakistani libraries. The Electronic Library. Retrieved from http://www. emeraldinsight.com/doi/pdf/10.1108/02640470910 979543

Randhawa, S. (2008). Open source software and libraries. arizona.openrepository.com. Retrieved from http:// arizona.openrepository.com/arizona/handle/10150/ 105743

Randhawa, S. (2013). Open Source Library Management Softwares. E-Library Science Research Journal. Retrieved from http://arizona.openrepository.com/arizona/ handle/10150/299575

Ransom, S. (2011). Improving Bhutan's academic libraries, recommendations from a situational analysis. The International Information & Library Review. Retrieved from http://www.tandfonline.com/doi/abs/10.1080/10572317.2011.10762900

Rapp, D. (2011). Open source reality check. dosen.narotama.ac.id.

Rayan, Z. (2015). Challenges and opportunities in migrating to web-based information services: a case study of Dhaka university library. repository.library.du.ac.bd. Retrieved from http://repository.library.du.ac.bd:8080/handle/123456789/693

Reddy, C. S. V. (2011). KOHA (Integrated Library Management Software): An Open Source Solution for Library Automation. sites.google.com.

Reddy, T. R., Kumari, C., & Reddy, M. E. (2012). Role of open source softwares and their impact on library and information centres: A study. International Journal of .... Retrieved from http://search.proquest.com/openview/fb3b2825a3bc1f71791051e48906362d/1?pq-origsite=gscholar

Reddy, T. R., & Kumar, K. (2013). Open source softwares and their impact on library and information centre: An overview. International Journal of Library and ....

Repanovici, A., & Cristea, L. (2011a). RFID-Application in Info-Documentary Systems. Designing and Deploying RFID .... Retrieved from http://eprints.rclis.org/handle/10760/16034

Repanovici, A., & Cristea, L. (2011b). RFID Technology used in Small Library-Case Study at Transilvania University. Romanian Review Precision Mechanics, Optics & ....

Richardson, J., & Hopkins, P. (2004). Selecting an ILMS for a future you can't imagine. VALA Conference Proceedings 2004.

Riewe, L. M. (2008). Survey of open source integrated library systems. scholarworks.sjsu.edu.

Riyaz, A., Rijal, N., Shrestha, S. R., & Nashfa, F. (2012). Bridging the information divide of the Maldives through library automation and digitisation. academia.edu.

Rodrigues, M. e. (2016). Open Source Software for Academic Libraries-The Creative Librarian. International Journal of Innovative Research and .... Retrieved from http://www.ijird.com/index.php/ijird/article/view/86083

Sajeer, S. L. M. (2012). Technology and services for library automation. ir.lib.seu.ac.lk. Retrieved from http://ir.lib.seu.ac.lk/handle/123456789/1289

Samyal, J. K., & Sumi, S. (2010). Creation of an Online Library using KOHA Open Source Software: A Case Study of Chitkara University. Open-Source Solutions in Education: Theory ....

Sanjailal, K. P., Padmavathi, T., & Seetharam, G. (2011). Design of a Next-Generation Library Catalogue using Web 2.0 Technologies and Faceted Navigation. ir.cftri.com. Retrieved from http://ir.cftri.com/9920/

Sarma, G. K. (2016). OPAC module in open source library management software: A comparative study. DESIDOC Journal of Library and Information Technology, 36(1), 56–61. http://doi.org/10.14429/djlit.36.1.9223

Satpathy, S. K., & Maharana, R. K. (2012). Awareness and adoption of open source software among LIS professionals of engineering colleges of Odisha. DESIDOC Journal of Library & .... Retrieved from http://search.proquest.com/openview/694df0550b633ce30b480e9755500074/1?pq-origsite=gscholar

Scott, D. (2014). Seeding structured data by default via open source library systems. Lecture Notes in Computer Science (including Subseries Lecture Notes in Artificial Intelligence and Lecture Notes in Bioinformatics), 8465 LNCS, 659–674. http://doi.org/10.1007/978-3-319-07443-6_44

Seitz, J. (2011). Koha at Peninsula Health Medical Library: A Case Study. Health. Retrieved from http://search.informit.com.au/documentSummary;dn= 928351508145658;res=IELHEA

Seshaiah, O., & Veeranjaneyulu, C. (2015). Implemetation of koha: An experience. Indian Journal of Science. Retrieved from http://www.indianjournals.com/ijor.aspx?target=ijor:ijs2&volume=21&issue=72&article=016

Shafi-Ullah, F., & Qutab, S. (2012). From LAMP to Koha: Case study of the Pakistan legislative assembly libraries.

Program, 46(1), 43–55. http://doi.org/10.1108/0033033 1211204557

Sharma, P., & Sharma, H. (n.d.). NewGenLib: Open Source Software from India. V3 Journal of Library and Information ScienceS.

Sharma, R. P. (2008). Application of information technology in catalogue and index: its retrieval aspects. 182.93.84.134. Retrieved from http://182.93.84.134:9991/nnl/handle/ 123456789/127

Shaw, A. K. (2013). Cloud Computing for Libraries: An Economic Strategy. eprints.rclis.org. Retrieved from http:// eprints.rclis.org/19359/

Sheehy, C. (n.d.). Open Source Library Automation Solutions: a Review of the Literature.

Sheeja, N. K. (2009). Adoption of Koha Open Source Software in Libraries: a Web Based Study. dspace.cusat.ac.in. Retrieved from http://dspace.cusat.ac.in/jspui/handle/ 123456789/6778

Sheeja, N. K., Mathew, S., Pillai, S. S., & Cherukodan, S. (2013). Collection and Assets management: one University Library's journey to the future. dspace.cusat.ac.in. Retrieved from http://dspace.cusat.ac.in/jspui/handle/ 123456789/6630

Shivaram, B. S. (2007). Library Automation: An overview. Dr. TB Rajashekar Memorial Seminar on Emerging.

Siddique, N., & Mahmood, K. (2014). Library software in Pakistan: A review of literature. Library Review. Retrieved from http://www.emeraldinsight.com/doi/abs/10.1108/ LR-04-2013-0048

Siddique, N., & Mahmood, K. (2015). Status of Library Software in Higher Education Institutions of Pakistan. International Information & Library .... Retrieved from http:// www.tandfonline.com/doi/abs/10.1080/10572317. 2015.1087796

Silvestre, J. J. R., da Cunha, L., Meur, J. L., & Šimko, T. (2010). An Integrated Library System on the CERN Document Server. librarytechnology.org.

Si, L., & Wanigasooriya, P. L. (n.d.). An Investigation and Analysis of Online Public Access Catalogues (OPACs) in University Libraries in Sri Lanka.

Singh, K. (2013). NewGenLib: open source software in Indian libraries. International Journal of Advanced Research in … .

Singh, M., & Sanaman, G. (2012). Open source integrated library management systems: Comparative analysis of Koha and NewGenLib. Electronic Library, 30(6), 809–832. http://doi.org/10.1108/02640471211282127

Singh, R. (2014). Open Source Initiative in Indian Library Automation Using Newgenlib and Koha: A Comparative Study. Indian Journal of Library and Information Science. Retrieved from http://search.proquest.com/openview/fc4955d12a9cf009817 42fdf10f52f1e/1?pq-origsite=gscholar

Singh, S. K., & Deka, P. K. (2008). Prospects of Open Source Software in LIS Area of Assam. INFLIBNET Centre.

Singh, V. (2010). Comparison of technical support for open source software versus proprietary software. Proceedings of the ASIST Annual Meeting, 47. http://doi.org/10.1002/meet.14504701437

Singh, V. (2013a). Experiences of migrating to an open-source integrated library system. Information Technology and Libraries (Online). Retrieved from http://search.proquest.com/openview/60a4c12c79d7d3f0ed76c79a6fccfa9e/1?pq-origsite=gscholar

Singh, V. (2013b). The Nuts and Bolts of Migration to Open Source ILS: Experiences and Recommendations from Librarians. Libri. Retrieved from http://www.degruyter.com/view/j/libr.2013.63.issue-2/libri-2013-0009/libri-2013-0009.xml

Singh, V. (2013c). Why migrate to an open source ILS? Librarians with adoption experience share their reasons and experiences. Libri. Retrieved from http://www.degruyter.com/view/j/libr.2013.63.issue-3/libri-2013-0016/libri-2013-0016.xml

Singh, V. (2014a). Expectations versus experiences: Librarians using open source integrated library systems. Electronic

Library, 32(5), 688–709. http://doi.org/10.1108/EL-10-2012-0129

Singh, V. (2014b). Open Source Software Use in Libraries: Implications for Social Justice? Qualitative & Quantitative Methods in Libraries.

Sklar, A. Y. (2003). Tribal college library web sites: provision of health information sources. ruby.ils.unc.edu.

Smet, E. D. (2010). Some ISIS-Software history and technical background on the new FOSS integrated library system ABCD. Liber Quarterly.

Smet, E., & Dhamdhere, S. N. (2010). ABCD: an open source automation tool for libraries. Pearl: A Journal of Library and .... Retrieved from http://www.indianjournals.com/ijor.aspx?target=ijor:pjolis&volume=4&issue=4&article=001

Somashekara, Y. L., Jagadeesha, B. M., & ... (2014). Library cataloging using KOHA software: a study of Mysore University library cataloguing experiences. E-Library Science .... Retrieved from http://eprints.uni-mysore.ac.in/17099/

Somashekara, Y. L., & Raju, C. (2013). KOHA cataloging module: a study of Mysore University library cataloging experiences. eprints.uni-mysore.ac.in.

Sonker, S. K. (2000). Implementation of Koha–An Open Source Library Management Software. National Center for Science Information Indian Institute ....

Sonker, S. K., & Jayakanth, F. (2003). KOHA: an open source integrated library automation system. SRELS Journal of Information Management. Retrieved from http://cat.inist.fr/?aModele=afficheN&cpsidt=15027366

Speirs, M. (2010). The Development of Information and Communication Technologies in Nigerian Libraries. eprints.rclis.org. Retrieved from http://eprints.rclis.org/handle/10760/14464

Srinivasaragavan, S. (2012). Bharathilibnet: An Online Union Catalogue Model for Bharathidasan University and its Affiliated Colleges. International Journal of Information Dissemination .... Retrieved from http://ijidt.com/index.php/ijidt/article/view/68

Steely, J. A. (2004). Open source software and resource sharing. Journal of Library Administration. Retrieved from http://www.tandfonline.com/doi/abs/10.1300/J111v40n01_05

Stilwell, C., & Hoskins, R. (2012). Integrated library management systems: a review of choices made and their sustainability in South Africa. Information Development. Retrieved from http://idv.sagepub.com/content/early/2012/07/12/0266666912454067.abstract

Stump, S. L., & Deegan, R. L. (2013). Open Source Opens Doors: Repurposing Library Software to Facilitate Faculty Research and Collaboration. Pennsylvania Libraries. Retrieved from http://search.proquest.com/openview/14d77c9305ef891636cc9886fcacef4c/1?pq-origsite=gscholar

Sunil, M. V. (2015). An analytical study of OSS Open Source Software for college libraries. shodhganga.inflibnet.ac.in.

Sunil, M. V., & Chandrappa, N. (2014). Next Generation of Catalogues: Comparative study of Five Indian Universities OPACs. sdmimd.ac.in.

Surulinathi, M., Abinaya, S., & Mahalakshmi, G. (2014). Smart Technologies for Library Services. 14.139.186.108. Retrieved from http://14.139.186.108/jspui/handle/123456789/14838

TechSource, A. L. A. (2008a). Evergreen Expands Into Academia. journals.ala.org.

TechSource, A. L. A. (2008b). Open Source ILS Gains Ground with Academic Libraries. journals.ala.org.

TechSource, A. L. A. (2009). EBSCO Sets Strategy for Discovery. journals.ala.org.

TechSource, A. L. A. (n.d.). LibLime Launches LibLime Enterprise Koha, or, Rift Splits the Koha Development Community. Journals.ala.org.

Thompson, K. J. (2012). Free as in Freedom, Not as in Beer: Free and Open Source Software ILS and the Library Community. B Sides. Retrieved from http://ir.uiowa.edu/bsides/23/

Tong, T. W. (2004). Free/open source software education. United

Nations Development Programme's Asia-Pacific .... .

Tramullas, J. (2012). Library Automation and OPAC 2.0: Information Access and Services in the 2.0 Landscape: Information Access and Services in the 2.0 Landscape. books.google.com.

Tyagi, A. K., & Senthil, V. (2015). Library automation in India: Assessment of library services platforms. DESIDOC Journal of Library and Information Technology, 35(6), 408–416.

Ukachi, N. B., Nwachukwu, V. N., & ... (2014). Library automation and use of open source software to maximize library effectivenss. Library Progress (.... Retrieved from http://www.indianjournals.com/ijor.aspx?target=ijor:bpaslp&volume=34&issue=2&article=002

Umaiyorubagam, R., JohnAnish, R., & Jeyapragash, B. (2015). E-GRANTHALAYA: LIBRARY INFORMATION SCIENCE OPEN SOURCE AUTOMATION SOFTWARE: AN OVERVIEW. eprints.rclis.org. Retrieved from http://eprints.rclis.org/24669/

Uzomba, E. C., Oyebola, O. J., & ... (2015). The Use and Application of Open Source Integrated Library System in Academic Libraries in Nigeria: Koha Example. Library Philosophy and .... Retrieved from http://search.proquest.com/openview/a3e36496a0dc3f0e0a878a1d01642905/1?pq-origsite=gscholar&cbl=54903

Vasupongayya, S., Keawneam, K., Sengloilaun, K., & ... (2011). Open source library management system software: a review. ... , Electrical, Automation, ...

Venus, R. (2012). DESIGN AND IMPLEMENTATION OF LIBRARY AUTOMATION USING KOHA (Open Source Software) AT BHARATHIDASAN UNIVERSITY COLLEGE, ... 14.139.186.108. Retrieved from http://14.139.186.108/jspui/handle/123456789/4992

Vrkiæ, D., Lisek, J., & Glavica, M. (2012). This summer she began to dance: Implementation of koha into the library system of the faculty of electrical engineering and computing: Part one [Zaplesala je ovo ljeto: Implementacija kohe u knjižnièni sustav fakulteta elektrotehnike i raèunarstva: Prvi dio]. Vjesnik Bibliotekara Hrvatske,

55(3-4), 1–16.

VV, B. (2014). Open Source Software Use in Indian Libraries: A Survey. International Journal of Advanced Research in .... Retrieved from http://eprints.rclis.org/23922/

Vyas, J. R. (2013). Open Source Library Management Software. Seva Sadan's College of Education, ...

Walls, I. (2011). Migrating from Innovative Interfaces' Millennium to Koha: The NYU Health Sciences Libraries' experiences. OCLC Systems and Services, 27(1), 51–56. http://doi.org/10.1108/10650751111106564

Wan, G. (2007). An open source alternative for libraries. oaktrust.library.tamu.edu. Retrieved from http://oaktrust.library.tamu.edu/handle/1969.1/6454

Wang, Z. (2009). Integrated library system (ILS) challenges and opportunities: a survey of US academic libraries with migration projects. The Journal of Academic Librarianship. Retrieved from http://www.sciencedirect.com/science/article/pii/S0099133309000275

Webber, D., & Peters, A. (2010). Integrated library systems: Planning, selecting, and implementing. books.google.com.

Wheeler, D. A. (2007). Why open source software/free software (OSS/FS, FLOSS, or FOSS)? Look at the numbers. dwheeler.com.

Whong, F. M., & Zakari, M. (2014). Application of Information and Communication Technologies (ICTs) to Library Operations and Routines in Selected Nigerian Federal University Libraries. Information Manager (The). Retrieved from http://www.ajol.info/index.php/tim/article/view/118029

Wijayaratne, A. (2005). Automation of library functions with special reference to circulation system adopted at the library of open university of Sri Lanka. Journal of the University Librarians Association of Sri .... Retrieved from http://jula.sljol.info/article/10.4038/jula.v9i0.311/

Williams, O. (n.d.). A Study of Software Evolution and Complexity Applied.

Wilson, K. (2006). Computers in libraries: an introduction for library technicians. books.google.com.

Xiaobin, C. (2013). VMware Virtual Machine-based Construction of Koha Open Source ILS. Information Research.

Yang, S. Q., & Hofmann, M. A. (2010). The next generation library catalog: A comparative study of the OPACs of Koha, Evergreen, and Voyager. Information Technology and Libraries, 29(3), 141–150.

Younker, J., & Ribaric, T. (2013). Beyond open source software: Solving common library problems using the open source hardware arduino platform. Partnership: The Canadian Journal of Library ....

Yuen, K. (2009). Can this economy support library changes to an open source software system? Preprint] Recuperado de Http://hdl. Handle. net/10760/ ....

Zeheimi, S. A., Zeki, A. M., Razi, M., & ... (2014). Perceptions of library and information science community towards open source software adoption in libraries of Oman. ... Technology for The .... Retrieved from http://ieeexplore.ieee.org/xpls/abs_all.jsp?arnumber=7020591

Zico, M. (2009). Developing an integrated library system (ILS) using open source software Koha. 123.49.46.157. Retrieved from http://123.49.46.157/handle/10361/755